The
Presidential Pulse
of Congressional
Elections

The Presidential Pulse of Congressional Elections

JAMES E. CAMPBELL

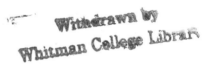

THE UNIVERSITY PRESS OF KENTUCKY

Copyright © 1993 by The University Press of Kentucky

Scholarly publisher for the Commonwealth,
serving Bellarmine College, Berea College, Centre
College of Kentucky, Eastern Kentucky University,
The Filson Club, Georgetown College, Kentucky
Historical Society, Kentucky State University,
Morehead State University, Murray State University,
Northern Kentucky University, Transylvania University,
University of Kentucky, University of Louisville,
and Western Kentucky University.

Editorial and Sales Offices: Lexington, Kentucky 40508-4008

Library of Congress Cataloging-in-Publication Data

Campbell, James E., 1952-
    The presidential pulse of congressional elections / James E.
  Campbell.
        p.   cm.
    Includes bibliographical references (p.   ) and index.
    ISBN 0-8131-1820-4 (acid-free paper) :
    1. United States.   Congress—Elections.   2. Elections—United
  States.   3. Voting—United States.   4. Political parties—United
  States.   5. Presidents—United States.   I. Title.
  JK1967.C25   1993
  324.973—dc20   93-12598

To my friends and teachers

Contents

Tables and Figures

Tables

Figures

Acknowledgments

Many people have contributed to this book. First, I have learned a great deal from the many political scientists who have worked and continue to work on this subject. Most of these are listed among the authors in the references at the end of the book. Two deserve special note. Although undoubtedly best remembered for *The American Voter*, Angus Campbell (no relation) also developed the original theory of surge and decline. Edward Tufte developed the referenda theory of midterms, which became the principal alternative explanation (though, as the following pages will show, Tufte's work actually foreshadowed the revised theory proposed here). Both were responsible for breaking new ground in research on congressional elections and my research owes much to both. I would also like to thank several election and congressional scholars who have read earlier versions of this research and provided me with their very valuable advice. In particular, I would like to thank Albert Cover, Morris Fiorina, Thomas Mann, and Richard Niemi. I also express thanks to the editors and anonymous reviewers of the several journals in which I reported early results of this research and to the staff of the University Press of Kentucky for the care they have given to the preparation of this manuscript for publication.

In addition, this book would not have been possible without the assemblage of a large body of election data. Several sources of these data deserve special acknowledgment: the National Election Studies conducted by the University of Michigan, Congressional Quarterly's *Guide to U.S. Elections* and its various editions of *Politics in America*, Michael Barone and his associates' various editions of *The Almanac of American Politics*, and Norm Ornstein, Tom Mann, and Michael Malbin's *Vital Statistics on Congress*.

Most of the analysis in this book is new. However, various portions of part two have appeared, in earlier incarnations, in several journal articles. The basic structure of the revised theory (chapter 5) first appeared in the *American Journal of Political Science* (1987). More limited analyses of the aggregate national evidence (chapter 6) first appeared also in the *American Journal of Political Science* (1986), in the *Journal of Politics* (1985), and in a chapter of Hertzke and Peters' *The Atomistic Congress* (1992). A more detailed discussion of the application of the surge and decline theory to state legislative elections (summarized briefly in chapter 9) can be found in the *American Political Science Review* (1986). I appreciate the advice of the editors and reviewers associated with these early reports of this research.

This book was written over several years spent on the political science faculties of the University of Georgia and Louisiana State University. I owe thanks to my former colleagues in the University of Georgia's Department of Political Science (especially Bob Grafstein, Chuck Bullock, Jerry Legge, Tom Lauth, and John Alford, now at Rice University) and the Institute for Behavioral Research (especially Doc Owens and Abe Tesser) for their support and advice over the years. I would like to thank my current colleagues in the Department of Political Science at Louisiana State University for their encouragement and advice (especially Ron Weber, Jim Garand, and Gene Wittkopf). Several research assistants have also contributed to this research. I have been especially fortunate to have had Darren Davis work on this project. Darren devoted long days to a good bit of the data collection and computer analysis necessary to complete this book. Mike Barr, Mark Baldwin, Steve Hanna, and Steve Procopio at LSU and Jean Kingston, Sae-jong Kim, and Kevin Lasher at the University of Georgia also provided valuable assistance on various parts of this project. The final preparation of the manuscript for publication was completed during my time as a program officer in the Political Science Program of the National Science Foundation. I would like to thank NSF and my colleague Frank Scioli for making it possible to bring the project to completion.

Since this is my first book, I would also like to acknowledge those who helped in my education: the schools of South Portland, Maine (especially Lorne Goodell); the faculty of Bowdoin College, who provided me with my undergraduate education (especially the late John Donovan); the Department of Political Science at Syracuse University, in which I received my graduate training (especially Tom Patterson, Bob McClure, Linda Fowler, Phil Beardsley, Jeff Stonecash, Bob DeVoursney, Jim Reynolds, and my graduate student colleagues, especially Karen Beckwith); and the American Political Science Association's Congressional Fellowship Program, which permitted me to learn firsthand about Congress in the offices of Representative Bill Frenzel (R-MN) and Senator Bob Packwood (R-OR). In different ways, each has contributed to this book.

I owe a great debt to my parents, my late father, Wallace J. Campbell, Jr., and my mom, Mary Campbell, and to my brothers, John, Bob, Dick, and Stephen. I also thank Margaret Reams for her encouragement during the writing of this book. Finally, I am grateful to Susan Porter for her kindness and her patience and to Danny, Annie, and Iggy for their friendship.

Introduction

This book is about congressional elections and the systematic differences between congressional elections that are held in presidential election years and those held in off-years or at the midterm of a presidency. The genesis of this book was in the 1982 midterm congressional election, in which the Republican party lost twenty-six seats in the House of Representatives. Using statistical models based on a theory of midterm elections that views the midterm vote as a referendum on the incumbent president, several political scientists made predictions about the 1982 election. In reviewing these predictions after the election, Evans Witt (1983) concluded that the models had performed quite poorly, forecasting Republicans to lose forty to forty-five seats. The natural question was why these predictions had been so far off target. Was 1982 an aberration, the result of greater insulation for incumbents, or was something more systematically wrong with the models used to generate these failed predictions?

The 1982 prediction errors caused me to reconsider an older theory of congressional elections, the theory of surge and decline. Originally formulated by Angus Campbell in 1960, this theory offers a clear alternative to the referenda perspective. Unlike the referenda theory, surge and decline explains midterm results as a repercussion of the prior presidential election. It offers a fairly well articulated theory of how microlevel voter behavior, in turnout and vote choice, causes a pattern of macrolevel election results. Because of the development and early success of the referenda model and because findings at the individual voter level contradicted the theory, surge and decline had fallen from the ranks of conventional wisdom in the early 1970s. However, in surveying the literature, aside from a few individual level studies, there was surprisingly little empirical work on which to evaluate the theory one way or the other.

The referenda model's problems with the 1982 midterm and the gap in the literature on surge and decline at the macrolevel persuaded me that the dismissal of surge and decline was at the very least premature and that it deserved a thorough reconsideration. This book reports that reconsideration, a reconsideration of both the theory's premises, its relationship with other theories of congressional elections, and the available evidence at the national, district, and individual levels. In the most general of terms, the empirical analysis indicates that at some points the data conform quite well to the theory but that at other points the theory falters.

In light of these mixed findings, I propose and examine a revised theory of surge and decline. The details of this revision will be left to chapter 5, but in broad terms the original theory is revised in three important respects. First, it is amended to include elements of the referenda theory. Second, the individual level foundations of the original theory are substantially changed. Third, as a consequence of the second change, the role of turnout in explaining midterm elections is modified. This revised theory is well supported by a wide variety of data.

In one sense, this book is about the relatively narrow subject of midterm elections. In another sense, however, it is a deceptively broad study, in both its theory and its evidence. It concerns a variety of different theories and evaluates a great deal of evidence of many different kinds—nearly a century of national elections, hundreds of congressional districts, and thousands of survey respondents. It is certainly about midterm congressional elections, but it is about congressional elections in presidential years as well. The primary focus is congressional, but the theme is presidential. It is concerned not only with questions of vote choice, but also with questions of voter turnout. Although it is principally concerned with mass political behavior, it is also concerned with the behavior of political elites and the functioning of political institutions. What follows is an integrated theory tested at both micro and macro levels of the effects of presidential elections on congressional elections, a thorough examination of the presidential pulse of congressional elections.

PART 1
Theories of Midterm Elections

1

The Midterm Question

In this world nothing is certain but death and taxes.
—Benjamin Franklin[1]

Whether the president is Republican or Democratic, serving in the nineteenth or twentieth century, midterm elections are almost always at the expense of his party. As V.O. Key wrote some time ago, "the president's party, whether it basks in public favor or is declining in public esteem, ordinarily loses House strength at midterm—a pattern that, save for one exception, has prevailed since the Civil War" (1958, 615). The pattern continues undisturbed since Key's observation. In thirty-two of the thirty-three midterm congressional elections since 1862 the party of the president has lost seats.[2] The sole break in this otherwise continuous string of losses was the 1934 midterm election, the first midterm of the New Deal realignment. While not as perfectly certain as either death or taxes, the loss of seats by the president's party in the U.S. House of Representatives as a result of midterm elections is a remarkably dependable event.

The size of these midterm seat losses typically has been substantial. Since the Civil War, the average midterm loss for the president's party is about forty seats. Although losses in recent years are not as great as they once were, they are often sizable. Since 1946 the president's party has lost in midterms an average of about twenty-six seats. Even more recently, since 1970, the presidential party's average midterm loss is about nineteen seats.

Nearly as impressive as the consistency of these midterm losses is their variability. While virtually always in the loss column, the magnitude of midterm losses for the president's party varies tremendously. In some midterms the president's party has suffered catastrophic losses. The president's party lost in excess of fifty seats in nine of the thirty-three midterms since 1860. The most devastating loss occurred in 1894, when more than one-half of the seats held by the president's party were lost. In that midterm, Grover Cleveland's Democratic party lost 116 seats in a House consisting of just 357 members. Seat losses in other midterms have been minuscule. In eleven of the thirty-three post-1860 midterms, the president's party lost fewer than fifteen seats. Aside from the 1934 aberration of a nine-seat gain and the phantom gain of 1902 when the president's party appeared to gain seats only because the total number of seats in the House increased in that election, the president's party sustained losses of fewer than five seats in just three midterms, two of which were the midterms during and immediately following the Civil War. In 1862 the incumbent Republican party lost just three seats and in 1866 a mere two seats. The third instance of minor midterm losses is Kennedy's 1962 midterm. In that midterm, just weeks after the Cuban missile crisis, the Democrats lost only four seats.

Both the tremendous variation in the extent of presidential losses in midterms and the remarkable consistency of these losses have attracted considerable scholarly attention. Why has the president's party regularly lost seats in midterms? Why are those losses severe in some midterms and minor in others?

This book explores several theories offering explanations of both the consistency and the variability of midterm losses. These theories are essentially of two types, differing by their focus on either the starting point or the ending point of the electoral change between presidential and midterm elections.

One school attributes midterm losses to the political conditions at the midterm itself. Midterm elections are viewed primarily as referenda on the performance of the president midway through his term. Public evaluations of the president are transferred to his party's congressional candidates. Several theories in this vein have become prominent in recent years and are addressed in some detail in the following pages.

A second type of midterm election theory, embodied in an earlier strain of research, explains midterm losses as a consequence of the prior presidential election. That is, the president's party is positioned to sustain losses at the midterm by its victory in the preceding presidential election. Presidential losses in midterm elections are repercussions of the prior election. Theories centered on presidential elections do not contend that the circumstances of the midterm itself are necessarily irrelevant, but they are also not systematically unfavorable to the president's party. The argument is that the circumstances of the presidential election produce a regularity in the interelection change and the systematic nature of this effect is stronger than the nonsystematic effects of the midterm. In short, the "action" that produces the pattern of midterm electoral change is in presidential elections.

The most prominent theory of midterms centered on presidential elections and the focal point for much of the analysis to follow is Angus Campbell's theory of surge and decline.[3] For those not already familiar with this theory a synopsis is in order. A more intensive examination of the foundations and premises of the theory follows in chapter 2.

The Theory of Surge and Decline

In originally setting forth his theory of surge and decline, Angus Campbell subtitled his article "A Study of Electoral Change." While the obvious purpose of the theory was to explain the midterm change in the electoral fortunes of the president's party, the theory was also concerned with another type of electoral change: the surge and decline of voter turnout from presidential to midterm elections. Turnout as well as support for the president's party drops in midterm elections. This decline has been even more dependable than the loss of seats. The turnout rate in midterm elections has declined from the prior presidential election without exception as long as reliable national turnout records have been kept. The typical turnout decline in recent elections has been about 12-14 percent of the voting age population or 20-25 percent of the prior presidential electorate. The turnout decline figures and seat loss figures for the last twelve midterm elections are displayed in table 1-1.

The fact that turnout rises and falls coincident with support for the president's party provided the critical clue in developing the theory of surge and decline. According to the theory, the coincidence of these regular electoral changes is no mere matter of chance. The decline in turnout and the loss of seats in midterm elections are linked. They are a consequence of another electoral decline, the decline in the prevailing short-term political forces of the prior presidential election campaign. As Angus Campbell put it, "Fluctuations in the turnout and partisanship of the vote in elections are primarily determined by short-term political forces which become important for the voter at election time. These forces move the turnout by adding stimulation to the underlying level of political interest of the electorate, and they move the partisanship of the vote from a baseline of 'standing commitments' to one or the other of the two parties" (Campbell et al. 1966, 41).

To understand more fully how short-term political forces of the presidential campaign cause the midterm decline in seats for the president's party as well as the midterm decline in turnout requires the introduction of two distinctions: one between different types of elections and the second between different types of voters.

The first distinction distinguishes between high-stimulus or "surge" elections and low-stimulus or "decline" elections. High-stimulus elections are characterized by relatively great amounts of campaign activity generating high levels of turnout. In general, presidential elections can be categorized as surge elections.[4] Low-stimulus elections involve relatively less energetic campaigns and thus precipitate lower levels of turnout. Midterm elections, for the most part, fall into this decline election category.

Table 1.1. Midterm Seat Losses for the President's Party and Congressional Election Turnout Decline, 1944-1990

Presidential and midterm election and winning pres. party		Seats held by the president's party			Congressional turnout as % of VAP		
		After presidential election	After midterm election	Change	In presidential election	In midterm election	Difference
1944-46	Dem.	243	188	−55	52.7	37.1	−15.6
1948-50	Dem.	263	234	−29	48.1	41.1	−7.0
1952-54	Rep.	221	203	−18	57.6	41.7	−15.9
1956-58	Rep.	201	153	−48	55.9	43.0	−12.9
1960-62	Dem.	262	258	−4	58.5	45.4	−13.1
1964-66	Dem.	295	248	−47	57.8	45.4	−12.4
1968-70	Rep.	192	180	−12	55.1	43.5	−11.6
1972-74	Rep.	192	144	−48	50.9	36.1	−14.8
1976-78	Dem.	292	277	−15	49.5	35.1	−14.4
1980-82	Rep.	192	167	−25	48.1	37.7	−10.4
1984-86	Rep.	182	177	−5	47.4	33.4	−14.0
1988-90	Rep.	175	167	−8	44.7	33.0	−11.7

SOURCES: Ornstein, Mann, and Malbin (1990, table 1.18 and 2.1), David Kaplan (1990, 3802), and Rhodes Cook (1991, 483-87). VAP: Voting age population

The theory's second distinction concerns voters. Again there are two types. The core voter is the habitual voter. Core voters have a strong and enduring interest in politics. Because of this interest, they vote regularly in elections, both presidential and midterm, and are likely to form a strong identification with one of the parties. The second voter type is the peripheral voter. The peripheral voter, as the name suggests, maintains only a passing interest in politics. The peripheral voter's intrinsic interest in politics is usually not enough to move him or her to vote. Peripheral voters need an extra push. With the greater stakes and the hoopla of the presidential contest, many peripheral voters get that extra push to the polls. In midterms, however, that extra stimulation is usually lacking and the peripherals stay home.

The above distinctions set the stage for the theory's explanation of what happens in presidential and midterm elections, how different voters behave in these elections in terms of both their vote choice and turnout decisions, and how the fortunes of congressional candidates of the president's party are affected by the cycle of presidential and midterm elections.

The key to understanding midterm losses for the president's party begins with an understanding of the effects of the previous presidential election. Presidential campaigns are well-financed, energizing, attention-grabbing, high-stimulus events contesting the nation's highest office. They are thus highly visible to all but the most apolitical citizen. Compared to low-stimulus midterm elections, presidential campaigns should have substantial effects on voters. The theory of surge and decline points to two important effects of these strong presidential campaign "short-term forces."

First, the strong surge of political information in a presidential campaign is likely to favor one of the parties more than the other. As Angus Campbell put it, "It is very unlikely that a political situation which heightens the public's sense of the importance of choosing one party-candidate alternative or another will favor the alternatives equally. The circumstances which create a high-stimulus election may be expected to create simultaneously a strong differential in the attractiveness of the vote alternatives" (Campbell et al. 1966, 44). One party, in nearly all cases, holds some advantage in a presidential election. In one election, the Republican presidential candidate might have personal qualities strongly admired by the public. In another, the most important issue may cut in favor of the Democrats. Whatever the source of the advantage, our national politics are competitive enough and presidential campaign short-term forces are strong enough (witness their effects on turnout) that a short-term or campaign advantage is generally decisive. The party holding the advantage is in a position not only to hold on to its own partisans but also to attract a disproportionate share of the independent vote and a healthy number of defectors from the opposition party. This not only results in the election of the advantaged party's presidential candidate but provides many of the party's congressional candidates with the extra boost they need to win their election or reelection.

The second effect of a presidential surge election is the stimulation of turnout. Campbell observed that "the general increase in the motivation to vote in such an election will . . . bring a surge of peripheral voters to the poll" (Campbell et al. 1966, 43). The mobilization of peripheral voters is significant both in numbers and in its political ramifications. In terms of numbers, roughly one-quarter of all presidential voters are peripheral voters.[5] These peripheral voters are important because they differ from core voters in a way that augments the advantage of the president's party. The politically important difference between peripheral and core voters is that peripheral voters are more susceptible to being influenced by the current campaign. Because of their greater interest in politics, core voters are likely to have strong commitments that outweigh the events of a particular campaign. Peripheral voters are more changeable or fluid. They lack a sustaining interest in politics and are less likely to have firmly rooted partisan attachments. Less stands in the way of the peripheral responding to just the events of the current campaign. Since these short-term forces generally determine the winner of the presidential contest, peripheral voters generally vote for the winning presidential candidate's party. If it is a good year for the Democrats, peripheral voters flock to the Democratic column. Conversely, if the Republicans are running strongly, peripheral voters flock to the Republicans. Since these short-term forces generally determine the winner of the presidential contest, peripheral voters generally vote for the winning presidential candidate's party. Given the intermittent nature of the peripherals' turnout, their vote could be thought of as a "bonus" vote for the president's party.

The advantages enjoyed by the congressional candidates of the president's party in presidential elections disappear or are at least greatly diluted in the following midterm election. First, as a low-stimulus election, the midterm campaign has less impact on the voter. Second, whereas the campaign information of the presidential election was, virtually by definition, advantageous to the winning party, this is not necessarily true for the president's party in the midterm campaign. A party must achieve some measure of popularity in order to win the presidency. In the midterm election that party may or may not be popular. Third, just as the turnout surge of the peripheral voters in the presidential election had not been neutral between the parties, the turnout decline in the midterm is also not neutral in its consequence. The president's congressional candidates in the midterm lose the "bonus" support that they had received from the peripheral voters mobilized in the prior presidential election. Without a high-stimulus campaign to pull them into the process, peripheral voters simply lack the motivation to turn out. They return to their prior inactive status. Since they had disproportionately supported the president's party in the presidential election, their absence in the midterm election is not neutral in its consequence. It is at the expense of the congressional candidates of the president's party. For some of these candidates the advantages of the presidential surge election were critical to their election. Without these advantages at the midterm election, some fail to win reelection.

Perhaps the best single summary of surge and decline comes from Angus Campbell himself:

In the relatively stimulating circumstances of a presidential election the turnout is high. . . . (R)egular voters whose intrinsic political interest is high enough to take them to the polls even under less stimulating conditions are joined by marginal voters who are less concerned with politics but may be activated if the stakes seem high. Ordinarily one of the two candidates standing for the presidency will be benefited by the political circumstances of the moment more clearly than the other, either because of embarrassments of the party in power, the personal

Figure 1.1. The Theory of Surge and Decline's Sequence

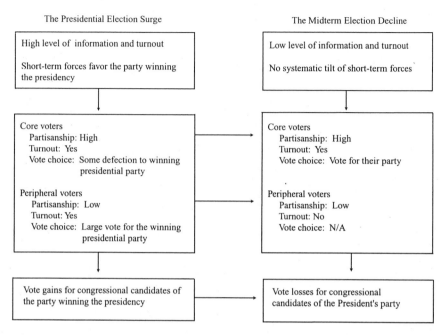

qualities of the candidates, domestic or international conditions, or for other reasons. The advantaged candidate will draw to him the votes of a majority of the marginal voters, who have relatively little party attachment and are responsive to such short-term influences. He will also profit from some defections by regular voters from the opposition party who are sufficiently tempted to break away from their usual party vote at least temporarily. In moving toward the advantaged candidate both the regular and the marginal voters, especially the latter, tend to support both the candidate and his party ticket. In the off-year election which follows, two movements occur. The regular voters who moved across party lines to support a presidential candidate they preferred are likely to move back to their usual party vote when that candidate is no longer on the ticket. The marginal voters who had given the winning candidate a majority of their votes in the presidential election do not vote in the election which follows. Both of these movements hurt the party of the candidate who benefited from the votes of the two groups in the presidential election. The loss of congressional seats is the result (1964, 750-51).

The essential elements of the theory of surge and decline are also sorted out in the diagram in figure 1.1. In the presidential election surge, both core and peripheral voters turn out and are pulled in the direction of the president's party. In the midterm election's decline, straying core voters return to their party and peripheral voters sit out the election.

Coattails and Midterms

The theory of surge and decline falls into the general category of theories that trace midterm losses to the prior presidential election. Surge and decline was not the first theory to do this. Before the development of the surge and decline theory, midterm seat losses for the president's party were explained by a less-sophisticated theory which accounted for midterm losses by the removal of presidential coattails.

The presidential coattail explanation of midterm losses might be regarded as a corollary to what became known throughout the Roosevelt era as Schorenstein's Law. Harold Lavine of *Newsweek* recounted the origins of this law: "the late Hyman Schorenstein, a leading Democratic politico in Brooklyn, propounded the law one afternoon when a young lawyer running for the New York State Assembly visited him to complain that 'the organization ain't doing anything for me.'

> 'Son,' said Hymie, 'did you ever watch a ferryboat coming into a slip?'
> 'Yes,' said the young lawyer.
> 'Son, did you notice how, as the ferryboat enters the slip, it drags in with it all sorts of debris, bits of wood, apple cores, banana peels?'
> 'Yes.'
> 'Son,' said Schorenstein, 'stop worrying. President Franklin D. Roosevelt is our ferryboat'" (Lavine 1956, 31-32).

Following along with Schorenstein's story, we might ask what happens when the ferryboat leaves the slip?

The basic thrust of the coattail (or ferryboat) explanation of midterms can be found in the work of Louis Bean (1948, 1950). According to Bean:

> The unanswered theological question of the Middle Ages: "How many angels can dance on the point of a needle?" has its counterpart in political discussion today: "How many Congressmen can ride into office on the President's coattail?" But this question we can answer definitely as a result of the discovery that the political tide is a duality. . . . The key lies in the fact that congressional elections in midterm are not strictly comparable with congressional elections in the more exciting presidential years. They must be studied separately. The congressional elections of 1928, 1932, 1940, and 1944 were part of presidential campaigns. They were influenced by the same national issues, personalities, and strategies that were the chief concern of both major parties in their efforts to elect their presidential candidates. In the mid-term elections, 1930, 1934, 1938, 1942, 1946, the congressional results were shaped by entirely different factors, largely local in character and lacking the nationwide interest that prevails in presidential elections. . . . About 26 to 30 Congressmen thus appear to have ridden into office on the President's coattail in 1932, 1936, 1940, and 1944. It may also be said that about as many Democratic congressional candidates were defeated in each of the mid-term

elections of 1930, 1934, 1938, and 1942 because they lacked presidential support (1948, 31-32).

The coattails theory is illustrated in figure 1.2 by consideration of a hypothetical congressional candidate of the president's party and the sources of his vote in a presidential and midterm election. In both the presidential and midterm elections the candidate receives many votes on the basis of party identification or issues or personal appeal or any of a variety of other factors. But in the presidential election the candidate receives some additional support from coattail voters making the difference between winning the presidential and losing the midterm election.

Bean's analysis of presidential coattails and their aftermath in midterm congressional elections foreshadowed the theory of surge and decline in several respects. Like surge and decline, Bean's coattail explanation distinguishes between congressional elections held in "the more exciting presidential years" and those held in midterm years. The former are part of the presidential campaign. The latter are "largely local in character." Like surge and decline, congressional candidates of the president's party benefit from running in the presidential election but lose their advantage when running in the next midterm. The crucial element of both theories is the premise that short-term forces in presidential elections consistently favor the winning president's party. These short-term forces, whether they be transmitted through the coattails of the president or otherwise, and whether amplified in some manner or not, sweep congressional candidates of the president's party into office in presidential elections and recede in the following midterm leaving these congressional candidates vulnerable to defeat. Like surge and decline, the coattails theory accounts for variation in midterm seat losses by the variation in the degree to which short-term forces in the presidential year favor the president's party. Midterm losses attributable to the withdrawal of coattails should be proportionate to the presidential election year gains attributable to the presence of coattails.

The coattail explanation of midterm seat losses is, of course, not identical to the theory of surge and decline. It can be distinguished on at least three grounds. First, the coattail explanation is silent about individual voting behavior. It does not explicitly explain how the behavior of individual voters produces the aggregate pattern of seat changes. Unlike surge and decline, the coattails theory does not identify which voters in the electorate provide and subsequently withdraw coattail support for congressional candidates of the president's party. The most we may surmise is that a more fully developed coattail explanation might look for coattail support from voters who otherwise would not have voted for the

Figure 1.2. The Presidential Coattail Explanation of Midterm Seat Losses

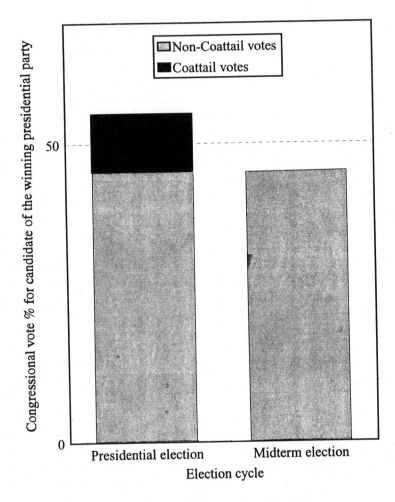

president's party, most probably independents and weak identifiers with the opposing party. As to the possible motivation of these coattail voters, apparently it is the converse of "guilt by association." Congressional candidates are given credit for being associated with an appealing presidential candidate. Voters who know little else about congressional candidates may judge them by the "company they keep."

Second, the coattail explanation, when contrasted with surge and decline, appears to focus more narrowly on the presidential candidates and their issues to account for the systematic tilt of presidential elections in favor of the winning president's party. Surge and decline includes these forces clearly linked with the presidential candidates' campaigns but also acknowledges all other short-term forces that may jointly benefit both the presidential candidate and those below him on the ticket.[6]

Third, the two theories differ in the role of turnout in electoral change. Whereas surge and decline partly explains the swing away from the president's party at the midterm by the turnout decline, the decline of turnout in midterms is not an element of the coattail explanation.

The Revised Theory of Surge and Decline

As clever and interesting as the theory of surge and decline is and as compelling as its reasoning appears, in this book I argue that in several ways the original theory is in error and incomplete, although its basic argument linking presidential election short-term forces and the pattern of midterm seat losses is well taken. Rather than accepting the original theory in its entirety, I argue that, using the framework of the original theory, a revised theory of surge and decline can be constructed and that this revised theory is strongly supported by the available evidence.

How does the revised theory of surge and decline compare to the original? First, like the original theory, the revised theory claims that the seeds of presidential midterm losses are sown in the prior presidential election. Unlike the original theory, the revised theory explicitly acknowledges that the extent of midterm losses is partially a function of political circumstances at the midterm itself, as well as an inverse function of the conditions favoring the president's party in the prior presidential election.

Second, as in the original theory, the difference in turnout between presidential and midterm elections plays a major role in the revised version. The claim that peripheral voters mobilized for the presidential election benefit the winning presidential candidate's party is reasserted in the revised theory. However, the original and revised theories make very different claims about who the peripheral voters are and why they contribute to the presidential election surge favoring the winning presidential candidate's party.

One point should be made clear from the outset: although the focus of the argument is unquestionably national and presidential in character, it in no way denies the crucial importance of local politics in congressional elections. Incumbency; campaign spending by congressional candidates; candidates' backgrounds, experience, issue positions, or personal traits; the partisan complexion of the district; and various other district political conditions undoubtedly weigh heavily in the vote. Local politics have always been important in congressional races and have probably never been more important than they are today. Despite the unquestionable importance of local politics, there are several reasons to examine the impact of national politics on congressional elections. First, although local politics are very important, national politics also have been and remain consequential in congressional elections. Voters respond to national politics, and there is no greater national political phenomenon than the election of the president. Second, while local political forces may be more important than national political forces in cross-sectional or static examinations of congressional elections, national politics may take on added importance in explaining electoral *change*. Many local factors, such as incumbency and the partisanship of the district, are usually unchanged from one election to the next and therefore are of limited use in explaining change. Finally, the examination of national political forces is especially important in examining *national* electoral change. Athough one party may win a net national advantage from local or district forces tilting its way in a particular election, in most cases shifts in party advantages at the local level "cancel out" across the country. In some areas local politics may tilt toward the Democrats but in other areas they may tilt toward the Republicans. Systematic national shifts in the parties' electoral fortunes may more likely result from evaluations of the presidential campaign and of the presidency itself, both of which provide an explicitly national political focus.

The Organization of the Book

This book is divided into two parts. The first explores existing midterm theories. It examines the foundations of and evidence pertaining to both the theory of surge and decline and the theory of the midterm referenda. Part 1 begins, in chapter 2, with a detailed discussion of the premises upon which the theory of surge and decline is based. This discussion examines much of the intellectual groundwork for surge and decline, groundwork provided by Philip Converse's work on the impact of political information storage and processing on voting behavior and by his work on the concept of the "normal vote." It also examines premises regarding the nature and effects of short-term forces in presidential and midterm elections.

Chapter 3 raises a number of specific hypotheses generated by, or at least commonly attributed to, the theory of surge and decline. The findings of pertinent prior research as well as new evidence are considered and evaluated for each individual hypothesis and, in the light of these findings, the status of the overall theory is then assessed.

Chapter 4 reviews various versions of the referenda theory of midterm elections, beginning with Edward Tufte's first statement of the referenda theory. Based on his analysis of the midterm vote, Tufte concluded that "the midterm is neither a mystery nor an automatic swing of the pendulum; the midterm vote is a referendum" (1975, 826). In the intervening years a number of scholars have elaborated, refined, or modified the referenda model. What all of these variations have in common is that they, in Tufte's words, "explain the *magnitude of the national midterm loss* by the President's party" (p. 813) in terms of political evaluations made by voters in the midterm itself, rather than in the prior presidential election. Each version of the referenda theory is critically analyzed and in several cases additional data are analyzed to evaluate the theory.

Part 2 considers the revised theory of surge and decline. The first of these chapters, chapter 5, sets forth the structure of the theory and identifies where the original and revised theories part company. The next four chapters of part 2 consider the evidence.

Chapter 6 examines the revised theory of surge and decline with national time-series data. National election returns, both the national congressional vote as well as seats won by the parties, since 1900 are examined to see how well the revised theory accounts for variation in presidential election gains for the president's party as well as midterm election losses. These data are also examined to determine how the cycles of surge and decline may have changed over the course of this century. This data analysis is then coupled with a discussion of two election cycles, 1952-54 and 1972-74. The 1952-54 elections are examined to demonstrate how the theory explains midterm losses in fairly typical election years. The 1972-74 pair of elections are discussed to illustrate occasional problems with detecting both surge and decline effects.

Chapter 7 brings the analysis down one step to a less aggregated level—the level of the congressional district. The presidential election year benefits to the president's party should be greatest in districts in which short-term forces ran most strongly in the party's favor. These should also be the districts that suffer the greatest losses as the forces recede at the midterm. In addition to a statistical analysis of districts in the 1976-78 and 1984-86 election years, two case studies are presented to illustrate the impact of surge and decline.

In chapter 8, the analysis drops a final notch to that of the individual voter. Several hypotheses of the revised theory of surge and decline about differences in the composition and behavior of presidential and midterm electorates are tested.

Evidence of surge and decline in elections to other offices is examined in chapter 9. I examine both state legislative and U.S. Senate elections for signs of surge and decline effects. These findings are joined with findings in House elections to complete the case. Finally, chapter 9 returns to the subject, raised in chapter 6, of the extent to which surge and decline effects are weaker now than at their historical levels. Several possible explanations for the weakening of surge and decline are explored.

In the concluding chapter, chapter 10, several implications of the surge and decline cycle are raised. I explore how it affects the interpretations of congressional election results, the evaluations of the competence and quality of the American voter, the functioning of elections as instruments for popular control of the government, the strength of political parties, the roll-call voting of congressmen, and the relationship between the president and Congress. Finally, I discuss the possible consequences of reforming the constitutional system to eliminate the midterm election and thereby eliminating the midterm decline for the president's party.

2

The Premises of
Surge and Decline

*The presidential election is the pulse of American politics.
The vote for state governors, for congressmen, local officers is
regularly higher in presidential than in "off" years.*
—E.E. Schattschneider (1942:150)

Like any theory, the theory of surge and decline is based upon certain premises. This chapter explores those premises, the foundation of surge and decline. Three elements of this foundation will be examined: the theory of how campaign information affects the vote choice; the premise that strong presidential short-term forces systematically favor the party winning the presidency; and the premise that support for the winning presidential candidate translates into support for his party's congressional candidates.

The Flow of Political Information

The theory of surge and decline is grounded to a large extent in a theory of political information. Accompanying surges and declines in turnout are surges and declines in political information or "short-term forces," which may affect the political behavior of both knowledgeable and not-so-knowledgeable citizens. A theory of political information suggests the nature of the effects of this surge and decline in political information: who will be affected and in what ways? Philip Converse's (1966a) theory of the effects of campaign information in "Information Flow and the Stability of Partisan Attitudes" provided the specific information processing theory underlying the argument of surge and decline.

Converse's theory relates the voters' past accumulation of information to their exposure and response to current campaign information. This information theory was adopted by Campbell and applied to the congressional election context. The theory of surge and decline logically followed. To appreciate the premises of surge and decline, we should examine this undergirding theory of information effects.

Before presenting Converse's political information theory, a few matters of definition must be addressed. We ought to be clear in what is meant generally by *information* and more particularly by *stored* or *accumulated* information. From the voter's or information receiver's standpoint, political information is any observation that is thought to be credible and relevant to evaluating the candidates and parties. It need not be accurate or meet any test of objective relevance. All political information, of course, is not of equal weight. The weight of a piece of information depends on the voter's assessment of both its credibility and relevance. Information that is stored or accumulated consists of the residual impressions left by past observations thought credible and relevant by the voter. Stored information need not be recalled in detail by the voter for it to have an effect on present deliberations. However, it would be fair to assume some discounting of stored information. Older information is likely to be of diminished importance in a voter's deliberations than comparable but recently received information.

Converse's theory begins with a recognition of the variable level of stored information in the electorate and then deduces the consequences of these different levels of stored information for the stability of partisan attitudes and the vote. Obviously, voters vary a good bit in the extent and depth of their political history. Some have a very rich history of political experience. Over a series of elections they have accumulated a substantial number of reflections and observations about politics and the parties. From this background, voters are likely to have formed definite political opinions and identifications. The weight of their history serves to anchor opinions quite firmly. Their partisan predispositions have been formed from and, in normal political times, have been reinforced by a variety of observations. Thus they have many reasons to feel quite confident that their partisan attitudes are justified and are not easily persuaded to stray from these predispositions.

At the other extreme are voters with little accumulated political information. Either because of their youth or because of simple inattentiveness to politics, they have few impressions about political events and actors. Their political background is at best sketchy. Whatever political opinions or identifications they have formed, and they may not have formed many, are likely to be lightly held or easily changed. They are prime candidates to be "floating voters." Unlike their knowledgeable counterparts, the relatively uninformed have opinions that are not deeply rooted in a wealth of accumulated political observations. These voters feel relatively unconstrained by whatever partisan predispositions they may have formed and, with only slight encouragement, may be persuaded to stray from these partisan leanings.[1]

Corresponding to the differences in the accumulation of prior political information are differences in the level of exposure to or absorption of current campaign information. At one extreme are the political junkies. They pay close attention to politics. They soak in as much information about the candidates and campaign as possible. At the other extreme are voters nearly oblivious to the campaign. They miss a good deal of what goes on. Even in very intense campaigns they are likely to be aware of only a small fraction of the available information. Their intake of current information is weak.

The amounts of stored information and currently processed information are related. People who are wealthy in their accumulation of *past* information tend to be also well attuned to *current* information. Likewise those generally having a poor or sparse political background are likely to remain ignorant or detached from current political events. The link between previously stored and currently processed information levels is the individual's enduring level of political involvement. This linkage is depicted in figure 2.1. Any voter motivated enough to have paid attention to past politics and campaigns is quite likely to pay a good bit of attention to current political developments. Conversely, there is little reason to suppose that someone who neglected or avoided politics in the past will do any differently in the present. In short, the already knowledgeable are likely to learn more than those who are not so knowledgeable.

What is the net effect of the information status of voters on the stability of their partisan attitudes and the likelihood of their straying from their party? Because the politically involved have amassed a good bit of prior information and as a result have developed stronger attachments to a party, their party loyalties are likely to remain strong. On the other hand, these well-informed voters are quite receptive to the information flow of the present and the current information climate may be at odds with their prior partisan predispositions. Converse's theory argues that though these voters are indeed more exposed to possibly destabilizing short-term or current information, usually the stored mass of past information sufficiently anchors their partisan opinions so they can withstand the force of the current campaign's information flow. Converse argues that the partisan opinions of voters with a good deal of stored information are stable in most campaigns. The ratio of newly acquired information to old information is fairly low for these voters even in heated campaigns generating a heavy flow of information to the electorate. Also contributing to the stability of these partisan attitudes is partisan bias in the perception and evaluation of newly acquired information. Since these very knowledgeable voters are likely to have reached definite conclusions about politics and the parties, if for no other reason than to organize the accumulated observations, new information is likely to be perceived from

Figure 2.1. Suspected Relationship of Political Involvement and
Information Storage and Acquisition

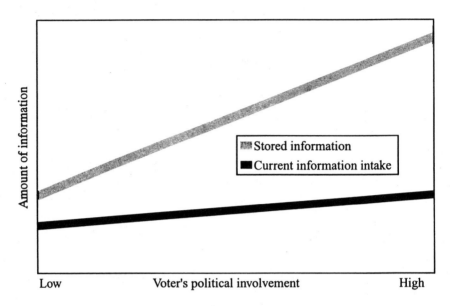

Source: Constructed by the author from Converse (1966a)

a partisan vantage point and is therefore more likely to be agreeable with
existing partisan opinions.

At the other end of the spectrum there is instability. Although the less
politically motivated are likely to be less cognizant of current campaign
information than those more politically attuned, the information that gets
through to these voters is likely to make more of a difference to their
opinions. The ratio of new to stored information, especially in more
intense campaigns, is higher for these voters than it is for the more
politically alert voters. Since their partisan opinions are not constrained
by a great mass of stored experience, they are more easily moved by
current observation. Of course, as Converse notes, in the extreme case of
those entirely ignorant of current politics one expects perfect stability
rather than instability. In this case the ratio of new to stored information is
zero, regardless of how little (nonzero) stored information the voter
possesses. Although this voter's partisan attitudes may be easily swayed,
they will remain undisturbed unless the voter becomes aware of at least
some new piece of information that would undermine them.

To this point, the description of Converse's theory of political information has focused exclusively on the voter and his or her political
involvement. In addition to recognizing the importance of voter motiva-

tion, Converse also acknowledged the considerable impact of the campaign on the voters' acquisition of new information. In some elections, information about the candidates and issues is in short supply. It is not that voters could not learn a good deal about these candidates and issues. They could. But to acquire much new information in these elections requires greater effort from the voters. There is only a weak flow of information in this "low-stimulus" type of election. With the candidates' campaigns and the media in low gear, voters must pay close attention to obtain new information. At the other extreme are "high-stimulus" elections. With candidates running aggressive and well-financed campaigns and the media continually and extensively reporting on the candidates and (at least occasionally) their positions, new information is easily accessible to the voters. Even the least politically minded are bound to hear or read something about the candidates and issues in these elections.

The impact of high- versus low-stimulus elections on partisan loyalties can be easily deduced. High-stimulus elections with their strong flow of information are more likely to pull people away from their partisan predispositions. The pulling power of high-stimulus elections is especially strong among weakly motivated voters, given their meager store of past information and potential volatility of partisan attitudes. Low-stimulus elections leave preexisting party loyalties undisturbed. Voters follow through with their standing decision to vote for the candidates of one party over those of the other party.

Put in terms of presidential year and midterm elections, the theory suggests that partisan loyalties should be somewhat greater in midterm elections. Presidential elections are high-stimulus elections. Voters confront a barrage of information that may divert them from their standing partisan decision. Midterm elections, by contrast, are low-stimulus elections. Without the excitement generated by a presidential contest, the information flow is weak, leaving most voters to act on their standing partisan commitments.

In proposing his theory of information flow and accumulation. Converse drew on a Newtonian metaphor, likening information levels to the concept of mass. Like physical mass, information mass was supposed to conform to certain laws. Partisan predispositions supported by a great mass of information had an inertia that could only be upset by the introduction of a considerable mass of new and contrary information. Partisan predispositions supported by a smaller mass of information could be more easily pushed. A mass of new information that might be insufficient to move predispositions in the former case might well be sufficient to make a difference in the later instance.

Figure 2.2 depicts the mass analogy. Four situations reflecting the combinations of two types of voters in two types of elections are illus-

Figure 2.2. The Mass of Stored and Acquired Information by Election Stimulus and Voter Interest

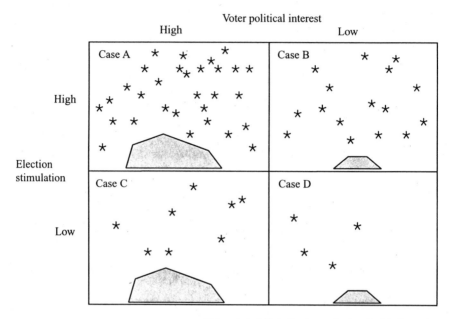

Note: Asterisks indicate newly acquired information and the shaded areas indicate stored information.

trated. The mounds represent the mass of stored information and the falling particles represent newly acquired information. For purposes of illustration we will assume that the new information acquired in each instance is not necessarily consistent with the preexisting store of information and the partisanship that it supports. Information consistent with partisan bias would in each case produce perfect stability regardless of the mix of stored and newly acquired information. Instability of partisan attitudes and the probability of partisan defection is reflected in the particles' ability to shift the center of gravity of the preexisting mass. Case B, a voter with a low level of political involvement and stored information in a high-stimulus election, is likely to defect. Cases A and D are mixed in that the ratio of new to old information is not lopsided. In situation A, the high-stimulus election's unsettling effect is set in some perspective by the voter's considerable political background. Situation D is the converse of this. While the poor background of the voter leaves him or her open to persuasion, there is little new information to cause a shift. The final situation, C, is one in which stability and partisan loyalty should be most evident. Neither the voter's background nor the information flow of the campaign make partisan defection very likely.

The basic structure of Converse's theory of political information may be displayed in a causal model. Such a model was constructed from his argument and is presented in figure 2.3. The hypothesized effects of both of the exogenous variables, the nature of the election (presidential or midterm) and the voter's level of political involvement, can be traced through the model. As previously stated, the effect of political involvement is primarily stabilizing. Political involvement brings one into greater contact with possibly disrupting new information, but it also provides a firm foundation for existing partisan attitudes, intensifies partisan commitments, and increases the perceptual and evaluative screen to protect partisan attitudes from dissonant new information. Also as has been stated, presidential elections generally have a destabilizing effect. With a greater flow of information in a presidential campaign, voters are likely to confront new information that may deflect them from their standing partisan decision.

Although not a major consideration in Converse's theory of political information, turnout is certainly a major consideration in Campbell's theory of surge and decline and can be placed within the information flow model to clarify the link between the two theories. As the model suggests, turnout and the likelihood of partisan defection are linked. The links are not a result of one causing the other, directly or indirectly, but of both being influenced by common causes.

How are turnout and partisan defection related? First, both are influenced by the voter's level of political involvement. Politically motivated voters turn out more regularly than other voters and also have enough stored information to secure their partisan attitudes and sustain their partisan loyalties, even though they are more open to new and possibly disruptive information. Second, the nature of the campaign—the level of office at stake and the volume of information flow—influences both turnout and partisan defection rates. The drawing power of presidential campaigns is obvious. Equally clear is the fact that presidential campaigns generate a tremendous amount of new information. To the extent that this new information conflicts with existing predispositions, it is likely to cause a great number of partisan defections. Moreover, to the extent that voters identify candidates with their parties, the same information that may stimulate a partisan defection at the presidential level of balloting may also cause a partisan defection at the congressional level.

Although both the nature of the election and the level of a voter's political involvement are thought to be potent causes of individual decisions to turn out, the nature of the election is considered to be the more important in affecting the variability of turnout in the aggregate. Political involvement is considered a long-term and stable disposition. An appetite for politics is not gained or lost overnight, so even with some

Figure 2.3. A Causal Model of "Information Flow and the Stability of Partisan Attitudes"

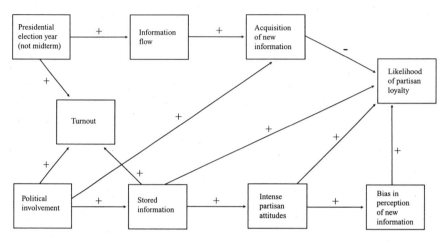

Source: Constructed by the author from Converse 1966a.

change in individual political involvement, there is little reason to suppose that these changes are substantial or systematic. As such, it is probable that public political involvement is nearly constant and thus could not contribute to changes in aggregate turnout or aggregate levels of partisan defection. The nature of the election, then, is what accounts for most of the connection between turnout and partisan defection observed in the aggregate. What this also means is that the peripheral voters attracted to the polls by a high-stimulus election are those who lacked enough political involvement to get to the polls on their own. As already noted, these are the voters whose partisan attitudes and loyalty are least stable, especially in a high-stimulus election.

The Short-term Force Advantage

The theory of political information proposed by Converse explains why partisan defections are more likely to be found in presidential elections than in midterms. It does not, however, account for why congressional candidates of the winning president's party necessarily are the beneficiaries of these defections. Why does the volatility of a presidential election benefit the president's party?

The direction and volume of short-term forces. The answer lies in the systematic tilt of short-term forces in presidential elections. A principal premise of surge and decline is that the direction of short-term forces, the general evaluations made of the candidates and their issue positions, favors the winning presidential candidate and, by association, his party. This is true virtually by definition. It is almost impossible for a presidential candidate to win election without the net effect of these short-term forces being favorable. There are only three possible circumstances under which a presidential candidate can win the election. The first two of these circumstances are consistent with the premise that short-term forces favor the winning presidential candidate in the presidential election, as expected by surge and decline. The third circumstance, however, is more problematic but, as I shall argue, does not pose a serious threat to the theory's premise.

In the first circumstance, the minority party's presidential candidate can win if and only if short-term forces are in his favor. Even then, he will win only if short-term forces are sufficiently in his favor to overcome his party's minority status. If a minority party's candidate faces short-term forces either against his candidacy or only very mildly in his favor, he may be unable to surmount his party's standing disadvantage.

In the second circumstance, the majority party's presidential candidate can win if the short-term forces are in his favor, even if only barely. It is important to note that it is even possible for the majority party's presidential candidate to win by less than the majority party's normal vote and still enjoy short-term forces in his favor. It is sometimes wrongly assumed that a majority party vote falling short of its normal vote indicates that short-term forces favor the minority party. This is not necessarily the case.[2] A majority party vote below its normal vote indicates only that short-term forces must be less positive for the majority party than are the long-term forces. The theory, however, does not require that the winning presidential party enjoy short-term forces that are more positive than long-term forces (the normal partisan vote). It requires only that short-term forces favor, in an absolute sense, the winning presidential candidate's party.[3]

In the third circumstance, the majority party candidate also can win if short-term forces are against him, so long as those forces are insufficient to overcome the party's majority status. While the first two circumstances of a presidential election are perfectly consistent with the theory's premise that short-term forces favor the winning presidential party, this third possible circumstance is not. The defense of the theory's premise that short-term forces favor the winning presidential candidate rests on the empirical evidence. While it is logically possible for a president to be elected with short-term forces running against him, is there any real chance of this logical possibility? The empirical evidence suggests that this is extremely unlikely—short-term forces very strongly influence the vote choice and, therefore, it is nearly impossible to assemble a majority vote without these short-term considerations behind a candidate.

The alternative to short-term influences on the vote are long-term influences, specifically partisanship. While the long-term influence of partisanship is unquestionably the strongest single influence on the individual vote choice, there are two reasons why partisanship is not determinative of presidential elections and was not even before the advent of partisan dealignment. First, the parties in the aggregate have been fairly competitive. The majority party usually holds a bare majority of popular support. For example, Converse's estimate of the normal partisan vote in the early 1960s, when Democrats appeared relatively strong, was a 54 percent Democratic presidential vote. If the estimated magnitude of this long-term advantage is accurate, much of the individual level impact of partisanship cancels itself out in the aggregate. If dyed-in-the-wool Democrats just barely outnumber dyed-in-the-wool Republicans, partisanship may be the strongest influence on the individual vote choice without being decisive to election outcomes. The impact of long-term forces may not be so overwhelming as to preclude short-term forces from regularly deciding presidential contests.[4]

Second, there is evidence to suggest that the effects of partisanship are largely mediated by short-term forces, as illustrated in figure 2.4. That is, partisanship more commonly influences the vote choice indirectly by shaping opinions about the presidential candidates' personal qualifications and policy positions than by triggering an automatic, "knee-jerk" direct party vote. Most comprehensive studies of the presidential vote choice find partisan effects on the vote to be substantially mediated. Even *The American Voter* study, commonly characterized as a study identifying partisanship to be of paramount importance in the presidential vote choice, argued that the effects of partisanship on the vote were primarily of an indirect nature through a group of six partisan attitudes that comprised short-term evaluations (Campbell et al., 1960, 137).[5] More recent and more methodologically sophisticated examinations of the presidential vote choice (Declercq, Hurley, and Luttbeg 1975; Pomper 1975, 202; Markus and Converse 1979, 1069; and Fiorina 1981) found a substantial portion of partisanship effects to be indirect. Moreover, the indirect nature of these effects are undoubtedly understated given the considerable difficulty of accurately measuring the enormous range of possible voter opinions about various issues and the variety of possible reactions to the many personal qualities of the candidates.[6]

The tremendous impact of short-term forces on the vote, even if reflecting the indirect influence of partisanship, is perhaps best demonstrated by Kelley and Mirer's "Voter's Decision Rule" (1974; see also Kelley 1983). Using responses to open-ended questions about the voter's

Figure 2.4. The Effects of Long-term and Short-term Forces on the
Presidential Vote

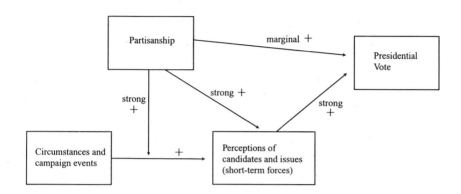

likes and dislikes about the candidates and parties (evaluations of short-
term forces) and the respondent's party identification, only in the few
cases in which the open-ended responses were indeterminant, the
Voter's Decision Rule proved extremely accurate in predicting the vote
choice (mean = 88 percent correct) (Kelley and Mirer 1974, 575-76). Given
that this index so accurately predicts the vote of individual voters and was
based almost exclusively on short-term forces, we might well expect that
short-term forces always favored the winning presidential candidate.

What does the evidence show? Table 2.1 presents the index of short-
term forces for each presidential election from 1952 to 1988. This index,
similar to the Voter's Decision Rule, is calculated from responses to the
open-ended questions regarding what voters like and dislike about the
presidential candidates.[7] As one might expect, when the margin of victory allows breathing room (as it has in all recent elections except the 1960
dead-heat), the evidence indicates that short-term forces consistently
favor the winning presidential candidate. Put differently, candidates
only win the presidency if short-term forces are in their favor. The
consistently favorable disposition of short-term forces for the president's
party is also indicated by an alternative measure of short-term forces, the
National Election Studies (NES) "thermometer" scores for the presidential candidates. Since the measures were adopted in 1968, respondents
have felt consistently warmer, on average, toward the candidate who
went on to win the presidency (Born 1990, table 4).

The evidence regarding the 1960 election, however, is inconclusive.
According to the mean short-term evaluations index, Nixon appears to
have lost to Kennedy despite short-term forces tipping slightly in the
Republican's favor. In this one instance, long-term forces may have
provided the winning presidential candidate with his slim margin of

Table 2.1. The Prevailing Short-Term Forces as Measured by the Mean of the Candidate Likes and Dislikes Index, 1952-1988

Election year	Winning presidential two-party vote %	Mean likes/dislikes candidate index		Short-term forces favored winning party?
		All respondents	Reported voters	
1952	55.4 R	.41 R	.58 R	Yes
1956	57.8 R	1.17 R	1.19 R	Yes
1960	50.1 D	.29 R	.34 R	No?
1964	61.3 D	1.67 D	1.50 D	Yes
1968	50.4 R	.17 R	.24 R	Yes
1972	61.8 R	1.07 R	1.16 R	Yes
1976	51.1 D	.15 D	.04 D	Yes
1980	55.3 R	.18 R	.43 R	Yes
1984	59.2 R	.04 R	.22 R	Yes
1988	53.9 R	.15 R	.29 R	Yes

NOTE: R indicates Republicans and D indicates Democrats. The likes/dislikes index is based on a count of responses to open-ended questions about the candidates. The index = ([like Dem + dislike Rep] - [like Rep + dislike Dem]). Respondents who offered no answers to any of the open-ended questions were dropped from the calculations. To minimize bias, respondents were weighted to the known national division of the two-party presidential vote.

victory. Given that this election is the closest presidential race on record and is one of only four elections since 1860 to be decided by a margin of less than two percentage points (51 percent to 49 percent), it is quite possible that 1960 was a rare exception to the rule of short-term forces being decisive.

However, even here, there is room to doubt that the short-term forces of 1960 actually favored Nixon. Aside from possible sampling and measurement error, doubts are raised by the fact that the median short-term evaluations were perfectly neutral. Moreover, if open-ended responses to party-image questions are also counted as short-term evaluations, short-term forces appear slightly to Kennedy's advantage. Perhaps most important is the fact that the open-ended questions used in computing the index are from a preelection survey that in some cases was conducted almost two months before election day, when more respondents strongly favored Nixon.[8] Thus, while it is difficult to determine which candidate was favored by short-term forces in an election decided by such a narrow margin, we can safely say one thing: whoever was favored was at most only slightly favored, and any surge or decline effects should be commensurately very slight (recall that the Democrats lost a mere four seats in the

1962 midterm following the 1960 dead-heat). Notwithstanding the complicated case of 1960, the evidence supports the theory's premise that short-term forces are to the winning presidential party's advantage.

While the question of whether short-term forces favor the winning presidential candidate in extremely close races remains open to question, the fact that the volume of short-term forces is greater in presidential than in midterm campaigns is beyond question. Presidential campaigns are the center-stage (some might say center-ring) events of American politics. Nothing commands the attention of voters like a presidential election. Nothing comes even close. As the single highest office in the nation and the only nationally elected official of the government, the election of the president is without a doubt, in the terminology of surge and decline, a "high-stimulus" election.

Because of the heavy information flow and turnout surge in presidential elections, the systematically advantageous nature of short-term forces for the winning presidential party is made all the more important. The heavy information flow of presidential elections amplifies whatever partisan advantage of short-term forces the winning presidential party enjoys. The issues and images of a campaign have a much more substantial impact when the volume of the campaign is turned up. Even if short-term forces appear only slightly to the winning presidential candidate's advantage, the sheer volume of the presidential campaign, with the greater attention it attracts, amplifies that slight advantage tremendously.[9]

The increased turnout of a presidential campaign also has the effect of amplifying the short-term force advantage of the winning presidential party. As already noted, the peripheral voters who turn out in the presidential election lack a stabilizing store of information and are thus more readily impressed by the issues and images of a particular campaign.

Short-term forces and the midterm. There are two important differences in midterm elections. First, there is no systematic tilt of short-term forces in favor of or opposed to the president's party.[10] Once a candidate wins the presidency there is no reason why he necessarily becomes more or less popular by the following midterm. The issues of the midterm may work to the advantage of the in-party or its opposition. It should be clear that the theory of surge and decline does not preclude the existence of significant short-term forces in midterm elections. The congressional vote in midterms may deviate from the normal partisan vote. What the theory argues is that these deviations are not systematically to the presidential party's disadvantage. Second, whatever the tilt of short-term forces in midterms, they are not amplified by the tremendous attention that a presidential campaign receives nor by the presence of highly impressionable peripheral voters.

The Presidential and Congressional Votes

One final assumption of the surge and decline theory should be made explicit. The theory assumes a linkage between presidential and congressional voting in presidential elections. The link between the two votes is based on the common party affiliations of presidential and congressional candidates. Short-term forces favorable to a presidential candidate of a party are also generally favorable to that party's congressional candidates. These short-term forces may even include evaluations of the presidential candidate himself. In other words, a good year for the Republican party helps Republicans at the congressional level as well as the Republican heading the ticket. Of course not all Republican candidates would benefit in a generally good Republican year; local conditions may deviate substantially from the national norm. Also, the congressional candidates who do benefit are unlikely to benefit equally. Nevertheless, when short-term forces nationally are running in a party's favor, its presidential candidate should stand a very good chance of winning and more of its congressional candidates should stand a better chance than usual of being elected.

As long as parties are salient labels to voters, the assumption that candidates of the same party are subject to similar trends seems quite safe. Only a dealignment of the parties would undermine this assumption. If voter reactions to candidates take on a less partisan cast, as they well might in a period of dealignment, the consequences of surge and decline would be blunted, though still in evidence.[11]

The Ticket-Splitting question. The threat of dealignment to presidential coattails or surge effects is not merely a hypothetical matter. There is a good deal of evidence to suggest that the party system has undergone some measure of dealignment since the mid-1960s and increased levels of split-ticket voting are commonly cited as evidence of this dealignment (Wattenberg 1990). It is presumed that the casting of a presidential vote for one party and a congressional vote for the other party is evidence that voters are not drawing partisan connections between the presidential and congressional candidates. Such partisan linkages are considered an absolute necessity to the operation of surge and decline. The common presumption is that split-ticket voting shortens the coattails of successful presidential candidates.

What should be made of the presumed threat of split-ticket voting to presidential coattails or the more broadly defined presidential election surge effects? The seriousness of the split-ticket threat to surge and decline would seem to depend on the extent of ticket-splitting. Certainly no one would contend that the theory would be in jeopardy if only a few voters split their tickets. However, the evidence suggests that ticket-splitting is not an uncommon practice and has become more frequent in recent years. One common, though flawed (Miller 1955; and Feigert 1979), indirect measure of split-ticket voting is the frequency of split-election outcomes in congressional districts—districts electing a congressman from one party and awarding a plurality of its presidential votes to the candidate of the other party. According to Ornstein, Mann, and Malbin (1990, 62) the percentage of districts with split results has increased substantially in this century. In the twelve presidential elections between 1900 and 1944, an average of only one in nine districts had split results. In the seven most recent presidential elections (1964 to 1988), split results were evident in more than one out of three districts (36 percent), and in some elections split-results were nearly as common as the same party winning district majorities for both offices (e.g., 1984 = 45 percent).

Survey data produces a more accurate and direct assessment of the extent of ticket-splitting. Using NES surveys, Wattenberg (1990, 165) calculated the extent of ticket-splitting between the presidential and House votes from the 1952 to 1988.[12] From 1952 to 1964, only 12 percent to 16 percent of all voters split their tickets in voting for president and congress. Ticket-splitting rose abruptly to 26 percent in 1968. Since 1968, it has ranged between 25 percent and 34 percent (mean 27.5 percent) of those voting, about twice its earlier level. While ticket-splitting between these two offices is much greater now relative to its former level and is significant in absolute terms, we should not forget that straight-ticket voting for president and congress continues to be the norm. At the very least, two out of three voters still vote for presidential and House candidates of the same party, and even in the dealigned system, three out of four voters usually cast a straight ticket.

Do these rates of ticket-splitting seriously erode or eliminate potential presidential election coattails or surge effects? Not necessarily. That is, while split-ticket voting may signal that voters are not linking presidential and congressional candidates together in partisan terms, it does not necessarily signal this uncoupling. In Born's (1984, 62) study of presidential coattails, he cleverly demonstrates with hypothetical data that it is logically possible for both coattail effects and split-ticket voting to increase simultaneously.

The relationship of split-ticket voting to the theory of surge and decline might be clarified by examining a few hypothetical voters and the impact of short-term forces on their presidential and congressional votes. Figure 2.5 presents diagrams depicting the effects of short-term forces on the presidential and congressional vote decisions of four hypothetical voters.[13] Each scale represents the likelihood of the voter casting a vote

Figure 2.5. The Effects of Short-term Forces on the Presidential and
Congressional Votes of Four Hypothetical Voters

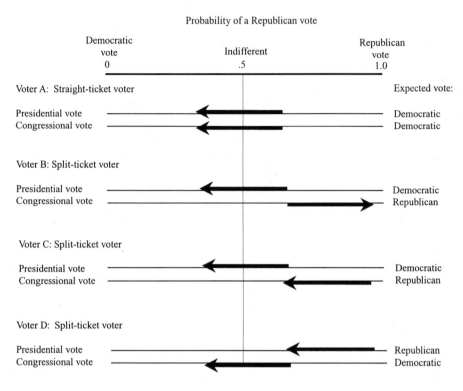

for the Republican candidate. The arrow on each scale reflects the impact
of short-term forces on the voter's deliberations. The first case, Case A, is
that of the straight-ticket voter moved by short-term forces from his initial
predisposition to vote for both the Republican presidential and congressional candidates to a straight-ticket for the Democrats. Case B is that of a
ticket-splitter. This case poses a real threat to surge and decline. The voter
in this instance is moved in one direction in his presidential vote and the
opposite direction in his congressional vote. If ticket-splitting necessarily
entailed this rupture of the forces affecting the presidential and congressional contests, it would indeed reflect a very serious threat to coattail
or surge effects. However, as the final two cases demonstrate, ticket-
splitting does not necessarily entail this break between the forces affecting the presidential vote and the forces affecting the congressional vote.

    Voters C and D are ticket-splitters whose presidential and congres-
sional votes reflect an equal partisan reaction to short-term forces. The
reason they are not straight-ticket voters is the difference in their initial
dispositions to vote for the Republican presidential and congressional

candidates. In considering both cases C and D together, we notice that even though both are ticket-splitters, the short-term forces favoring the Democratic candidates gained the Democratic party one of the two presidential votes and one of the two congressional votes over what they probably would have received without short-term forces in its favor. Split-tickets of this sort do not pose a threat to presidential surge effects. The effects of the presidential election surge may be dampened by this ticket-splitting, but this is a consequence of independent factors influencing the congressional vote rather than a breaking or even weakening of the association voters see among candidates of the same party.

Summary

In exploring the premises of surge and decline, this chapter finds the theory to rest on a firm foundation. First, it is based on a well-constructed and highly plausible theory of information effects in political campaigns. Surge and decline applies Converse's theory of information flow, linking voter knowledge and partisanship to campaign conversion effects. It applies the theory to the different circumstances of high-stimulus, high-turnout presidential election years and low-stimulus, low-turnout midterm election years. This application explains why peripheral voters, the add-on voters of the presidential electorate, might be especially open to persuasion by the short-term forces of the presidential campaign. Second, the theory's premises that short-term forces in presidential campaigns are especially strong and favor the party winning the presidency appear to be well founded. There is little question that presidential campaigns are higher visibility events than midterm campaigns. Survey evidence also indicates that short-term forces consistently favor the eventual winning presidential candidate. Third, the theory's premise that the short-term advantage for the winning presidential candidate spills over to the benefit of the party's congressional candidates also appears to be well grounded. While the rise in split-ticket voting suggests some deterioration in this relationship, the theory's expectation that congressional candidates benefit from a popular presidential candidate heading the ticket remains intact.

Of course, a theory is not necessarily true just because its premises are true. The theory of surge and decline is not the only theory that might be built on the above foundational premises. Moreover, there may well be other well-grounded premises on which to build a theory of congressional interelection change. In the next chapter, we turn to the evidence regarding the theory. How well supported is the theory itself?

3

The Propositions and Evidence of Surge and Decline

Swings away from the basic division of party loyalties in high-turnout elections tend to swing back in the low turnout elections which follow.

—Angus Campbell (1966:62)

Although carefully crafted and widely accepted, for some time the theory of surge and decline failed to generate much empirical investigation. As Cover observed, "Campbell's seminal article was not closely examined for over a decade after its original publication (1985, 607)." Even then, only parts of the theory were studied. The general lack of research into the theory is all the more remarkable given the relatively scant evidence offered in its behalf by Campbell's original article. Campbell examined evidence at only one level, that of the individual voter, and restricted that analysis to a single pair of presidential and midterm elections, 1956 and 1958.[1] Moreover, even this limited analysis did not at all points support the theory.[2]

This initial lack of empirical research should not suggest that the theory is not open to testing or is even difficult to test. In the last few years a number of hypotheses have been extracted from the theory and set against available evidence. The purpose of this chapter is to identify the specific hypotheses drawn from surge and decline and to consider the evidence and analysis offered as tests of these propositions.

The various hypotheses or propositions can be grouped into three sets corresponding to three levels of analysis—the national level, the congressional district level, and the individual citizen level. Each proposition is not equally important to the theory. Some are vital and if disproved would at best require a substantial revision of the theory or, at worst, would leave it beyond repair. The national level proposition regarding variation in midterm seat losses, which we will address first, is a proposition of this gravity. Other propositions, such as those regarding the demographic composition of the electorates (also to be considered later) are not so vital. They are best characterized as suggesting circumstantial evidence for or against the theory. The theory can survive intact even if evidence fails to support a proposition of this sort.

The National Level Hypotheses

The natural starting point of an analysis of surge and decline is at the national level. After all, it was in response to the regularity of national midterm seat losses by the president's party that the theory of surge and decline was first constructed. Since the president's party won the prior presidential election, the surge and decline explanation for the president's party consistently sustaining losses in midterms is not open to empirical verification. However, several other national level propositions can be extracted from the theory for examination.

The first national level hypothesis of the theory concerns its explanation of variation in midterm seat losses. The extent of midterm losses should be proportionate to the advantage the party enjoyed in the presidential election. This hypothesis is the most obvious and most central to the theory. More specifically:

Proposition 1: In midterm elections,the president's party loses congressional seats and votes in proportion to the short-term forces in its favor in the prior presidential election, all other things being equal.

The withdrawal of short-term forces systematically to the advantage of the president's party should have repercussions at the midterm for congressional candidates of the president's party. The breadth and depth of these negative repercussions depends upon the strength of the original positive short-term forces. If it can be assumed that long-term forces have remained essentially stable over a series of elections, fluctuations in the presidential vote should reflect the tilt of the partisan direction of short-term forces. The extent of midterm losses, therefore, should correspond to the prior presidential vote. Midterm losses should be especially large following the landslide election of the president. Conversely, midterm losses should be relatively minor following a narrow presidential election victory.

The second national level hypothesis takes a step back two years before the midterm. If the theory of surge and decline is true, there ought to be evidence of a surge effect in presidential elections as well as the decline effect in midterms. Losses should be expected at the midterm only because gains induced by favorable short-term forces were made at the presidential election. Although short-term forces consistently favor the president's party in presidential elections, they do not necessarily favor the presidential party equally in each presidential election. This variation should be reflected in the congressional election outcomes in presidential years:

Proposition 2: In presidential election years, the winning presidential party gains congressional seats and votes in proportion to the short-term forces in its favor, all other things being equal.

A presidential landslide, itself reflecting strongly positive short-term forces, should translate into relatively large seat gains for the winning presidential party. Conversely, a narrow presidential victory, reflecting only weakly positive short-term forces, should translate into minor seat gains for the winning presidential party.

Evidence. To assess the evidence pertaining to the national-level surge and decline propositions requires some national measure of the net partisan balance of short-term forces in presidential election year. A fairly rough but very simple summary measure of national short-term forces is whether or not the president won in a landslide election. It is safe to claim that short-term forces strongly favored the president's party, whether that party was the majority or minority party, if the president defeated his opponent by a very wide margin.[3] Conversely, narrow presidential victories can be interpreted reasonably as a sign of short-term forces being a more restrained benefit to the winning presidential candidate and party.

In examining the two-party presidential votes in this century (excluding 1912 because of the complications involved in the second-place finish of Teddy Roosevelt's third-party candidacy), the elections can be divided neatly into two groups of nearly equal size. A gap of almost two and one-half percentage points separates the landslide and nonlandslide presidential elections. The two sets of elections, ranked by the two-party presidential vote, and the midterm seat losses following the presidential election are presented in table 3.1.

The data reveal a stark difference between midterm seat losses following presidential landslides and those following more competitive presidential elections. This difference is quite in keeping with the first national-level proposition of surge and decline. As Hinckley observed in a similar examination of midterms from 1920 to 1962, "the largest net midterm losses tend to follow large presidential victories" (1971, 20). The median seat loss following presidential landslides in this century is nearly forty-nine seats. In six of the ten postlandslide midterms, the president's party lost in excess of forty seats. The three exceptions, moreover, can be explained as a consequence of realignment (1932 and perhaps 1984) or by the complicating presence of a strong third-party candidacy (La Follette in

Table 3.1. Midterm Seat Losses by Margin of Prior Presidential Victory, 1902-1990

Narrow to moderate size presidential victories (50.0% to 56.9% of the pres. vote)			Presidential landslides (57.0% or more of the pres. vote)		
Year	Presidential vote %	Seat loss	Year	Presidential vote %	Seat loss
1954	55.4	− 19	1926	65.2	− 11
1982	55.3	− 25	1922	63.8	− 75
1942	55.0	− 46	1938	62.5	− 76
1910	54.5	− 63	1974	61.8	− 49
1990	53.9	− 8	1966	61.3	− 48
1946	53.8	− 56	1906	60.0	− 32
1902	53.2	− 12	1934	59.2	+ 12
1950	52.3	− 29	1986	59.2	− 5
1918	51.6	− 20	1930	58.8	− 51
1978	51.1	− 15	1958	57.8	− 49
1970	50.4	− 12			
1962	50.1	− 4			
Median Seat Loss = − 19.5			Median Seat Loss = − 48.5		

Note: The presidential vote is the percentage of the two-party vote from the election two years before the midterm. Seat losses prior to 1912 are calculated as though there were a constant House size of 435. The 1912-14 pair of elections were omitted because of the unusually strong showing of the third party presidential candidate, Theodore Roosevelt.

1924). Less severe losses were generally sustained in midterms following nonlandslide presidential elections. The median midterm seat loss for the president's party following presidential election victories of small or moderate proportions was just nineteen seats, less than one-half the median seat loss incurred after presidential landslides. The president's party lost more than forty seats in only three of the eleven midterms in this century that followed nonlandslide presidential elections.

The second aggregate-level proposition is addressed by an examination of presidential election year seat gains for the party winning the presidency. Seat gains in landslide and nonlandslide presidential elections are presented in table 3.2. While the principal purpose of this table is an examination of differences in seat gains, we should first observe that seat gains for the president's party in presidential election years are quite common, whether the president has been elected in a landslide or not. Seat gains are evident in seventeen of the twenty-two presidential elections. If the president's party were actually as likely to gain as lose seats in presidential elections, by the binomial distribution, there would be less

Table 3.2. Presidential Election Year Seat Gains by Margin of Presidential Victory, 1900-1988

Narrow to moderate size presidential victories (50.0% to 56.9% of the pres. vote)			Presidential landslides (57.0% or more of the pres. vote)		
Year	Presidential vote %	Seat gain	Year	Presidential vote %	Seat gain
1952	55.4	+ 22	1924	65.2	+ 23
1980	55.3	+ 34	1920	63.8	+ 61
1940	55.0	+ 6	1936	62.5	+ 13
1908	54.5	− 7	1972	61.8	+ 13
1988	53.9	− 2	1964	61.3	+ 37
1944	53.8	+ 20	1904	60.0	+ 48
1900	53.2	+ 14	1932	59.2	+ 99
1948	52.3	+ 75	1984	59.2	+ 15
1916	51.6	− 22	1928	58.8	+ 31
1976	51.1	+ 1	1956	57.8	− 2
1968	50.4	+ 4			
1960	50.1	− 21			
Median Seat Gain = + 6			Median Seat Gain = + 27		

Note: The presidential vote is the percentage of the two-party vote. Seat gains prior to 1912 are calculated as though there were a constant House size of 435. The 1912 election is omitted because of the usually strong showing of the third party presidential candidate, Theodore Roosevelt.

than eight chances in one thousand of the party gaining seats in seventeen (or more) of the twenty-two elections. Evidently, much as the theory of surge and decline proposes, the winning president's party regularly enjoys short-term forces in its favor and gains some number of seats as a result.

The real purpose of table 3.2 is not to examine the consistency of presidential election seat gains but the variation between landslide and nonlandslide presidential elections. The second surge and decline proposition hypothesizes greater seat gains in landslide presidential elections, when there is little doubt about the direction and intensity of short-term forces. This is precisely the pattern. As expected, presidential election year seat gains have been substantially greater in presidential landslides. The median seat gain in landslide election years is almost five times that of nonlandslide years. In half of the landslide elections the president's party gained thirty or more seats. The president's party achieved gains of this magnitude in only two of the eleven nonlandslide election years. At the other extreme, the president's party actually sustained losses or gained only a few seats (less than ten) in seven of the eleven non-landslides but in only one of the ten landslides. The presidential election of 1988 also fits this pattern nicely—a nonlandslide presidential election in which the winning presidential party actually sustained minor seat losses.

Of course, this analysis of the first two surge and decline propositions is not very sophisticated. A more sophisticated analysis and an examination of similar propositions offered by a revised theory will be discussed in chapter 6. However, it does not require sophisticated data analysis to see that the data generally support the national-level propositions of surge and decline. The president's party gains seats in presidential election years and loses seats in midterm election years and the data give us good reason to suppose that these gains and subsequent losses are proportionate to the short-term forces favoring the president's party in the presidential election—exactly as the theory of surge and decline proposes.

The District Level

Originally designed to explain aggregate changes in partisan seat holdings, the theory of surge and decline does not stop there. It not only explains the consistency and extent of the presidential party's gains and losses but identifies their location as well. That is, the theory specifies the congressional districts in which the president's party is most likely to make gains in the presidential election year and to suffer losses in the following midterm. Two congressional district level propositions can be extracted from the theory.

The first proposition concerns the location of congressional vote losses for the president's party in midterm elections. It is unlikely that the president's party would lose support equally across all congressional districts. The withdrawal of presidential election short-term forces should have a greater fallout in some districts than in others:

Proposition 3: All things being equal, in a midterm election the congressional vote for the president's party in a district decreases in proportion to the short-term forces in the district favoring that party in the prior presidential election, especially to the degree that turnout in the district declines.

Congressional candidates who had the good fortune of running on a ticket with a presidential candidate who was unusually popular in their district should feel a greater loss when they run next without this advantage. As in the comparison of different presidential elections, a bigger bust follows on the tail of a bigger boom.

The second district-level proposition concerns the district surge effects that preceded the midterm decline. If candidates of the president's party suffer midterm losses because of the evaporation of short-term forces previously in their favor, there ought to be evidence that these prior short-term forces actually helped these congressional candidates in the presidential election. As in the case of the midterm decline, the short-term forces of the presidential surge should be felt more strongly in some districts:

Proposition 4: All things being equal, in a presidential election year the vote for a congressional candidate of the winning presidential party increases in proportion to the short-term forces in the district favoring that party, especially to the degree that turnout in the district increases.

Before discussing what is already known about these two propositions, two points deserve note. First, both propositions recognize the amplifying effects of the surge and decline of turnout in a district. Whatever short-term forces are present in a district during a presidential election should be magnified if the campaign is intense enough to draw a large number of peripheral voters to the polls. Second, the phrase "all things being equal" draws attention to the fact that a variety of local factors must be taken into account in examining congressional elections at the district level. Probably the two most important of these local considerations are the partisan composition of the district and the relative quality of the congressional candidates. The advantage of incumbents has been amply demonstrated and, along with various other local circumstances, should be taken into account in assessing district level surge and decline effects.

Evidence. In evaluating the revised theory of surge and decline in chapter 7, a district-level analysis will address propositions three and four. That analysis will generally support these hypotheses, but not in their entirety. Previous research is rather sparse. However, three previous studies at the district level are relevant. All three are supportive of the propositions, but again only in part.

Hinckley's (1967) study of midterm losses for the president's party most closely addresses proposition 3, the first district-level proposition. Hinckley examined the relative vote strength of the president compared to his party's congressional candidates and whether the president ran ahead or behind his congressional candidates. The difference was related to congressional seat losses in the 1954, 1958, and 1962 midterm elections. She concluded: "We found that midterm loss was concentrated in districts where the president ran ahead at the preceding election and we clarified this relationship by linking midterm loss to those marginal districts where the president ran ahead. . . . Fluctuations in midterm loss may be explained in terms of the scale set by the preceding presidential-year election. As the victorious presidential candidate wins by larger pluralities, the number of districts where the president runs ahead markedly increases" (p. 699). Hinckley's measure of short-term forces, the deviation of the presidential vote from the contemporaneous congressional vote, is certainly a far cry from an ideal measure, as she acknowledged (p. 698), as Miller (1955) previously argued, and as will become clear in our later discussion of the measurement of short-term forces. For instance, a presidential candidate could, quite conceivably, outpace the lower part of his ticket and still be have short-term forces running against him and his party in a district election if his party had nominated an especially weak congressional candidate. Nevertheless, as flawed as the vote gap measure is, it probably is related to the tilt of short-term forces, and Hinckley's findings may be considered as at least tentative support for the district midterm loss proposition (proposition 3).[4]

The second study relevant to the district-level propositions is Born's (1984) study of coattails in presidential elections.[5] Contrary to Edwards's (1979) earlier district-level study of presidential coattails and the outcomes of congressional elections,[6] Born's study of the congressional vote at the congressional district level from 1952 to 1980 revealed that presidential coattails were a consistently substantial influence in each of the eight presidential election years examined. In repeated multivariate analyses, taking incumbency status, the prior congressional vote, and (in post-1972 elections) campaign expenditures into account, the presidential vote had a strong and statistically significant effect on the congressional vote. While the present analysis takes issue with using the prior congressional vote in lieu of a district's normal vote, Born's analysis is quite sound and, as expected, finds that short-term forces (as measured in the presidential vote) affect the congressional vote. His congressional vote equations account for between 80 percent and 90 percent of the variance and quite consistently estimate coattail effects in the range of .3 to .4 (Edwards 1979, table 2, p. 70 and table 3, p. 75), indicating that 30 percent to 40 percent of a presidential candidate's share of the vote carries over to his congressional candidate.

The third district-level analysis also bearing on presidential year gains as stated in proposition four, is part of a broader congressional elections study by Ferejohn and Fiorina (1985, 107). They examined the vote for Democratic incumbents in 1980 and 1984. In their multivariate analysis, including the prior vote for the incumbent and the challenger's campaign expenditures and experience, they found the presidential vote to be a significant influence on the congressional vote. Moreover, the magnitude of the presidential vote influence was similar to that found in Born's analysis. In both years, coattail effects were equal to 40 percent of the presidential vote.

The findings of the above two studies, like Hinckley's before, should be taken as at least tentative evidence in behalf of the surge and decline proposition concerning on-year gains by the victorious presidential party (proposition 4). None of the above three studies, however, addresses the suspected role of turnout in the surge and decline propositions. Both district-level propositions suppose that the impact of short-term forces is heightened by large fluctuations in turnout, indicating a significance presence of peripheral voters in the presidential electorate. As the analysis in chapter 7 will indicate, while the district propositions are generally supported by the evidence, turnout fluctuations do not appear to have the kind of amplifying effects that the theory supposes.

The Electorates

The theory of surge and decline offers a number of propositions regarding the electorates of presidential and midterm elections. The voting public in midterm elections is supposed to differ from the voting public in presidential election years. These suspected differences reflect differences the theory supposes between core and peripheral voters. By definition, the midterm electorate is composed entirely of core voters. The larger presidential electorate, on the other hand, is composed of transitory peripheral voters as well as dependable core voters. Differences between core and peripheral voters should, thus, appear as differences between the presidential and midterm electorates, with the presidential electorate exhibiting more of the characteristics of the peripheral voters. Since both electorates have core voters in common, the difference between presidential and midterm electorates will be a muted version of the difference between core and peripheral voters.

The hypothesized differences between peripheral and core voters, or midterm and presidential electorates, are of three sorts. First, midterm and presidential electorates are alleged to differ in their demographic and personal background compositions. Although Campbell (1966, 52) himself investigated several of these suspected differences in his original analysis, the existence of these differences is of relatively little gravity to the theory's validity. That is, these suspected differences are essentially tangential to the theory. Second, midterm and presidential electorates are supposed to differ in their mix of political attitudes, principally their political interest and partisanship. Finally, the electorates are supposed to differ in their actual voting behavior—the vote choice of independents and the defection rates of partisans.

The theory suggests that the midterm electorate is not merely a scaled-down version of the presidential electorate. Since various demographic and personal background characteristics are known to be associated with certain political motivations and turnout patterns, demographic and background differences are suspected, though the theory does not require that these differences exist. In particular, core and peripheral voters are presumed to differ on two demographic characteristics: age and education.[7] Core voters are thought to be older and more educated than peripheral voters. Thus:

Proposition 5: All things being equal, midterm electorates are older than presidential electorates.
Proposition 6: All things being equal, midterm electorates are more highly educated than presidential electorates.

Why should midterm electorates be somewhat older and more educated than presidential electorates? As to age, older voters are more likely to have established roots in a community, to have fewer distractions, and therefore to have developed habits of paying attention to political matters and of turning out to vote regularly. They have also lived through more political history and, therefore, are likely to have stored more information from their political experiences. Greater experience may engender greater confidence in their vote decision and less hesitance in expressing that decision at the polls. Education is likewise a factor stimulating political involvement, knowledge, and undoubtedly turnout (Wolfinger and Rosenstone 1980). The more educated are more likely to have developed strong political opinions and the desire to express them at the polls. They are also likely to have developed greater cognitive skills useful in making sense of political events. In short, older and better-educated citizens are good candidates to be core voters who participate regardless of the campaign's intensity. Younger and less-educated citizens are less likely to be core voters and more likely be peripheral voters, needing the added push of a high-stimulus presidential campaign.

Although neither the age nor educational difference is strictly required by the theory, both mesh well with its contention that the presidential electorate is less stable in its preferences than the midterm electorate. As to age, younger voters are thought to be more sensitive to the events of the immediate campaign than older voters, who fit the campaign into their historical framework. Moreover, as Converse (1976) well documents, partisanship tends to strengthen with age. As partisans grow older, their identifications become more intense, and presumably, this produces greater loyalty. The association of age and partisanship also comports well with Fiorina's (1981, 84-105) theory of party identification.[8]

According to Fiorina, partisan bonds are formed through experience as well as through socialization. So long as experience consistently points a voter toward the same party, and for real as well as perceptual reasons this is generally the case, it reinforces and strengthens party attachments. Voters with more political experience, therefore, tend to form stronger partisan bonds, and quite naturally these more experienced voters tend to be older voters.

A similar argument can be made linking education with stable preferences. Educated voters should have accumulated a greater store of information. This should restrain the influence of the current campaign, though they may also be somewhat more attentive to the current campaign than their less-educated counterparts. If true and if core voters are more educated, the educational differences would contribute to the greater stability of preferences in midterm electorates and to the greater volatility of preferences in presidential electorates.

The second set of supposed differences between midterm and presidential electorates concern attitudes. The proposition concerning the relative political interest of the two electorates is undoubtedly the most explicit hypothesis in Campbell's original exposition of the theory. According to Campbell (1966, 42-43), compared to core voters, peripheral voters have a less intense interest in politics. Set in terms of the two electorates:

Proposition 7: All things being equal, voters with a deep and sustained interest in politics compose a larger segment of midterm electorates than of presidential electorates.

Peripheral voters are only brought into the presidential electorate because of the motivation externally induced by high-stimulus presidential campaigns. Their own interest by itself is not enough to spur peripherals to political activity. As a result, their inclusion in presidential electorates and absence from midterm electorates should make the presidential electorate as a whole appear less politically involved.

Although somewhat less central to the theory than the claim of a difference in levels of political interest, the theory also suggests that the two electorates differ in the general strength of partisanship:

Proposition 8: All things being equal, voters with a strong party identification compose a larger segment of midterm electorates than of presidential electorates.

Conversely, independents comprise a larger share of presidential electorates than of midterm electorates. The basis for this proposition is that peripheral voters, lacking a rich political background, are less likely to make strong standing commitments. Their sporadic and shallow attention to political matters makes it less likely that they will form durable and general political attachments. Core voters, on the other hand, have enough interest and information to form firm partisan attachments. Since core voters constitute the entire midterm electorate but only a portion of the presidential electorate, it follows that the midterm electorate should be somewhat more partisan than the presidential electorate.

There are two caveats to this proposition. First, Campbell never suggested that the partisan difference between the electorates was extreme. Core voters as well as peripheral voters may be independents. Both may adopt an independent identification or simply fail to adopt a party identification if they regard the parties as being of roughly equal merit. However, peripheral voters, unlike core voters, have a second route to independence. Because of their minimal interest in politics some peripherals may be independents simply because they failed to consider seriously the relative merits of the parties.

The second caveat concerns the importance of the partisan difference proposition to the surge and decline explanation of midterm losses. The difference is not vital to the explanation. The theory of surge and decline could survive without the partisan difference between electorates, but the supposed partisan difference does contribute to the theory's account of midterm losses.

An important claim of the theory is that presidential electorates are more open to the influence of short-term forces than are midterm electorates. The partisan difference may heighten this volatility difference. Independents, as Campbell noted (in Campbell et al. 1960, 42), are "less stable in their partisan positions from year to year." Voters with strong partisan attachments, on the other hand, are prone to stand by their party commitments and are less subject to short-term forces. The greater presence of partisans in the midterm electorate thus adds to its stability whereas the relatively greater presence of independents in the presidential electorate adds to that electorate's volatility.

Finally, presidential and midterm electorates are supposed to differ in their actual voting behavior. These differences are very important to the theory. It is the contention of the theory that presidential electorates, by their composition and exposure to a more intense campaign, are more volatile in their voting patterns than midterm electorates and that this volatility works to the advantage of the president's party and its congressional candidates. Since partisanship plays such a central role in influencing the vote choice, the behavior of partisans and independents can be considered separately.

The theory hypothesizes a pattern to partisan defections in presidential and midterm electorates:

Proposition 9: Partisan defections from the disadvantaged party (i.e., the party losing the presidential race) in presidential elections are greater than in midterm elections and are proportionate to the short-term forces favoring the president's party.

There are two reasons for this suspected defection difference. First, the presidential electorate contains a number of undependable peripheral partisans who are easily induced to defect. Second, the presidential electorate is subjected to the heavy information flow of the presidential campaign. Even usually loyal, core partisans may defect if a campaign sharply exposes failings in their party and its candidates.

The independent vote is similarly subject to more pronounced swings in favor of the president's party in presidential elections:

Proposition 10: The independent vote for the president's party in presidential elections is greater than in midterm elections and is proportionate to the short-term forces favoring the president's party.

The rationale for the independent vote proposition is similar to that of the party defection proposition. The independent vote should especially favor the president's party in presidential elections. This should be true because of the presence of persuadable peripheral independents in addition to core independents and the systematic tilt of high-volume short-term forces favoring (to a greater or lesser degree) the president's party, a factor that may affect the votes of core independents as well as the peripherals.

Evidence. Compared to research at the national and district levels, research concerning the individual characteristics, attitudes, and vote choices of presidential and midterm electorates has been extensive. As already noted, several of the propositions at this level are not vital to the theory, and as will be noted, some of the research concerning properties of the two electorates has missed the mark. Generally speaking, the findings have not been very supportive and, unfortunately, have led many to dismiss the entire theory.

The first of the five propositions claiming that the compositions of the two electorates differ with respect to age, that midterm electorates are somewhat older than presidential electorates, has generally been confirmed. Both Campbell (in Campbell et al. 1966, 52) and Wolfinger, Rosenstone, and McIntosh (1981) found evidence that presidential electorates are younger than the midterm electorates. As Wolfinger, Rosenstone, and McIntosh conclude midterm elections "have many fewer younger voters" (p. 254).

Figure 3.1. Median Age of Presidential and Midterm Electorates, 1956-90

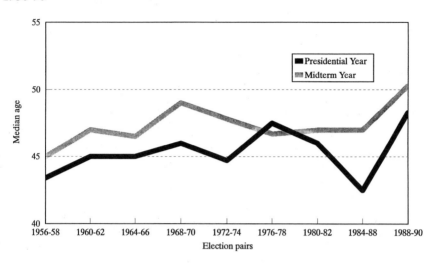

Although these authors each based their observations on only a single pair of presidential and midterm electorates (1956-58 and 1972-74 respectively), an examination of pairs of electorates from 1956 to 1990 also indicates that presidential electorates are younger.[9] The median age of these electorates are charted in figure 3.1. In eight of the nine election pairs the median age of the midterm electorate was greater than that of the presidential electorate. As one would expect, given the great overlap in the two electorates of core voters, the age gap is not large. However, if the one deviating election pair (1976-78) is set aside and the median age of peripheral voters is calculated algebraically,[10] the age gap between core and peripheral voters looks somewhat larger. The typical peripheral voter in these seven election pairs was anywhere from seven to thirteen years younger than the typical core voter.[11]

The second electorate level proposition, proposition 6, hypothesized an educational gap between presidential and midterm electorates, with midterm electorates being more highly educated. Past research reached slightly different conclusions on the education gap. Campbell (in Campbell et al. 1966, 52) originally noted a gap but also characterized it as a small difference. Wolfinger, Rosenstone, and McIntosh (1981, 253) noted that "the educational and occupational composition of the two groups is virtually the same."

The educational attainments of both types of electorates are presented in figures 3.2 and 3.3. Figure 3.2 charts the percentage of each electorate having graduated from high school and figure 3.3 charts the percentage having graduated from college. At first glance, it would

Figure 3.2. Percent of Presidential and Midterm Electorates Having
Graduated from High School, 1956-1990

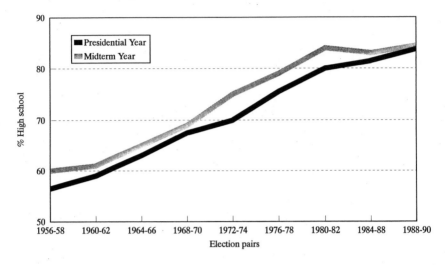

Figure 3.3. Percent of Presidential and Midterm Electorates Having
Graduated from College, 1956-1990

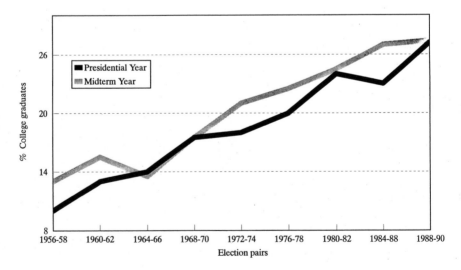

appear that there is a consistent, though modest, educational gap between midterm and presidential electorates. There is a slight but consistent difference in the percentage of high school graduates between presidential and midterm electorates. Moreover, a similar difference with respect to college graduates was found in six of the nine election pairs examined, with only one pair of electorates barely deviating from the pattern.

At least initially, the educational gap might be construed as supporting surge and decline's view of the electorate. An educational difference may reasonably be the basis for a motivational difference between core and peripheral voters. If a greater educational background reflects greater general involvement, socializes a greater sense of civic duty, and instills a long-term interest in politics, core voters should be among the better educated.

The educational gap, however, does not reflect this motivational difference. The gap is actually an artifact caused by a general trend over the years toward a more highly educated public. While it is true that voters in presidential elections are less educated than voters in the following midterm, it is also true that those midterm voters as a group are less educated than voters in the next presidential election. For example, high school graduates compose 59 percent of the 1960 presidential electorate and 61 percent of the 1962 midterm electorate. However, the 1964 presidential electorate includes an even greater percentage (63 percent) of high school graduates. Generally, presidential electorates were more educated than the prior midterm electorate in six of the eight comparisons using the high school graduation standard and in four of the eight comparisons using the college graduation standard, and were nearly equal in two of the remaining comparisons.

Turning to the political interest proposition, are midterm electorates in fact more interested in politics than more inclusive presidential electorates as stated in proposition 7? Although the supposed political interest difference is central to the theory, it has received surprisingly little attention. However, the evidence we will consider suggests marginal support at best for there being a significant and consistent difference in the political interest of presidential and midterm electorates.

NES surveys have regularly asked voters about their interest in political campaigns. In figure 3.4 the percentages of presidential and midterm election voters claiming that they are very much interested in the political campaign are charted for elections from 1956 to 1990, with the single exception of the 1974 midterm when the political interest question was not asked. The results do not fit the expected pattern. According to these data, midterm electorates are not regularly more interested in politics than presidential electorates. The expected difference is observed

Figure 3.4. Political Interest of the Presidential and Midterm
Electorates, 1956-1990

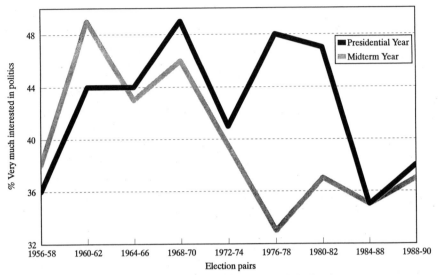

Note: The political interest question was not asked in the 1974 study.

in only two of the eight elections pairs examined (1956-58 and 1960-62).
In more recent pairs of elections, the midterm electorates are actually less
politically interested than the presidential electorates.

It is tempting to conclude from this evidence that the suspected
political interest difference proposed by surge and decline does not in fact
exist. However, there is a problem with the data that stops us short of that
conclusion. The surge and decline thesis argues that there ought to be a
difference between core and peripheral voters' internal sense of interest
in politics, not necessarily in their reactions to a particular campaign
(Campbell et al. 1966, 53). Political interest is thought of as an attribute of
the voter rather than a condition induced by external and, quite likely,
transient events. Responses to the political interest question do not,
unfortunately, allow for this very important distinction. Two voters may
claim great interest in a campaign for very different reasons. One may be
deeply interested because he is always interested in politics. Another
may be interested because the particular campaign has jarred him from
his usual indifference. Moreover, election induced interest may have a
greater effect on those lacking their own long-standing political interest,
since those who were already very much interested in politics probably
cannot be much more interested than they already were. In other words,
there may be a ceiling effect for self-motivated voters. Given this likely
contamination of the interest measure charted in figure 3.4, we should
not expect this figure to show the predicted pattern of differences in

political interest. This makes the pattern in figure 3.4 less telling than first supposed.

While drawing conclusions from the direct political interest questions is problematic, two related examinations do raise doubts about the supposed political interest difference. First, panel data permit an examination in which the contamination of political interest responses based on the stimulation of the current campaign is reduced, if not eliminated. The less contaminated data are drawn from the NES's 1972-74-76 panel survey in which respondents were asked about their general interest in public affairs, rather than about their interest in the specific election at hand.[12] More importantly, since the data are from a multiyear panel, responses can be examined at a common point in time, in the 1974 midterm election when short-term forces are presumably at their ebb. If proposition 7 is true, we should observe that those who indicated a strong general interest in public affairs (in 1974) make up a larger share of the 1974 midterm electorate than they did of the 1972 presidential electorate. The data reveal only a small difference in the expected direction. The midterm electorate contained 4 percent more voters who claimed to follow public affairs than did the prior presidential electorate (47 percent of the 1972 electorate and 51 percent of the 1974 electorate).[13] Raising further suspicions about the political interest difference is the fact that these attentive voters composed a slightly larger share (52 percent) of the 1976 electorate than the prior midterm electorate. In short, the panel data on general interest in public affairs along with campaign political interest data tracked over time do not reveal the consistent and large political interest differences between the two electorates suggested by the theory.

Second, a number of voter qualities other than political interest were also examined under the assumption that they might be less sensitive to contamination by the election at hand. Included were responses to questions about the respondents' trust in government, their impression of the responsiveness of government, their sense of political efficacy, and their knowledge about which party controlled the House of Representatives. There was no evidence of a consistently "higher quality" midterm electorate by any of these measures.

The evidence against the partisan composition of midterm and presidential electorates as stated in proposition 8 is indisputable. Where the theory led us to suppose a greater partisan presence in midterm electorates, no such systematic difference has been found. As previously noted, the theory did not suppose an extreme partisan difference and the suspected difference was not of vital importance to the thrust of the theory's argument. Nevertheless, the failure of the evidence to support the theory's contention has done more to undermine the theory's credibility than any other finding.

Table 3.3. Strong Partisans in Presidential and Midterm Electorates,
1956-1990

Election years	% Strong partisans		Difference consistent with theory?
	Presidential electorate	Midterm electorate	
1956-58	40	45	Yes
1960-62	40	42	Yes
1964-66	43	36	No
1968-70	35	36	Yes
1972-74	30	35	Yes
1976-78	32	32	No
1980-82	32	38	Yes
1984-86	35	37	Yes
1988-90	39	41	Yes

SOURCE: National Election Studies.

Evidence from both ends of the partisan intensity spectrum bear on the partisan turnout proposition. That is, if the proposition is valid, we ought to observe a greater presence of strong partisans, either Democratic or Republican, in midterm elections and a greater presence of pure independents in the turnout surge of the presidential election.[14] An examination of the presence of strong partisans in the two electorates indicates that they usually do compose a larger portion of the midterm electorate, but the gap is not observed with perfect regularity. Table 3.3 offers a comparison of the portion of presidential and midterm electorates from 1956 to 1990 composed of strong partisans. Consistent with the proposition, strong partisans were a larger component of the midterm electorate than the prior presidential electorate in seven of these nine electorate pairs. However, the difference observed in the 1964-66 comparison ran strongly in the opposite direction and the differences in four of the seven consistent pairs of electorates (1960-62, 1968-70, 1984-86 and 1988-90) were of only modest magnitude (2.5 percent or less).

Evidence at the other end of the partisan intensity scale has been more frequently cited and unambiguously contradicts the hypothesis of a partisan turnout difference. The data's discrepancy with the proposition was first documented by Arseneau and Wolfinger (1973) and was later repeated by Kernell (1977, 46), Hinckley (1981, 120-121) and others. The proportions of the two electorates composed of pure independents for elections from 1956 to 1990 are presented in table 3.4. The difference is

Table 3.4. Independents in Presidential and Midterm Electorates, 1956-1990

Election years	% Pure independents		Difference consistent with theory?
	Presidential electorate	Midterm electorate	
1956-58	9	5	Yes
1960-62	8	6	Yes
1964-66	5	8	No
1968-70	7	8	No
1972-74	8	8	No
1976-78	9	9	No
1980-82	8	6	Yes
1984-86	7	6	Yes
1988-90	7	5	Yes

SOURCE: Ornstein, Mann, and Malbin (1992, table 2.17).

anything but consistent. Four pairs of electorates flatly fail to support the proposition that independents play a greater role in presidential elections. Of the five remaining electorate pairs consistent with the theory, a substantial expected difference is found in only one instance (1956-58). There simply is no consistent disproportionate surge in the turnout of independents from which the winning presidential party can gain an advantage and later lose at the next midterm.

Unfortunately, the initial research concerning surge and decline's thesis in proposition 9 of a partisan defection difference between the two electorates addressed a proposition critically different from that raised here, a defection proposition more central to the theory. Arseneau and Wolfinger (1973) compared overall partisan defection rates between presidential and midterm electorates and found no consistent pattern of greater defections in presidential election years. By casting their analysis in terms of partisan defections of all partisans rather than in terms of only defections by partisans of the disadvantaged party, their research considers the proposition that the greater stimulation of the presidential election campaign should be generally disruptive of normal party allegiances. While one might draw from the theory a proposition about the gross amount of partisan defections along these lines, such a proposition is by no means central to the theory's explanation of midterm losses. Moreover, by examining gross rather than net partisan defections this prior work neglects a principal element of the theory: the net partisan short-term forces favors the president's party in the presidential election. More recent research, however, has shown that the presidential vote does influence the congressional vote choice. Fiorina (1990, 125), Born (1990), and Mondak (1990), using very different multivariate specifications, have found that presidential short-term forces significantly affect the congressional vote choice.

The partisan defection proposition set forth earlier in this chapter (proposition 9) addresses itself to the theory's contention that presidential elections, unlike midterms, systematically benefit the president's party by stimulating greater defections from the opposing party's ranks. This proposition is essentially of two parts: the first, comparing the opposition party's defections in presidential and midterm elections, and the second, concerning the association between the extent of the presidential year defections in the opposing party and the strength of short-term forces favoring that party. These two components can be examined separately.

Table 3.5 presents the partisan defection rates (with respect to defection on the congressional vote) for nine pairs of presidential and midterm elections. The partisans are grouped according to whether their party had been advantaged by or disadvantaged by short-term forces in the presidential election. The key columns in the table are the defection rates of partisans of the disadvantaged party. The proposition claims that because of the systematic pull of short-term forces in favor of the president's party these defection rates should be greater in the presidential election year than in the midterm. While this is true in six of the nine election pairs, sizable differences in defection rates are found in only two of the nine cases.

The advantaged partisans in these election pairs are included as a control group of sorts. As such, we would expect no differences in their defection rates in the two elections. For the most part they should be reinforced in their partisan loyalty by the favorable short-term forces of the presidential year and undisturbed in those loyalties in the next midterm. As expected, the actual defection rates of advantaged partisans were not systematically greater in either presidential and midterm elections.

While the comparison of partisan defection rates for advantaged and disadvantaged partisans in presidential and midterm elections yields some evidence in behalf of surge and decline, the evidence pertaining to the second part of the partisan defection proposition fails to offer even modest support. The extent of a party's defections in a presidential election year is not proportionate to the short-term forces favoring the party. In the ten presidential election years from 1952 to 1988, the correlations between the congressional vote defections of both Republicans and Democrats and a measure of short-term forces were examined. The

Table 3.5. Partisan Defection Rates in Presidential and Midterm Elections for Partisans of the Advantaged and Disadvantaged Parties, 1956-1990

Election years and advantaged party		Disadvantaged partisans			Advantaged partisans		
		Presidential election %	Midterm %	Difference consistent with theory?	Presidential election %	Midterm %	Difference consistent with theory?
1956-58	Rep	11.0	10.9	*	9.2	13.5	Yes
1960-62	Dem	13.6	11.9	Yes	11.4	12.8	Yes
1964-66	Dem	18.5	16.2	Yes	15.9	20.3	Yes
1968-70	Rep	23.4	17.4	Yes	16.1	16.1	No
1972-74	Rep	17.2	15.6	Yes	19.9	24.1	Yes
1976-78	Dem	24.8	26.7	No	18.2	24.9	Yes
1980-82	Rep	23.8	17.9	Yes	25.6	19.9	No
1984-86	Rep	22.2	21.7	Yes	26.6	26.1	No
1988-90	Rep	16.8	18.5	No	24.8	22.5	No

NOTE: Differences in the expected direction of less than one-half percentage point were not considered as supportive of the theory and are indicated by an asterisk. The percentages are calculated from National Election Study data after adjusting it to reflect the actual partisan division of the national congressional vote (see, chapter 8, note 7). Among disadvantaged partisans, defection rates are hypothesized to be greater in the presidential election year. Among advantaged partisans, defection rates are hypothesized to be lower in presidential election years.

proposition suggests a significant positive correlation between Republican defections and the Democratic presidential vote and a significant negative correlation between Democratic defections and the party's presidential vote. In both cases the correlations were very weak and not statistically significant (Republican defection $r = -.04$, wrong sign; and Democratic defection $r = -.14$, $p = .35$, one-tail).

To summarize, whether examining gross or net defections, the partisan defection findings as a whole offer little support for the theory. The brightest spot to emerge is in the comparison of defection rates for advantaged and disadvantaged partisans. But even here all is not so bright; it is difficult to imagine that a pattern as strong and as consistent as the midterm seat and vote loss rests on the observed marginal and somewhat erratic defection differences. Moreover, the second element of the proposition, that defection rates in the disadvantaged party are supposed to be proportionate to the strength of short-term forces favoring the advantaged party and thus stimulating defection, simply fails to materialize. In short, the analysis of the partisan defection proposition yields at best mixed results and raises further doubts about the theory's soundness.[15]

With the prevailing short-term forces in its favor, the winning presidential party in presidential elections should be more attractive than usual to all groups of voters. The theory of surge and decline suggests in

Figure 3.5. Effect of Short-term Forces on the Congressional Vote of
Independents in Presidential Elections, 1952-1988

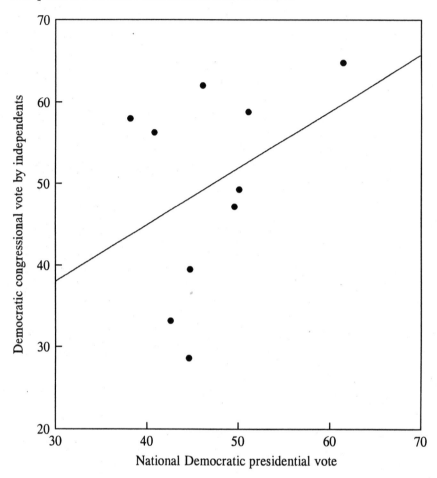

proposition 10 that the party winning the presidency should be especially
attractive to independent voters. This is not only because they lack
identifications anchoring them to one of the parties, but because a larger
portion of independents are supposed to be highly persuadable peripheral voters. However, as the evidence pertaining to proposition 8
attests, this premise is false. Independent voters in presidential elections
are not disproportionately peripheral voters. The independent vote proposition is still worth investigating, however, because it does not rest
solely on the premise that these independent voters are largely peripherals. We might continue to suppose that short-term forces would
strongly affect independent voters only because independent voters,
unlike partisans, lack a prior disposition to vote for one of the parties.

The independent vote for Democratic congressional candidates in the ten presidential election years from 1952 to 1988 is plotted against the national Democratic presidential vote in those years (an indicator of the direction and magnitude of short-term forces) in figure 3.5. The positive association between the two measures (b = .70, r = .37) suggests that the independent vote in presidential elections is sensitive to the prevailing short-term forces.[16] When short-term forces favor the Democratic party, as indicated by a large presidential vote for the Democratic presidential candidate, independent voters are much more likely to vote for Democratic congressional candidates than when short-term forces favor the Republican party.

Before leaving proposition 10, it should be noted that one of its underlying premises—that peripheral voters are particularly swayed by the short-term forces of the presidential campaign—has been addressed by three previous studies. All three concluded that peripherals are in fact more frequently persuaded to vote in accord with the prevailing short-term forces. DeNardo (1980, 1986) found in a study of over 300 congressional district level elections between 1938 and 1966 that "the rates of defection in each party increase as the level of turnout among peripheral voters increases" (1980, 415). Petrocik (1981), in an individual-level study based on surveys conducted in seven presidential elections between 1952 and 1976 and five "straw polls" in 1974, found that irregular or peripheral voters responded "very sharply to the partisan forces of the moment" (p. 166). Finally, Kenney (1988) found in the 1984 election that voters who did not care much about congressional elections (presumably peripheral voters) were more likely to use their presidential vote choice as a cue in casting their congressional vote.

A Brief Detour: A Question of Variance

Before reviewing the above evidence, a hypothesis related to the partisan defection proposition that has been attributed to surge and decline should be addressed. It concerns the relative magnitude of the congressional vote variance in presidential and midterm elections. Jacobson and Kernell (1981, 63) suggest that surge and decline supposes that the variance of the congressional vote should be greater in presidential elections than in midterm elections. This hypothesis, like the defection proposition, is based on the premise that the magnitude of short-term forces in presidential campaigns should be more generally disruptive of partisan voting. Jacobson and Kernell's investigation of this hypothesis does not find the expected difference. In fact, contrary to the hypothesis, they observe somewhat greater variation in midterm elections. They concluded that, "Modern midterm elections have as a set exhibited greater variation in the two-party division of the vote than congressional elections during the presumably more volatile, coattailish presidential elections. Since 1944 the standard deviation in the congressional vote has been 3.9 percentage points at the midterm and only 2.4 points during presidential elections" (p. 63). Erikson (1988, 1020) offers this comparison as a major reason for rejecting the surge and decline theory.

Two different defenses of surge and decline can be offered on this score. First, the theory of surge and decline implies a general decline to the normal vote in midterms, but a simple comparison of presidential year and midterm vote variances is an inadequate test of this notion. Such a comparison implicitly assumes two separate and unchanging normal votes, one for presidential years (the mean vote in these elections) and a second for midterms (the mean midterm vote). This is clearly erroneous. Examining deviations of the congressional vote from an adjusted normal vote, Cover (1985, 611) reaches somewhat different conclusions from Jacobson and Kernell. Though the difference was not great, Cover found the congressional vote deviation from the normal vote was greater in presidential election years, as expected.

An examination of presidential year and midterm congressional vote variation from the normal vote (1900 to 1986) also conflicts with the Jacobson and Kernell findings. As in Tufte's (1975) analysis, the normal vote was calculated as the mean congressional vote of the eight congressional elections preceding the presidential election. Standard deviations computed from this normal vote "mean" indicate greater variation in presidential election years (5.81 in presidential years and 4.23 in midterms), though since 1944 there has been about the same amount of variation in midterms (std. dev. = 2.82) as in presidential years (std. dev. = 2.84). In terms of the consistency of a midterm-presidential election difference, deviations from the normal vote have been greater in the presidential election year in fifteen of the twenty-two pairs of presidential and midterm elections.[17]

The second defense to the comparative variation hypothesis is that a comparison of the raw variance of the congressional vote in midterm and presidential years, even from a properly identified normal vote, is not essential to the theory of surge and decline. The theory argues only that the variance, of whatever magnitude, in the on-year congressional vote is systematically associated with evaluations favorable to the party winning the presidency. Variance in the congressional midterm vote, again of whatever magnitude, is not supposed to be as systematically associated to national conditions and, more importantly, is not supposed to be as consistently favorable to the presidential party.[18]

Table 3.6. Review of the Evidence: Ten Surge and Decline Propositions

Proposition and Level	Subject of Proposition	Evaluation of Proposition
1. National	Midterm vote and seat losses	Supported
2. National	Presidential year vote and seat gains	Supported
3. District	District midterm vote losses	Generally supported
4. District	District presidential year vote gains	Generally supported
5. Electorate	Age of two electorates	Supported
6. Electorate	Education of two electorates	Not supported
7. Electorate	Political interest of two electorates	Partially supported
8. Electorate	Partisanship of two electorates	Not supported
9. Electorate	Party defections of two electorates	Not supported
10. Electorate	Independent vote of two electorates	Supported

Evaluating the Theory

After considering all the evidence, where does the theory of surge and decline stand? Table 3.6 offers a report card for the ten propositions. What emerges from a review of the evidence is that while the theory fails on several counts, it is also supported in some very important respects. There is little trouble with what the theory has to say about election outcomes at either the national or district levels in either presidential or midterm elections. Where deficiencies emerge are in its propositions about the presidential and midterm electorates. Neither the composition nor the behavior of voters in the presidential and midterm electorates is quite what the theory leads us to expect. The failed proposition regarding the education gap (proposition 6) is not especially troubling, but the lack of support for the propositions concerning political interest, partisanship, and partisan defections is quite another matter.

These results, then, present a puzzle. *How is it that the theory stands up quite well to tests involving national and district level election returns but stumbles in examinations of propositions it raises about the midterm and presidential electorates?*

Beginning in chapter 5, I suggest a solution to this puzzle of contradictory evidence. In brief, the proposed explanation is that while the original theory of surge and decline is correct in many of its basic tenets, it is incorrect in its explanation of how these electoral forces play themselves out within the electorate. The theory is correct in its assertion that the systematic tilt of short-term forces in favor of the winning presidential party in presidential elections is responsible for the systematic loss of seats for that party in midterm elections. It also correctly identifies turnout as playing a role in the explanation of midterm losses. The flaw in the theory is in its identification of who in the potential voting public is affected by the short-term advantage of the president's party and in its explanation of how different elements of the potential voting public are affected. In other words, the original theory of surge and decline correctly specified the basic ingredients at work in presidential and midterm elections but incorrectly specified the mechanisms by which these ingredients are translated into midterm losses for the president's party.

Before offering a revised version of surge and decline to address the original's shortcomings, we turn next to an alternative perspective on midterm elections, a perspective that interprets midterm elections as referenda on the performance of the incumbent president and his party.

4

The Theory of the Midterm Referendum

The midterm is neither a mystery nor an automatic swing of the pendulum; the midterm vote is a referendum.
—Edward R. Tufte (1975:862)

Referenda theories of midterm elections stand in sharp contrast to the theories centered on presidential elections. Rather than focusing on the circumstances of the presidential election, referenda theories attempt to explain midterm losses by conditions at the midterm itself. The results of midterm elections can be interpreted, from this perspective, as the voting public's judgment of the current administration's effectiveness on the job.

Since its introduction in the mid-1970s the referenda theory has replaced the theory of surge and decline as the accepted wisdom regarding national forces in midterm elections. In reviewing the congressional elections literature, Barbara Hinckley commented that the presidential election centered explanations of midterms are "no longer widely accepted by political scientists" (1981, 115), and Gary Jacobson and Samuel Kernell observed that "the surge and decline view of midterm elections has been eclipsed by the more fashionable economic voting theory" (1981, 64)—the economic voting theory being one aspect of the more general referenda theory. In another overview of the field Herbert Asher after briefly reviewing the surge-and-decline theory, concluded that "today the dominant portrait of congressional elections is far different" (1983, 368). Assessments of individual midterm elections, such as the 1982 midterm (Mann and Ornstein 1983, 138-140), are now almost entirely conducted from the referenda theory's viewpoint. The theory has even been applied successfully outside the American context. In a study of government vote losses in British midterm by-elections from 1950 to 1983, Mughan concluded that "by-elections can quite legitimately be interpreted as national referendums on government performance" (1986, 773). The final testimony to the displacement of surge and decline is, as we will shortly see, the shear volume of research devoted to testing, refining, and otherwise modifying the basic referenda model.

The Basic Referenda Theory

Edward Tufte (1975, 1978) authored the seminal work espousing the referenda theory of midterm elections. Tufte first presented his referenda model in "Determinants of the Outcomes of Midterm Congressional Elections" (1975) and shortly thereafter extended his analysis in *Political Control of the Economy* (1978, chap. 5). Together these reports constitute the centerpiece of work in the referenda strain of midterm elections research.

Two aspects of Tufte's analysis require discussion. First, I address the specification of the referenda model itself, the initial evidence marshaled in its behalf, and the more recent analysis raising questions about the model. Second, and just as importantly, I examine Tufte's claims about his model and its relationship to surge and decline.

Tufte succinctly states the rationale for the referenda theory as follows: "Because there are no other targets available at the midterm, it is not unreasonable to expect that some voters opposed to the president might take out their dissatisfaction with the incumbent administration on the congressional candidates of the president's party" (1975, 813). The extent of voter displeasure with the incumbent administration may of course vary from one midterm to the next, thus accounting for variation in the extent of midterm losses.

What might indicate the extent of public satisfaction or dissatisfaction with the president at the midterm? Tufte proposed two indicators. The first indicator is quite straightforward: the public's expression of approval for the incumbent president's handling of his job as measured in national surveys. Since the late 1930s the Gallup poll on nearly a monthly basis has asked a national sample of citizens whether they approved of the president's job performance. The standard question's wording since 1945 is "Do you approve or disapprove of the way (the incumbent) is handling his job as president?" The percentage of the sample indicating approval of the president's job performance in September before the November election, his approval rating, is the aggregate indicator of midterm satisfaction. The second indicator of sentiment for or against the administration is an economic index, the annual change in real disposable personal income per capita between the year of the midterm and the previous year (1975, 817). Following the work of Kramer (1971) and others, Tufte hypothesized that a midterm verdict would be at least partly a verdict on the adequacy of economic progress made under the administration. With these two indicators of public satisfaction, Tufte offered a joint hypothesis: "the lower the approval rating of the incumbent president and the less prosperous the economy, the greater the loss of support for the president's party in midterm congressional elections" (1975, 817).

Two aspects of Tufte's construction of the dependent variable in his analysis deserve note. First, he elected to conduct his analysis in two steps. The first step sought to explain the congressional vote in terms of presidential popularity and economic conditions. The second step translated the congressional votes into seats via a swing-ratio. This is somewhat problematic since the swing-ratio fluctuates a good bit over time. Second, Tufte's measure of the congressional vote was a "standardized vote loss by president's party" in the midterm. The standardized vote loss measure was computed as the difference between the party's national congressional vote and the party's normal congressional vote. A party's normal congressional vote was computed as the average of its vote in the preceding eight elections. Tufte examines deviations from the normal vote in order to control for the varying strength of the Democratic and Republican parties over time. Some control for the normal vote is required so that judgments at the midterm would not be confused with standing commitments to the parties. Without this standardization or deviation measure, a majority party would appear to receive a greater vote than it deserves from the public's referenda judgment and the minority party would appear to receive a smaller vote than the referenda judgment would merit. The standardized vote loss predicted by the economy and popularity variables can be translated into a predicted vote for the party by adding the normal vote to the standardized vote loss.[1]

With the referenda equation of midterm vote losses specified, Tufte proceeded to conduct a very thorough analysis yielding findings strongly supportive of the referenda theory. He produced five findings in behalf of the referenda explanation: (1) The two referenda independent variables—presidential popularity and economic change—accounted for 91 percent of the variance (adjusted $R^2 = .88$) in the standardized vote loss in midterms between 1938 and 1970, excluding the 1942 midterm for lack of a presidential popularity reading (Tufte 1975, table 2, p. 818). The equation estimates are presented in table 4.1. (2) The coefficients for both variables were statistically significant (at .01 level) and consistent with estimates independently arrived at by Kramer (in the case of the economic variable) and Kernell (in the case of the presidential popularity variable). (3) These coefficients and the overall fit of the model were shown not to be overly sensitive to particular midterms in the analysis. Reestimating the equation with different midterms omitted from the analysis showed the model to be quite stable (p. 819). (4) The postdictions, or after-the-fact expected votes based on the equation, proved to be quite accurate. The average absolute error of these postdictions was only .6 percentage points, a good deal more accurate than Gallup's direct measure of the national congressional vote (table 3, p. 819). (5) The equation also yielded quite accurate predictions. Tufte generated predic-

Table 4.1. Referenda Equations of Midterm Losses

Independent variables	Dependent variables and midterms included				
	(1.) Std. vote loss (1946-70)*	(2.) Std. vote loss (1946-74)	(3.) Std. vote loss (1946-90)	(4.) Cong. vote (1946-90)	(5.) Seat loss (1946-90)
Constant	−11.08	−10.74	−9.14	−.10	−86.15
Presidential popularity	.13 (4.03)	.13 (3.00)	.12 (2.19)	.10 (1.62)	1.07 (2.44)
Economic conditions	.04 (5.83)	.62 (3.75)	.51 (2.46)	.59 (2.54)	2.27 (1.37)
Normal vote (8 election ave.)	—	—	—	.84 (4.24)	—
Number of cases	8	8	12	12	12
R^2	.91	.83	.59	.84	.50
Adjusted R^2	.88	—	.50	.77	.39

SOURCE: Equation 1 is from Tufte 1975 (table 2). This equation also includes the 1938 midterm. Equation 2 is from Tufte 1978 (table 5.2). Equations 3, 4 and 5 were estimated by the author. Note: The t-ratios are in parentheses.

tions for the five more recent midterms in his study from the equation estimated only with data from midterms prior to the one being predicted. The average absolute error of these predictions was only 1.3 percentage points, again better than Gallup's direct measure (table 4, p. 820).

Since Tufte's initial exposition of the referenda theory there has been some erosion in the evidence supporting it. The first indication that the referenda equation was not as complete an explanation of midterm elections as Tufte's original analysis suggested was apparent in Tufte's own reanalysis of the equation (1978, 112). In this reanalysis Tufte dropped the 1938 midterm case (because the wording of the Gallup presidential popularity question deviated from the standard wording that year) and added the 1974 midterm case. After substituting the 1974 case for the 1938 case, the fit of the equation dropped considerably (see equation 2 in table 4.1), from accounting for 91 percent to 83 percent of the variance. The percentage of the variance in the standardized vote loss accounted for by the economy and presidential popularity measures declines still further with the addition of the 1978, 1982, 1986, and 1990 midterms (equation 3 in table 4.1). The equation accounts for about 60 percent of the variance for midterms from 1946 to 1990 (adjusted $R^2 = .50$).

Tufte's equation appears somewhat stronger over the period from 1946 to 1990 when the actual congressional vote is examined as the dependent variable (as opposed to standardized vote loss or vote change) and the normal vote is included separately as an independent variable. This equation, including presidential popularity, economic change, and the normal vote, is estimated as equation 4. As specified, this equation accounts for 84 percent (adjusted $R^2 = .77$) of the variation in the midterm congressional vote for the president's party, though presidential popularity surprisingly falls short of conventional levels of statistical significance.

In its focus on the vote loss at the midterm, Tufte's analysis stopped short of explaining variance in seat losses. The analysis examined how votes translated into seats, noting a highly erratic and generally declining swing ratio, but did not attempt to explain seat losses directly. The referenda equation constructed by Tufte has been used, nevertheless, to generate seat loss predictions. These predictions in several recent midterms have been significantly off the mark (see Jacobson 1983b, 6; Mann and Ornstein 1983, 140; Witt 1983, 49). The strength of the referenda equation in explaining midterm seat losses can be assessed more systematically by respecifying the equation so that it accounts directly for seat losses rather than for the standardized vote loss. Such an equation has been constructed and estimated. The results appear as equation 5 in table 4.1. The referenda equation adapted to account for seat losses directly seems to be a modest success. It explains about half the variance (adjusted $R^2 = .39$) in midterm seat losses between 1946 and 1990. However, in five of the twelve midterms the equation was more than fifteen seats in error. In the 1958 midterm, for instance, the equation yielded an expected seat loss that was twenty-two seats less than the actual loss (-26 expected vs. -48 actual). The average absolute error over these twelve midterms was 10.7 seats.

Despite these recently apparent shortcomings, the point emerging from the reanalysis of Tufte's referenda theory is not that the theory now fails to be supported by the data. On the contrary, the evidence continues to show that midterms are, to some significant degree, referenda on the administration's performance. However, the theory as originally operationalized does not appear quite as strong as it did in Tufte's original analysis. While considerable effort has been devoted to strengthening the specification of the referenda theory, I will argue that, however revised or modified, a purely referenda explanation of midterm losses is at best a seriously incomplete explanation.[2]

What is the relationship between Tufte's referenda theory and Angus Campbell's surge and decline theory of midterm elections? Obviously they both explain midterm outcomes in terms of national political forces but disagree as to whether the relevant forces are at the midterm or at the prior presidential election. But should these theories be seen as competing with one another, as complementing one another, or as basically addressing different questions about the nature of midterm election outcomes? Tufte offered some interesting observations about the relationship of the referenda theory to the theory of surge and decline.

According to Tufte, the two theories address essentially two separate and distinct questions about midterm elections. Surge and decline, as interpreted by Tufte, explains why the president's party consistently loses votes and seats in midterm elections. In Tufte's own words, "(i)t explains why the president's party should almost always be operating in the loss column, it does not account for the number of votes and seats lost by the president's party. In statistical parlance, the adjustment model [author's note: surge and decline] of midterm congressional elections explains the location of the mean rather than variability about the mean" (1975, 813). In contrast, the referenda theory sought to explain the variability of midterm losses, though in his conclusion Tufte speculated that the referenda theory is also a partial explanation of the consistency of presidential party midterm losses. Two reasons presidents do not do well in midterm elections is that their popularity generally "has declined since the prior on-year election and because the economy is performing less well at the time of the midterm than it was two years earlier during the presidential election" (Tufte 1975, 826). He went on to speculate that, "a satisfactory explanation of why the president's party always operates in the loss column in off-years will grow from a combination of the midterm model [author's note: the referenda model of midterms] and a revised version of Campbell's 'surge and decline' model (which, in revision, might place more emphasis on the surge and decline of coattail effects and less on turnout effects" (1975, 826). In effect, Tufte suggested that the two theories might well be considered as complementary in answering the consistency question about midterm losses.

While his speculation about the complementary nature of the two theories with respect to explaining the consistency of midterm losses is an important insight, there is one major flaw in Tufte's analysis of the relationship between the two theories. Tufte mistakenly interpreted the theory of surge and decline as only speaking to the question of the consistency of midterm losses and not to the question of their variability. But all surges are not equal. There are surges, and then there are *surges*. Losses following a narrow presidential victory should be small compared to those following a landslide presidential election.

The Development of the Referenda Theory

Tufte's seminal work on the referenda theory of midterm elections laid the foundation for a great deal of research. The character of this research varied. Some scholars attempted to reconfirm and extend the initial findings or offered minor refinements. Others attempted to elaborate or to amend more significantly the original theory. In this section I will address five efforts to improve upon the original referenda model.

The negative voting hypothesis. Writing at about the same time as Tufte, Samuel Kernell (1977) offered an intriguing amendment to or elaboration of the referenda theory. Based on findings of *The American Voter* (Campbell et al. 1960, 554-556) and more generally on social psychology, he argued that negative impressions are more salient to voters than positive impressions. As applied to midterm elections, this means that the referendum on the administration's performance in office is not an unbiased one; it is biased against the president's party. This negative bias plays itself out in three ways: (1) The negativity thesis hypothesizes, as Mueller (1973) and Stimson (1976) found and Tufte (1975, 826) also observed, that the popularity of the president tends to decline by the time of the midterm.[3] It is generally suspected that the public becomes disenchanted when the high expectations raised in the administration's initial honeymoon period are not met. In addition, Kernell hypothesizes that the public has a tendency to focus on incumbents' failures. Achievements by incumbents are taken for granted. (2) The negativity thesis also hypothesizes that disgruntled potential voters are more likely to turn out at the midterm than potential voters satisfied with the administration's performance. Displeasure with the current administration activates voters while satisfaction engenders complacency. (3) Finally, the negativity thesis hypothesizes that the greater salience of negative evaluations affects defection rates. Partisans of the president's party who disapprove of the president's performance are more prone to defect than approving partisans of the opposition party.[4]

Kernell finds evidence generally supporting the negativity hypotheses in an analysis of six midterm election polls from 1946 to 1966. As expected, those disapproving of the president at the midterm turned out and defected at greater rates. Further research, however, has not been so supportive. Cover (1986b) performed a multivariate test of the negativity hypotheses with NES data from the 1974, 1978, and 1982 midterm surveys. Although a multivariate analysis is discussed by Kernell in an appendix to his article, most of the evidence he presented in behalf of the hypotheses is in the nature of contingency table analysis. Contrary to Kernell's analysis, Cover found that "negative evaluations of the president do not appear to motivate voters to turn out in disproportionately higher numbers in midterm congressional elections" (1986b, 800) and found only "some support for the notion that disapproving partisans are less likely to vote for the in-party's congressional candidates than are other partisans" (1986b, 795-96).[5]

Although Cover's analysis fails to support strongly the negativity hypotheses, Erikson's (1988) analysis concludes in favor of the negative voting theory. Erikson examined a variety of theories about the relationship between the congressional vote in succeeding presidential and midterm elections. For the ten midterms from 1946 to 1982, Erikson estimates that negative voting cost the president's party between 9 and 10 percentage points of the national congressional vote. Extending the analysis back to the 1904 midterm (n = 21), he calculates that negative voting costs the president's party about 7.7 percent of the midterm vote. The equation explains the Democratic midterm congressional vote as a function of the prior presidential year Democratic congressional vote and a dummy variable for the president's party (equal to one for Democratic administrations). Erikson interpreted the coefficient for party dummy variable as the in-party penalty attributable to negative voting. The equation accounts for 70 percent of the variance in the midterm congressional vote for Democrats.

There are two major problems with Erikson's analysis. First, the significance of the simple dummy variable for the president's party is consistent with several different interpretations of midterm elections besides the negative voting interpretation. The dummy only reveals the average midterm vote loss for the president's party. Erikson's equation links the party dummy to a decline in the midterm vote. Or in other words, the party holding the presidency loses votes at the midterm. But this is just what all the various theories, surge and decline as well as the negative voting theory, seek to explain. The equation does not indicate in any way whether the average midterm vote loss is due to negative voting or to any other cause or set of causes, including those suggested by surge and decline. In fact, as one might well expect, the presidential vote—the principal indicator and independent variable in the aggregate model of surge and decline—is strongly and positively related to Erikson's party control dummy variable (r = .84 from 1900 to 1984).

Second, while Erikson specifies the impact of negative voting as a constant by using a dummy variable for the in-party penalty, Kernell's theory of negative voting suggested that the negative voting penalty was variable. The extent to which the in-party is penalized should depend on the popularity of the president, and presidents are not equally popular or unpopular with midterm electorates. As Kernell wrote, "High presidential popularity reduces the deleterious consequences largely to the degree that it limits the number of voters who are dissatisfied (or at least attribute blame and are thus likely to engage in negative voting). . . . Low popularity, according to this model, indicates that a large proportion of the electorate may be disposed toward negative voting" (1977, 52). That is, the negative voting thesis according to Kernell is not an alternative to the presidential popularity/economy referendum interpretation of midterm losses as Erikson perceives it, but a variant of the basic referenda model.[6]

Although still in dispute, the negative voting theory is an interesting elaboration of the referenda theory of midterms. Like surge and decline, the referenda theory with the negative voting thesis traces the developments of the midterm election to turnout decisions as well as to partisan defection decisions. Perhaps more importantly, though the negative voting thesis does not alter the referenda model's explanation of why some midterm losses are greater than others, it does help the referenda theory explain why the president's party consistently operates in the loss column. In a presidential election the public reacts to both parties and the greater salience of negative impressions affects the parties about evenly. In midterms the focus is only on the president's party and whatever shortcomings the president is perceived as having are magnified by the greater salience of the negative.[7]

The strategic politician. Gary Jacobson and Samuel Kernell (1981) offer a very interesting and quite different revision to the referenda theory. They argue that the referenda theory as originally formulated "is deficient for failing to recognize the prior, independent role of politicians in systematically structuring voters' choices" (1981, 65). That is, the original referenda theory—and for that matter the theory of surge and decline—explains midterm election outcomes entirely in terms of the voters' behavior. The decisions of politicians are ignored. Jacobson and Kernell argue that this is a major oversight. Politicians make decisions that influence midterm outcomes, and there is reason to suspect that the strategic behavior of potential congressional candidates systematically affects aggregate midterm election results. In essence, Jacobson and Kernell offer an elite version of the referenda theory.

The core of their argument concerns candidate recruitment, the decision of potential congressional candidates of whether or not to throw their hats into the ring. Given the tremendous investment of time, energy, and money needed to run a serious congressional campaign, potential candidates, as a group, are quite deliberate in making the decision to run. It is not a decision to be made lightly or without a careful reading of the political climate. While rationality and information assumptions may apply broadly to potential candidates, all potential candidates are not equal and will not necessarily make the same decision to run under the same circumstances. Some are more savvy than others. Some have more to lose than others. Some would run a stronger campaign than others. Jacobson and Kernell (1981) hypothesize a pattern: "Ambitious career politicians looking to enter or move up the hierarchy of elective offices are likely to be the most formidable challengers. But they also have the most to risk in the attempt; defeat is at best a setback, at worst ends the career. Thus the best candidates will also be the most cautious in deciding when to run for higher office. They will be most sensitive to the odds on winning and most aware of the factors that affect those odds" (p. 424).

When conditions appear favorable for a party, more of the stronger potential congressional candidates from that party may be tempted to take the plunge. The prospects that their party label may provide more of a help than a hindrance, or more of a help than it would be in other election years, may entice some candidates to run who wouldn't take the gamble under other circumstances. Campaign activists and contributors might make similar calculations, choosing to work harder or contribute more when there is reason to be optimistic about the party's chance of victory. Conversely, when conditions look bleak for a party, strong potential candidates may be more inclined to postpone making the run until the partisan climate appears more favorable. Similarly, campaign workers and contributors may be reluctant to invest their time and money in a campaign fighting such an uphill battle. In short, the political climate of a campaign may encourage or discourage strong candidates from entering the field.

What are the measures of the political climate in midterm elections? What national factors might potential candidates believe would affect their odds of winning the election? Like Tufte, Jacobson and Kernell claimed that the political climate could be measured by the popularity of the president and the condition of the economy. When all things are being equal—such as the efforts and financing of the national parties (1982, 428-430)—and when the president is popular and the economy is healthy, the president's party will find it easier to recruit strong candidates to the ticket and the opposition party will find it more difficult. As Jacobson and Kernell put it, "the party expected to have a good year will field a larger proportion of high-quality challengers with well-financed campaigns, while the opposing party is stuck with a disproportionate number of feeble challengers lacking the resources for a serious campaign" (1982, 425).

Initially, Jacobson and Kernell offered only an indirect test of the thesis. Since potential candidates must decide whether or not to run well before voters must decide for whom they will vote, they hypothesized that if the real referenda is being conducted at the candidate rather than voter level, earlier rather than later indicators of the political climate should be more strongly associated with midterm results. They constructed and examined three referenda equations: one with political climate variables (economic change and presidential popularity) in the fall just before the midterm, one with the political climate in the spring when candidates would be deciding to run, and one with both spring and fall indicators. Although they concluded that the analysis "presents strong evidence for the counterintuitive prediction that the more distant spring political environment will have a greater effect on the election" and therefore supports the strategic politician revision, the evidence is ambiguous. While the spring model accounts for a greater portion of the variance in the standardized vote loss measure than the fall model, the difference is not very large (adjusted $R^2 = .72$ and .65, respectively). Moreover, though the economy in the spring matters more than in the fall, just the reverse is true of presidential popularity. The fall presidential popularity measure is stronger than the earlier spring measure, contrary to the strategic politician hypothesis but in accord with the voter referenda hypothesis.

Born's examination of the strategic politician thesis reached a very different conclusion. Examining aggregate data from 1946 to 1982 and individual-level data from 1966 to 1982, Born concluded that "the theory does not stand up to empirical investigation" (1986, 599). Born's adjustment to Tufte's original referendum model, looking at economic change over eighteen months rather than a year and averaging presidential popularity over the three final months of the campaign, accounted for a greater percentage of variance in the standardized vote loss than the strategic politician referendum model (adjusted $R^2 = .643$ and .594, respectively). The individual-level analysis also failed to support the strategic politician thesis. The quality of the challenger, as measured by his having previously held elective office, did not significantly affect the vote choice in any of the five midterms examined.

Since his original analysis and Born's counterfindings, Jacobson produced additional support for the thesis (1982, 1989). Measuring candidate quality by whether or not the candidate had ever held elective office, he found evidence of two critical links in the strategic politician thesis in both aggregate and district analyses of elections from 1946 to 1986. First, like Bond, Covington, and Fleisher's (1985) analysis of challenger quality in the 1980 elections, Jacobson (1989, 779-80) found that the national political climate affected a party's attraction of quality challengers, though this effect was not significant for Republicans. Second, he found that the relative quality of the parties' challengers significantly affects both vote margins and election outcomes (Jacobson 1982; 1989, 781-87).

Although the status of the strategic politician thesis is still open to question, the evidence on balance suggests that candidate recruitment is sensitive to political conditions and has an impact on election results. As such, and as specified in Jacobson's (1989) analysis, the thesis would appear to supplement the original referendum theory based on voter reactions. It is important to bear in mind that the decisions of strategic politicians magnify the consequences of the political climate rather than entirely displace voters as judges of midterm conditions. If candidates behave in ways that anticipate voter reactions that never materialize, the strategic politician thesis amounts to a fragile self-fulfilling prophecy of supposedly well-informed and strategic politicians systematically making career decisions on the faulty premise that midterm conditions really matter to voters. If voters don't react to the political climate, there is little reason for well-informed strategic politicians to enter anticipated reactions into their deliberations. If politicians are not fools, they will only anticipate voter reactions that ultimately will affect the vote.[8]

Party competence evaluations. In a series of articles Albert Cover and his colleagues (Cover 1986a, 1986b; Abramowitz, Cover, and Norpoth 1986) suggest that the referenda model as originally specified omitted an important variable, the public evaluations of party competence, the party's relative ability to handle the nation's most serious problems. These party competence evaluations, according to Abramowitz, Cover, and Norpoth, "are the linchpin of the midterm election model" (p. 570).

In their revised referenda model, party competence evaluations mediate the effects of the two principal exogenous variables, the economic growth variable and the presidential popularity variable, on the ultimate dependent variable, the standardized vote loss measure employed by Tufte (1975). There is considerable empirical support for the party competence referenda model. In examining the nine midterms from 1946 to 1982 (excluding 1954 because of missing data), Abramowitz, Cover, and Norpoth found: (1) that the exogenous variables of the economy and presidential popularity strongly affect evaluations of party competence (beta's of .54 and .52, respectively) and (2) that party competence evaluations are a very strong influence on the standardized vote loss (beta of .88). They also found that party competence evaluations helped to explain the greater losses that had been sustained by presidents serving in their second term. Evidence supporting the importance of party competence evaluations is also found in an examination of individual level survey data. Determinants of the congressional vote choice are examined by a probit analysis of the NES of 1974, 1978, and 1982. Party evaluation effects on the vote choice are found to be statistically significant in two of the three elections (1974 and 1982). Cover (1986a) extended the analysis to include presidential year elections and found further evidence of the impact of party competence evaluations. Party competence continued to have a strong direct effect on the standardized vote loss in the aggregate time series analysis and was significant in five of the six (1972 to 1982) individual-level, cross-sectional probit analyses of the vote choice (the sole exception again being 1978).

In evaluating the party competence amendment to the original referenda model a few points should be kept in mind. First, the addition of party competence evaluations to the model does not alter the model in any basic sense. That is, since party competence evaluations are inserted as an intervening variable between the exogenous variables and the election outcome variable, its role is to elaborate the mechanism by which economic growth and presidential popularity are translated into congressional vote choices.[9] Second, the causal standing of party competence evaluations is open to question. Advocates for the incorporation of these evaluations in the referenda model assume that these evaluations affect the vote choice and are not affected by the vote choice. It is quite plausible, however, that party competence evaluations may in part be rationalizations of the vote. That is, voters who have decided to vote for a party's congressional candidate may be inclined to report that party is the most able to solve the most important national problem, simply out of a desire for consistency. Last, although the inclusion of party competence evaluations improves the fit of the referenda model, the improvement is not dramatic. Over the nine midterms considered, party competence evaluations directly account for 78 percent of the variance (adjusted $R^2 = .74$) in the standardized vote loss. As a point of comparison, over the same set of nine midterms from 1946 to 1982 (also excluding 1954), the original version of the referenda model with the state of the economy and presidential popularity accounts for 71 percent of the variance (adjusted $R^2 = .61$).

Despite these reservations about the value of introducing party competence evaluations into the midterm referendum model, the party competence variable may still shed some light on the public's referendum judgment. In particular it may help to illuminate the role of the economy in that judgment. In a separate piece of research and using somewhat different terminology, Petrocik and Steeper (1986) reach a conclusion about the need of an overall subjective evaluation of performance that in many ways is similar to the Cover (1986a) argument. Examining the 1982 midterm election, Petrocik and Steeper argue that many voters did not fully attribute the blame for the 1982 economic recession to President Reagan and the Republican party. Some voters believed that Reagan had inherited an economic mess from the Carter administration. Any analysis that just examined the cold economic figures in 1982 would miss how they were being politically translated by the public. A model using only objective economic change data would incorrectly assume that a first-term Reagan presidency would be punished as much for a 1982 recession as a second-term Carter presidency.[10]

The exposure thesis. Bruce Oppenheimer, James Stimson, and Richard Waterman (1986; Waterman 1990; Waterman, Oppenheimer, and Stimson 1991) have offered another modification to the referenda theory: the exposure thesis. The exposure thesis adapts the referenda theory to explain the loss of seats at the midterm by the president's party rather than the standardized vote loss and introduces a new variable into the referenda equation, the exposure variable. The exposure variable is a measure of the extent to which a party's preelection seat holdings exceed or fall short of its normal share of seats. If a party typically has held 254 of the 435 House seats, as Oppenheimer, Stimson, and Waterman calculate the Democrats have held since 1938, then if it held fewer than 254 going into an election it would be underexposed by the difference. Conversely, if the party held more than the 254, it would be overexposed.

According to the exposure thesis, all things being equal, a party that is underexposed should find it easier to gain seats than a party overexposed. An underexposed party has a number of seats to gain back that it normally holds. This is a much easier job than that faced by the overexposed party. A party that holds seats in excess of its usual number would do well simply to preserve the status quo. Generally, the overexposed party should expect to lose some of its surplus at the next election as the system returns to equilibrium.

Oppenheimer, Stimson, and Waterman conducted an aggregate analysis of the impact of a party's exposure on its seat change in both on-year and midterm elections from 1938 to 1984. They examined equations with the exposure variable alone, in conjunction with a midterm dummy variable and incorporated it into both Tufte's and Jacobson and Kernell's (earlier measures) referenda equations. In each case the exposure variable proved strongly negative and statistically significant as expected by the thesis. The exposure variable alone accounted for nearly one-half of the variance in seat changes in the twenty-four congressional election years examined from 1938 to 1984 (adjusted R^2 of .46). Moreover, it substantially improved the fit of the two differently timed referenda equations. The addition of the exposure variable to the Tufte equation, using fall measures of the political climate, improves the proportion of explained variance in seat changes from 27 to 78 percent (adjusted R^2). Similarly, the addition of the exposure variable to the Jacobson and Kernell version of the referenda equation, using the earlier spring measures increases the proportion of variance explained from 21 percent to 64 percent (adjusted R^2).

Although the exposure thesis is quite plausible, there are real questions about the extent and nature of its actual contribution to explaining midterm losses.[11] First, the explanatory power of exposure is less impressive when more recent elections are considered. The second equation in table 4.2 updates the "exposure alone" equation for elections from 1944 to 1990. While the estimated effects of exposure remain negative and

Table 4.2. Seat Changes Explained by the Exposure Thesis

Dependent variable: Seat changes for the presidential party

Independent variables	Presidential and midterm election years		Only midterm elections (1946-1990)		
	1938-84	1944-90	Only exposure	Tufte model	Referenda & exposure
Constant	−8.05	−4.60	−24.95	−86.15	−86.92
Exposure	−.71	−.64	−.09	—	−.40
	(4.47)	(2.96)	(.27)		(1.55)
Presidential popularity	—	—	—	1.07	1.18
				(2.44)	(2.85)
Economic conditions	—	—	—	2.27	3.06
				(1.37)	(1.88)
Number of cases	24	24	12	12	12
R^2	.48	.28	.01	.50	.62
Adjusted R^2	.46	.25	.00	.39	.48

SOURCES: The estimates for the regression in the first column are from table 2 of Oppenheimer, Stimson, and Waterman (1986, 237). The other regressions were calculated by the author. Note: The t-ratios are in parentheses.

statistically significant, exposure now accounts for a bit more than one-quarter of the variation in seat change rather than the half estimated in the original analysis of the elections from 1938 to 1984. Second, Oppenheimer, Stimson, and Waterman's original test of the thesis was conducted on all congressional election years without distinguishing those held in presidential election years from those held in midterms, except for the inclusion of a midterm dummy variable in one version of the equation.[12] The implicit assumption is that exposure matters equally in on-year and midterm congressional elections. But this need not be and apparently is not the case. In their analysis of the equation explaining seat changes in terms only of the party's exposure, Oppenheimer, Stimson, and Waterman examined the residuals for the twelve midterm elections in their series (1986, table 3). The absolute magnitude of these errors indicate that, at least in this bivariate analysis, the exposure variable contributes little, if anything, to explaining variation in midterm seat losses in the president's party. In one midterm, 1946, the exposure alone equation was nearly fifty-five seats in error. In six of the twelve midterms the error in the exposure alone equation exceeded nineteen seats. The average absolute error for the equation over the twelve midterms from 1938 to 1982 was nearly nineteen seats, and even though its prediction for 1986 of a seven-seat loss was only two seats off the mark, the average error for the last six midterms (1966-86) was still thirteen seats. As a benchmark, consider that the average absolute error produced by simply predicting the average midterm seat loss would be just eighteen seats (from 1938-82). Reanalyzing the "exposure only" model by conducting a regression analysis on only midterm elections from 1946 to 1990, presented in table 4.2, confirms the suspicions. *Exposure alone actually fails to account for any variance in midterm seat losses.* Moreover, when the exposure variable is added to the conventional referenda equation, the variable's effects fall short of statistical significance though the explanatory power of the equation is increased a bit (the adjusted R^2 increases from .39 to .48).[13]

Where the exposure variable may contribute to understanding midterm elections is in the consistency, rather than variability, of presidential party losses. Although Oppenheimer, Stimson, and Waterman do not make mention of it in their analysis, the president's party was overexposed and therefore more vulnerable to seat losses in eleven of the twelve midterm elections they considered.[14] Why is the president's party regularly overexposed going into a midterm? The answer would seem to reside with the events of the prior presidential election. The president's party is overexposed going into the midterm because the political climate in the prior presidential election favored that party. Favorable short-term forces in the prior election determined which party won the presidency and spilled over to help that party win more than its normal share of seats. In essence, the exposure thesis amounts to a partial elaboration of surge and decline or, perhaps, some other presidential election theory of midterm election losses.[15]

The lagged referendum. Michael Lewis-Beck and Tom Rice (1984) have constructed a version of Tufte's referenda equation with the purpose of making it more useful for forecasting purposes. Since the two political climate variables are not available until very close to the midterm election or, in the case of the economic measure, actually well after the midterm, the original referenda equation is not useful for forecasting midterm election outcomes before the fact. Lewis-Beck and Rice modified the original equation to make it useful for forecasting by taking earlier measurements of the political climate independent variables (measuring the president's popularity and the growth rate in the economy six months prior to the midterm) and by directly predicting seat losses rather than by converting standardized vote losses into seat losses with an estimated swing-ratio. The early measurement not only resulted in an equation yielding forecasts but also an equation somewhat more accurate in its predictions than the original version modified to predict seat losses directly. Whereas the original equation erred on average by about eleven seats from 1950 to 1982, the lagged equation erred on average by just eight seats over this same period. Still, an average error of plus or minus eight seats is a sizeable spread and on occasions the equation has been off by eighteen and nineteen seats. Although the lagged referendum equation is more accurate than the original, there is certainly room for further improvement.

An Assessment of the Referenda Theory

Although the particulars of several of the suggested revisions to the referenda theory are still matters in dispute and although the evidence of recent midterms has not been as kind to the theory as the evidence of prior midterms examined by Tufte, the basic argument and opera-tionalization of the theory seem now to be well confirmed. As Jacobson and Kernell and Lewis-Beck and Rice have separately shown, the timing of referenda decisions occurs somewhat earlier than originally envi-sioned, but there is little doubt that the decisions expressed in the midterm at least partially reflect the voters' and, most probably, potential candidates judgments about the performance of the president. As Tufte claimed, "the midterm vote is a referendum" (1975; 862).

Despite the significant evidence in its behalf, the referenda theory is flawed. In concentrating exclusively on the midterm itself and the short-term forces of that campaign, the theory fails to take into account the full context of the election. With the single exception of the exposure thesis variation on the theory (a variation which has its own problems), the referenda theory ignores the political events of the preceding election. While this is a more glaring omission for those versions of the theory explicitly looking at change from the presidential election to the midterm (e.g., Lewis-Beck and Rice 1984), it is a problem inherent in the narrow focus of the referenda theory. The outcomes of midterm elections reflect referenda-like judgments by the voting public, but this is not all that they entail. The referenda story of midterm elections is an incomplete story. The story of a midterm election really begins in the prior presidential election.

PART 2
The Presidential Pulse

5

The Revised Theory
of Surge and Decline

> *I suspect that a satisfactory explanation of why the presi-*
> *dent's party always operates in the loss column in off-years*
> *will grow from a combination of the midterm model and a*
> *revised version of Campbell's "surge and decline" model*
> *(which, in revision, might place greater emphasis on the*
> *surge and decline of coattail effects and less on turnout*
> *effects).*
>
> —Edward R. Tufte (1975:826).[1]

In light of the analysis of Part 1, Tufte's suspicion of what a complete explanation for the consistency of midterm losses might entail seems well worth pursuing. In what follows, I argue that Tufte was basically on the right track. A revised version of the theory of surge and decline provides a more complete explanation for both the consistency and variation in midterm seat losses and is also sustained by evidence of the composition and behavior of the presidential and midterm electorates.

As the analysis and discussion in chapter 3 indicates, the original theory of surge and decline is supported on many important points (at the national and district levels), but fails in other respects. This suggests the possibility that the theory may be fundamentally sound but in need of revision. How should the original theory of surge and decline be revised? The obvious starting point is to address the weaknesses in the theory that have been discovered by subsequent research. In what respects has the theory of surge and decline proven deficient and how might it be amended to correct for these deficiencies?

Weaknesses of the Original Theory

Based on the review of research on midterm elections in the previous chapters, the original theory of surge and decline seems to suffer from two shortcomings. First, the theory was found in several respects to be in error in its claims about the characteristics and behavior of the presidential and midterm electorate. Second, a different sort of problem for the original theory emerges from the consideration of the alternative theory, that midterm elections are referenda on the president's performance in office. Although plagued by problems of its own, as the review of the evidence in chapter 4 finds, the referenda theory has merit. This referenda aspect of midterm congressional elections was entirely neglected by the original theory of surge and decline and amounts to an implicit deficiency in the original theory. Fortunately, the problem posed by the referenda theory's challenge can be addressed relatively easily by simply acknowledging that the midterm pattern of electoral change may to some degree be a function of public evaluations of the president's party at the midterm itself. As Tufte suggested in the above epigraph, the two theories ought to be regarded as complementary rather than as antagonistic to one another.[2]

The original theory's problems in explaining individual behavior in the electorate are not so easily explained or resolved. Two errors—one of commission and one of omission—would seem to account for the original theory being misleading about how short-term forces work on different segments of the public. First, the original theory went astray in its understanding of the link between partisanship and turnout (an error of commission). Second, it failed to take cross-pressures into account in evaluating the impact of short-term forces (an error of omission).

Partisanship and turnout. The error of commission is the exaggerated difference in the quality of independents and partisans and the faulty inference drawn from this supposed difference. The notion that partisans comprise a larger portion of the midterm than presidential electorates (proposition 8) is based on the premise that partisans are better informed and more politically involved than independents. Political interest is supposed to stimulate and maintain partisan allegiances, and they in turn are supposed to sustain and fuel further interest. These politically interested partisans are the dependable voters. Independence from party, on the other hand, is supposed to reflect and promote political indifference and apathy. Only the jolt of a presidential campaign, the theory argues, can push these politically inattentive independents to the polls.

Unquestionably partisanship is related to turnout and strong partisans in particular are more inclined to turn out than are weak partisans, independents leaning in favor of one of the parties, or pure independents (Verba and Nie 1972, 210-212). Strong partisanship is also positively associated with psychological involvement in politics (Abramson 1983, 81-81). However, these associations are not especially strong. Nonparametric correlations between intensity of partisanship and turnout for presidential and midterm elections from 1952 to 1988 are displayed in table 5.1.[3] While these correlations are consistently positive, they are not

Table 5.1. Nonparametric Correlations between Reported Turnout and Intensity of Partisanship, 1952-1988

Presidential elections		Midterm elections	
1952	.08	1954	—
1956	.05	1958	.13
1960	.05	1962	.13
1964	.08	1966	.17
1968	.09	1970	.16
1972	.05	1974	.04
1976	.16	1978	.19
1980	.15	1982	.23
1984	.15	1986	.20
1988	.19		

NOTE: The correlations are asymmetric Somer's d with turnout as the dependent variable. Intensity of partisanship was coded as three categories with "not strong partisans" and "independent leaners" grouped together.

especially strong. Partisans are somewhat more likely to vote than independents, but a great many independents do vote and a great many partisans fail to vote. In midterm elections the pool of nonvoting independents and weak partisans is proportionately larger than the pool of nonvoting strong partisans, but the difference is not very great. As a result, the presidential election increase in turnout rates pulls in many peripheral partisans along with the peripheral independents.

Even though the difference in nonvoting partisans and independents is only marginal, one might suppose that it would still produce a consistent but small difference in the partisan composition of presidential and midterm electorates. With proportionately more independents not voting in the midterm, there is more room to expand their ranks in the presidential electorate. But they don't. The reason would seem to be that while the pool of nonvoting independents is proportionately larger than the pool of nonvoting partisans in midterms, it is more difficult to draw independents not voting in the midterm into the presidential electorate. Nonvoting partisans in midterms may be closer to the activation threshold than nonvoting independents. A number of independents, as Miller and Wattenberg have documented (1983), are not just neutral between the parties but largely removed from politics. This type of independent may require more stimulation to vote than even a presidential election campaign can muster. In effect, since partisans are a bit more likely to vote than independents, they are more likely than independents to be core voters but they are also more likely than independents to be peripheral voters. As a result, core and peripheral voters do not systematically differ in their degree of partisanship.

Cross-Pressures. The original theory's error of omission was in failing to take fully into account the potential conflict many face between their reaction to a presidential campaign's short-term forces and their long-standing partisan commitments. Cross-pressures of this sort may have significant consequences for the behavior of voters or potential voters beyond those suggested by the original theory.

The original theory considered only how conflict between short-term forces and party identification would affect how voters would vote (the question of vote choice) and not how this conflict would affect whether potential voters would vote (the question of turnout). In terms of the vote choice, the theory suggested that a surge of information favorable to a party would draw votes from independents and cause increased defection from the opposing party. The question of turnout was treated as almost an entirely separate matter. According to the theory, the gross volume of the information surge in presidential campaigns stimulates an increase in turnout, drawing peripheral partisans of both parties and especially peripheral independents to the polls. The net partisan message or the substance of this information surge was not hypothesized to have any effect on turnout.

To understand why the conflict of short-term campaign forces and long-held partisan predispositions might affect turnout, a brief review of the theory of cross-pressures is in order.

As a concept, cross-pressures identifies a situation in which an individual is confronted with cues or influences recommending conflicting decisions or behavior. These cues or influences may be implicit and remote, such as different social background characteristics associated with different courses of action. For instance, an individual's economic and religious background may indicate different political responses. A wealthy Catholic may feel pressures to vote for a Republican because of his economic status as well as pressures to vote for a Democrat because of the traditional links of his church to the Democratic party. Conflicting cues may also be more explicitly and directly political. An individual may hold some political opinions that favor one party and at the same time hold other opinions that favor the opposing party. For instance, an individual may simultaneously agree with the Democrats' domestic policies and the Republicans' foreign policies. While both types of cross-pressures can generate internal conflict for an individual, politically explicit cross-pressures of opinions would seem to have the greater potential of creating anxiety and turmoil in the individual's deliberations.

How do people respond to the conflict posed by cross-pressures? One response, suggested by cognitive consistency theories in general and by cognitive dissonance theory (Festinger 1957) more particularly, is to relieve the stress associated with dissonance by rationalizing attitudes so that they are more comfortably consistent with each other.[4] Accordingly, if someone initially favoring the Democrats domestically but the Republicans in foreign affairs eventually decides to vote for the Republicans, he or she may revise or rationalize evaluations of Republican domestic policy to put them in a more favorable light. These revised views of domestic and foreign policies might then be more consistent, or at least less inconsistent, in their support for the Republican choice than the initial more dissonant opinions. Going one step further, the psychological processes of selective perception and selective evaluation may prevent or retard the initial creation of cross-pressures. If voters screen new information that might challenge or upset previously held opinions, they may be able to preserve consistency in their opinions and avoid the unpleasantness associated with conflicting cross-pressures.

Cognitive dissonance reduction, however, is no cure-all. Social characteristics in conflict cannot be rationalized into consistency, and voters may be constrained in rationalizing away attitudinal conflicts. Some may determine one cue to be more important than the other, follow the more important cue, and simply tolerate the continuing cross-pressures. Another reaction or response to this conflict is suggested by the theory of cross-pressures. That reaction is withdrawal. Much of the unpleasantness of a cross-pressured decision may be avoided if the decision itself can be avoided. As Flanigan and Zingale observe in their review of cross-pressure research: "The responses to cross-pressures predicted by the hypothesis are avoidance reactions—efforts to avoid or to minimize the anxiety produced by conflict" (1987, 66). Cross-pressures make for an unpleasant choice, because whatever course of action is chosen, that choice will conflict with some relevant cue. By withdrawing from or downgrading the importance of the decision, the anxiety of the unpleasant choice can be reduced. At the extreme, cross-pressures induce abstention, a complete avoidance of the cross-pressured choice.

The first major electoral studies to investigate carefully the effects of cross-pressures were the Columbia voting studies of the 1940 and 1944 presidential elections, *The People's Choice* (Lazarsfeld, Berelson, and Gaudet 1944) and *Voting* (Berelson, Lazarsfeld, and McPhee 1954). Their investigations concluded that cross-pressures diminish interest in the campaign causing some to postpone their decisions, causing others to vacillate in their decisions, and causing still others to abstain from voting altogether (1954, 284). The major Michigan election studies (Campbell et. al. 1960, 77-88) basically concurred with these findings that attitudinal cross-pressures are "associated with nonvoting, indecision[,] and indifference toward the election" (Flanigan and Zingale, 1987, 68).

From both a theoretical and an empirical standpoint Sperlich (1971) provided the single most thorough analysis of cross-pressures to date. Although critical of the simple cross-pressures thesis, Sperlich offered a set of revisions to it. Essentially these revisions specified cross-pressure effects to be conditional rather than across-the-board. According to Sperlich's analysis, cross-pressure effects depend upon the extent or magnitude of the cross-pressures, the centrality or importance of the decision being cross-pressured, and the individual's willingness and ability to tolerate cross-pressure stress.[5] This conditional cross-pressures theory was strongly supported by Sperlich's analysis of data from the 1952 and 1956 NES.[6]

Whether across-the-board or conditional, most research that focuses directly on cross-pressures has found some withdrawal effect. The precise mechanism or mechanisms by which cross-pressures induce this effect is less clear. At least two reasons for this cross-pressure effect seem plausible—indifference and uncertainty.[7]

First, cross-pressures may weaken voter preferences, leaving the potential voter indifferent or nearly indifferent between the candidates. If some factors provide reasons for a Democratic vote and other factors provide somewhat more compelling reasons for a Republican vote, the voter might end up preferring the Republican, but only at the margin. If voters are nearly indifferent between the two candidates, they may choose not to expend the effort to vote. In their study of turnout in the 1968 election, Brody and Page (1973) found evidence that indifference was related to low turnout. They concluded that "(t)hose who saw no difference between the candidates were likely to stay away from the polls; the greater the discrepancy in one's feelings about opposing candidates, the more likely one is to vote" (1973, 5). In a subsequent analysis of turnout decline, Brody also suggested that "the complete indifference of these citizens to the choices offered to them by the parties reduces their likelihood of voting" (1978, 310). Frohlich, Oppenheimer, Smith, and Young (1978), testing Downs' (1957) calculus of voting with data from the 1964 presidential election, likewise found indifference to depress turnout.[8] Zipp's (1985) extensive multivariate analysis of turnout in the four presidential elections between 1968 and 1980 supports Brody's and Page's claim of indifference effects. In fact, according to Zipp's analysis, the abstention effect of indifference, possibly created by cross-pressures, was greater than the abstention effect attributed to alienation from the two candidates.

Contrary to the above studies, however, Weisberg and Grofman (1981) dispute the effects of indifference on turnout.[9] Based on their examination of potential voter indifference in the 1976 election, Weisberg and Grofman conclude that "indifference does not decrease turnout" (1981, 207). Their analysis, however, does not take into account many background factors known to be related to turnout (education, among others) and employs a very restrictive definition of indifference. They count as indifferent only those respondents who rated both candidates equally on the NES "feeling thermometer" scales.[10] Quite conceivably, voters may be basically indifferent to the candidates without being perfectly indifferent. They may see "a dime's worth of difference," but no more. Very minor differences in evaluations may not warrant the effort of making a choice or expressing it at the polls.

Aside from indifference, the conflict endemic to cross-pressures may itself cause potential voters to stay home. With conflicting signals and uncertainty as to how heavily to weigh them in ultimately deciding a vote choice, potential voters simply may find their decision too risky to make.[11] They may feel so uncomfortable with their choice that they simply opt not to vote rather than risk a decision that they might later come to regret. There is some research that finds evidence of this effect. Measuring uncertainty by respondents' willingness to identify candidate issue positions, Gant (1983) found that uncertainty had a substantial effect in inhibiting turnout in a multivariate analysis of the 1980 election.

A comparison of two voting situations, illustrated in figure 5.1, may clarify this point. Potential voter A prefers one candidate over the other, but only narrowly, after considering several cues that consistently but weakly support that preference. Thus the preference function is concentrated on candidate X's side of the dimension (the distribution is of smaller variance) but the center of the function is only barely past the neutral point. Like potential voter A, potential voter B is nearly indifferent to the candidates. B slightly prefers one candidate over the other but arrived at this preference only after comparing and weighing some cues that favored one candidate and others that favored the second candidate. Voter B's preference function also is centered on candidate X's side of the scale, but is more dispersed, suggesting less certainty about the preferred candidate. The potential voter in this situation may be more uneasy about his choice because of the uncertainty involved in determining the import of each cue in order to combine them into a single preference. (The risk to voter B of making the wrong choice is indicated by the cross-hatched area under the preference curve.) Since the cues in a cross-pressure situation indicate different vote choices, the uncertainty involved in gauging the relative weights of each cue raise more doubts about the reliability and satisfaction with the decision based on these cues.[12] For instance, a voter might be uncertain how heavily to count evaluations of the candidates' themselves, their personal qualities and

Figure 5.1. Subjective Probability Distribution of Satisfaction with Vote Cast for a Candidate under Conditions of Consistent Cues and Cross-Pressures

Voter A. Consistent but weak cues: Near indifference but low risk of regret

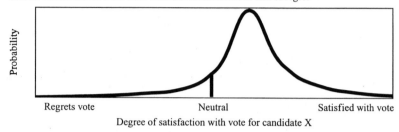

Degree of satisfaction with vote for candidate X

Voter B. Cross-pressured cues: Near indifference and high risk of regret

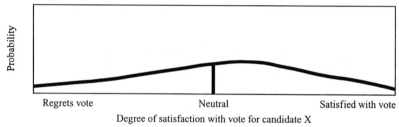

Degree of satisfaction with vote for candidate X

Note: The area under the curve to the left of the neutral bar indicates the likelihood of regretting a vote for candidate X. Observe that this area is greater under the cross-pressure conditions of voter B.

issue positions, in their overall preference. The voter might choose one candidate if these candidate considerations weigh in heavily but decide in favor of the opponent if they are given less weight. Of course, few voters ever feel entirely certain that they have made the right choice. Information is imperfect and incomplete and candidates once in office often act in unanticipated ways. Cross-pressured voters, however, bear an added burden. If they vote, they must go into the voting booth with doubts already in place about the relative merits of their chosen candidate.[13]

From the perspective of the theory of surge and decline the most important source of cross-pressures evident in presidential elections is between long-term and short-term forces. It is inevitable in a presidential campaign that many partisans encounter short-term forces—the issue positions or character traits of candidates—that conflict with their long-term partisan predispositions. A conservative Democrat may be irritated by the liberal positions of his party's nominee or a Republican may find the apparent leadership strengths of the Democratic party's candidate especially appealing. In any particular election there are a variety of ways in which a partisan may be either displeased by his party's nominee or

Figure 5.2. Impediments to Cross-pressures between Long-term and Short-term Evaluations

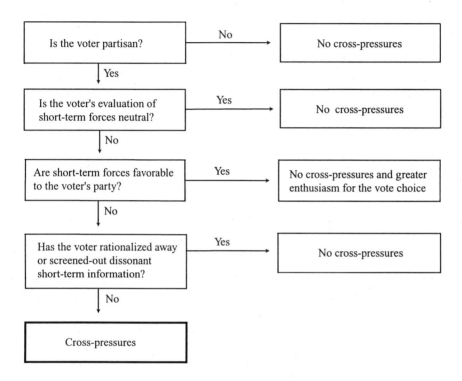

especially pleased by the opposition's nominee, cross-pressuring the partisan.

There are, of course, impediments to conflict between these long-term and short-term evaluations. Several such impediments to the development of cross-pressures are illustrated in the flow chart of figure 5.2. To begin with, cross-pressures between long-term and short-term evaluations require that neither of these evaluations be neutral. If the voter is truly independent, having no general long-term predisposition for or against either party, cross-pressures between short-term and long-term evaluations are impossible. The independent can feel free to vote according to his or her assessment of the short-term aspects of the campaign—the candidates, their records, their philosophies, and their promises—without the added doubts raised by cross-pressures. Similarly, cross-pressures are impossible for voters whose evaluations of short-term forces in a campaign are neutral.[14] Their standing partisan preferences stand unchallenged.

A third impediment to the development of cross-pressures is that the new information generated in a campaign may be consonant with the voters' long-term partisan preference. To some degree the consistency of short-term forces with long-term evaluations is attributable to inertia. As long as voters and parties maintain some continuity with their pasts, voters who preferred a party in past elections should prefer the same party in future elections. Also, to some degree, many changes in the voter or by the party serve to reinforce rather than to contest the voter's predisposition in favor of a party. As a contest with a single winner, the news in an election campaign cannot be bad for everyone. News that cuts in favor of one of the parties should be welcomed by its partisans as supporting prior views. Rather than feeling cross-pressured, these partisans should be reinvigorated in their party loyalty and some who might not have otherwise voted may be moved to turn out because of their greater enthusiasm for their vote choice.[15]

Even if the news about a party and its candidates is not good by some objective standard, the psychology of cognitive dissonance reduction, as we have already discussed, may screen out or reinterpret the bad news to avoid or undo the cross-pressure dilemma. It is well documented that campaign information is at least partially observed through partisan lenses (see for instance Campbell et al. 1960,133; Lodge and Hamill 1986; Nie, Verba, and Petrocik, 1986,114). The considerable rationalization of issue opinions and impressions of the candidates leadership abilities is also well documented (see for instance Meier and Campbell 1979; Campbell 1983; Shaffer 1981). Beyond the distortion of short-term information for the sake of consistency, there is also evidence that presumably long-term partisan identifications are, to some measure, revised to conform better with appraisals of the current campaign (Meier 1975; Fiorina 1981, chap. 5; Allsop and Weisberg 1988). Some who find their impressions of the current campaign to be at odds with their party identification apparently are willing to resolve the conflict by adjusting their party identification, at least to a point.

The caveat "to a point" is what leaves room for cross-pressures. Dissonance reduction has its limits. Reasonable perceptions of the campaign must be tied to reality. While the vague nature of candidate and campaign information permits varying and often self-serving interpretations, these interpretations generally cannot stray too far from the actual facts of the campaign. Shadings are possible, but evidence of a candidate's weakness generally cannot be remade into an observation of strength, ineptitude into competence, or callousness into compassion. Rationalization about candidate issue positions is even more constrained by reality. The records and statements of any candidate are certainly not precisely clear on all points at all times, but they are somewhat less malleable than fairly distant impressions of the candidate's character.

Given these limitations to dissonance reduction, some partisans find themselves cross-pressured.

The cross-pressured partisan has three possible choices. The first option is to remain loyal to the party. The temptation to defect and vote for the relatively more appealing candidate of the opposition party may be resisted out of party loyalty. A life-long Democrat, for instance, may find it difficult to vote for a Republican candidate even when he thinks the Republican is a much better candidate. Out of party loyalty he may "hold his nose" and vote Democratic. The second option is to set aside party loyalties and vote for the preferred candidate in the election at hand. The original theory of surge and decline claimed that a substantial number of cross-pressured partisans would exercise this defection option. Given a choice between voting one way because of past party loyalty or voting the other way because of assessments of the current candidates and issues, it is quite understandable why many would decide to cast their vote in the current election according to their assessments of the current candidates and issues.[16]

While both continued loyalty and partisan defection are understandable responses to cross-pressures on partisans, neither is a very pleasant option. A voter must either vote against his own party's candidate or vote contrary to his own evaluation of the candidates running in the particular election. The unpleasantness of the first two options is what may cause some cross-pressured partisans to adopt the third option: abstention. In abstaining, the cross-pressured partisan can avoid the unpleasantness of either defecting from his party or voting against his preferred candidate.

The Electorate in Three Parts

In dividing up the public for the purpose of explaining where the votes for the president's party come from in presidential election years and where these votes go in midterm years, there is a segment of the public that can be dismissed at the outset. These are the habitually inactive. While there are a significant number of people who, for any one of the variety of reasons, might not vote in any given election, the inactives consistently fail to vote. For this group there is not even a remote possibility of their voting. They are removed from politics altogether. As such, they are of no relevance in explaining the midterm pattern. They do not vote for or against the president's party in either presidential or midterm elections.

With the completely inactive portion of the public set aside, the remainder can be divided into three groups to explain the gains made by the president's party in presidential election years and losses in subsequent midterms. The three pertinent groups are independents, partisans of the advantaged party in the presidential election, and partisans of the disadvantaged party in the presidential election. The theory argues that the consistency of midterm losses and, in large part, their variation are a consequence of a particular mix of turnout and vote choice decisions of these three groups. The revised theory of surge and decline contends that each of these groups, either by their turnout or vote choice or both, contributes to the congressional vote and seat gains of the winning presidential party in the presidential election year and sets up that party for a fall at the next midterm.

Independents. A group's contribution to any election outcome is a function of three variables: the group's size, its turnout rate, and its vote choice (Axelrod 1972). Although independents have been and continue to be a relatively small segment of the American public, even well into a period of partisan dealignment, they play an important role in the change in election outcomes between presidential and midterm years.[17] According to the revised theory, *independents contribute to this electoral change through the change in their vote choice between the two elections.* Contrary to the original theory, the revised theory contends that the turnout of independents is not important to explaining the midterm pattern.

Without a standing partisan commitment going into the election, nothing stands in the way of independents voting for the candidate that on balance they prefer in a particular presidential election. While independents may recognize strengths and weaknesses in both parties candidates, there is no possibility of serious conflict between their overall long-term and short-term views of the parties. The neutral long-term evaluations allow independents to be guided entirely by their short-term evaluations. Although some voting independents may decide in favor of the losing presidential candidate, most should vote for the winning presidential candidate given that prevailing short-term forces are advantageous to the party winning the presidency, as demonstrated earlier in chapter 2. The combination of independents lacking a long-term countervailing partisan predisposition and the systematic tilt of short-term forces in the direction of the winning presidential party should produce an independent vote that contributes to the winning presidential party's margin in the presidential contest. And as the original version of the theory also contends (proposition 10), the greater clarity in the winning presidential party's short-term advantage, the greater the independent's contribution to the president's vote margin. To the degree that even independents link one candidate to another through their respective party affiliations, the independent vote for the winning presidential candidate should spill over to help that party's lesser known candidates further down the ticket.

Unlike presidential election years, the independent vote in midterms does not systematically favor the president's party. Nor is the independent vote systematically against the president's party at the midterm, though as the negative voting theory contends, there may be some tendency for voters at the midterm to be disappointed by unfulfilled expectations of the president's performance. While undoubtedly the independent midterm vote is in part a referendum on the president, the revised theory contends that it reflects national and presidential forces less than the independent vote in presidential election years. Without the presidential candidates actually seeking office and running attention-grabbing national campaigns, the independent midterm vote naturally focuses more on local politics and the congressional candidates themselves.

With the independent vote in presidential elections focused more on national presidential politics to the benefit of the winning presidential party and in midterms focused more on the local congressional contests (less systematically to one party's advantage), the difference in the presidential and midterm votes of independents contributes to the general pattern of midterm vote loss for the president's party.

As to the turnout of independents, the revised theory argues that it is of no particular bearing for the midterm pattern. Independents turn out in greater numbers in presidential elections than in midterms, but not disproportionately so. Many peripheral voters who happen to be independents, like those who identify with either of the parties, are pulled into the presidential electorate by the excitement of the presidential campaign and the higher office at stake. These peripheral independents are no more or less likely than core independents to respond to the prevailing short-term forces at work in a campaign. Because they lack partisan predispositions, neither is likely to rationalize or misperceive short-term factors for the sake of cognitive consistency and neither is vulnerable to the turnout inhibiting effects of cross-pressures.

Advantaged partisans. Advantaged partisans are those who identify with the party having short-term forces generally in its favor in the presidential election year. Given the potency of short-term forces in a presidential election campaign and the long-term competitive balance between the two major parties, the party that enjoys the general advantage of short-term forces in its favor is the party that wins the presidential election.

It is the contention of the revised theory that *advantaged partisans contribute to the midterm pattern primarily through their turnout rather than their vote choice.* The reason that advantaged partisans contribute to the midterm pattern by their turnout is that they tend to be consistent partisans in presidential election years but not in midterm years. By consistent partisans I mean partisans whose impressions of the campaign are consistent with or supportive of their party, the opposite of a cross-pressured partisan. As noted earlier, consistent partisans have reason to be more enthusiastic about their vote preference and, as a result, may be more inclined to turn out. Of course, like others, advantaged partisans are more likely to go to the polls in presidential elections simply because of the added excitement and higher stakes involved. But beyond this, the fact that their long-term partisan predispositions have been reinforced by evaluations of the current campaign should encourage even the least politically involved advantaged partisans to vote. As a consequence, the presidential electorate should be disproportionately composed of partisans of the winning presidential party.

Advantaged partisans tend to be consistent partisans in presidential election years for several reasons. Like all partisans, there is certainly the psychological impetus for finding consistency. Partisan bias may affect how the campaign is perceived and evaluated. But beyond partisan bias, most advantaged partisans may have good reason to evaluate the campaign as being favorable to their party. As already shown, from most points of view short-term forces in a presidential election cut in favor of the advantaged or winning presidential party. Therefore, most advantaged partisans should quite accurately assess short-term factors as being consistent with their long-term partisan attachments.

Of course not all advantaged partisans are necessarily pleased by their party's performance in the campaign. With different values, priorities, and experiences, some advantaged partisans may find themselves at odds with their party and its candidates. Rather than consistency, there are cross-pressures. Of this group of advantaged partisans, some may stick by their party and other may just "sit out" the election. Still others, presumably with weaker partisan ties or stronger negative reactions to the campaign, may defect to vote for the opposition. The basic point, however, is that this group of cross-pressured advantaged partisans is a comparatively small group. This point is illustrated by figure 5.3. Given the psychological pressure for perceiving consistency coupled with the generally favorable political climate for their party, most advantaged partisans should find the campaign quite hospitable to their partisan predispositions.

The advantaged partisans of the presidential election year are likely to find themselves in a very different situation in the midterm election. Compared to the presidential election year, short-term forces in the midterm are less systematic with respect to the president's party and generally are somewhat weaker in their effects one way or the other. Since the determination of the president's party does not hinge on midterm short-term forces as it does on presidential election short-term

Figure 5.3. The Revised Theory of Surge and Decline's Division of
Partisans by Their Evaluations of Short-term Forces in Presidential
Elections

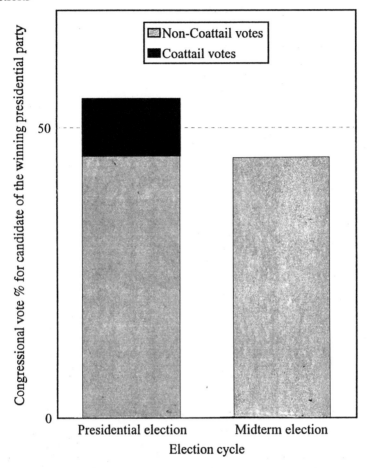

forces, the political climate at midterm may be either favorable or unfavorable for the president's party. Moreover, whichever way the midterm winds are blowing, they are less forceful than the winds of the
presidential election year. Without the focus and energy of a presidential
campaign, short-term forces at the midterm simply pack less of a punch.
Even though they in part revolve around evaluations of the sitting president, without the national focus demanded by the waging of a presidential contest, midterm elections are influenced to a relatively greater extent
by a variety of local factors.

The difference between short-term forces in presidential and midterm election years accounts for the advantaged partisans' contributions
to the pattern of midterm change. Although most advantaged partisans

will find that short-term conditions favor their standing partisan decision in both the presidential and midterm elections, they are somewhat less likely to be consistent partisans in the midterm. To the extent that previously consistent partisans find themselves cross-pressured, whether the cross-pressures are of national or local origin, they may drop out of the midterm electorate. In addition, even if advantaged partisans continue to assess the midterm political climate as favorable to their party, because of the more restrained nature of the midterm campaign this consistency may not engender the same level of enthusiasm that propelled some advantaged partisans to the polls in the presidential year. In short, there are good reasons to suppose that the turnout of advantaged partisans should drop off disproportionately between the presidential and midterm elections. Since these advantaged partisans were predominantly consistent and loyal partisans in the presidential election, the decline of their turnout in the midterm is at the expense of the president's party.

As to the vote choice of advantaged partisans, it is hypothesized to be of secondary importance in accounting for the pattern of midterm change. Since they are predominantly consistent partisans in the presidential election year, there is every reason to believe that advantaged partisans generally will loyally vote for their party's candidate, unless some particularly important and contrary local factor intervenes. At the midterm, many of the advantaged partisans will undoubtedly remain consistent partisans and loyally vote for their party, if they vote at all. Of the advantaged partisans who are cross-pressured at the midterm, some may stick by their party, but others may opt to stay home. The more drastic option of defection may only be expected of the few advantaged partisans with fairly weak partisan attachments who are either quite upset with their party's performance at the midterm or convinced by local conditions that the opposition offers the better alternative. Thus, while midterm defections by advantaged partisans may contribute to the losses by the president's party, they are neither essential to these losses nor are they expected to be the principal means by which advantaged partisans contribute to the midterm loss pattern.

Disadvantaged partisans. If one party is advantaged by short-term forces in a presidential campaign, its opposite is obviously disadvantaged. Given the intensity of the presidential campaign and the general competitiveness of the two parties on the national level, the party disadvantaged by an unfriendly political climate is the party that loses the election.

It is the contention of the revised theory that *disadvantaged partisans, like their advantaged counterparts, contribute to the pattern of presidential midterm losses principally through their turnout rather than by means of their vote choice.* The circumstances encountered by disadvantaged partisans, as one might expect, are in several key respects the mirror image of those faced by advantaged partisans. Most importantly, while short-term forces of the presidential election provide advantaged partisans with an extra incentive to vote, they have the effect of discouraging some disadvantaged partisans from voting.

Disadvantaged partisans turn out in presidential elections in fewer numbers than one might suppose because they are more likely to be subjected to cross-pressures. Compared to advantaged partisans, disadvantaged partisans are more likely to be dissatisfied with their own party or attracted to the candidates or issue positions of the opposition party. With short-term forces generally in favor of the opposing party, many disadvantaged partisans may develop short-term partisan assessments at odds with their long-term party attachments. These cross-pressures may be a countervailing force to the drawing power of the presidential campaign. Some cross-pressured partisans of the disadvantaged party may opt not to vote rather than to make the hard choice between their party and their preference in the particular election.

It is *not* the contention of the revised theory that all or even most disadvantaged partisans in a presidential election are cross-pressured (see figure 5.3). Given different perspectives and values, different experiences and observations, and the drive to find or manufacture consistency, many disadvantaged partisans may be consistent partisans, actually preferring their own party's presidential candidate in the particular election. These consistent but disadvantaged partisans should vote loyally for their party's presidential candidate and (barring the intervention of strong reasons to the contrary at the local level) for their party's congressional candidate. Whether or not these consistent and loyal partisans outnumber cross-pressured partisans in the disadvantaged party in the presidential year is not at issue. The claim of the revised theory is only that the proportion of cross-pressured partisans is greater in the disadvantaged party than in the advantaged party in the presidential election year. This cross-pressure difference between the parties should translate into a turnout difference in favor of the advantaged party.

Circumstances at the midterm are different for disadvantaged partisans. With weaker and less systematic short-term forces working for or against the party, both the likelihood and the force of cross-pressures among partisans of the previously disadvantaged party decline. Midterm turnout among disadvantaged partisans, like the advantaged partisans, would decline in any case because of the absence of the presidential campaign spectacle. However, the disadvantaged partisans' midterm decline in turnout should be less precipitous because cross-pressures of the presidential year had reduced their turnout in the last election.

To this point the focus with respect to disadvantaged partisans has been on their turnout. What of their vote choice? With the prevailing political winds against their party, certainly some disadvantaged partisans can be expected to defect and vote for the opposition in the presidential year. In the following midterm, when short-term forces are weaker and more variable in which party they help or hurt, many defectors can return and loyally vote with their party.

While the rise and fall of defections in the disadvantaged party would contribute to the midterm pattern, according to the revised theory this is not the principal means by which disadvantaged partisans contribute. Defection is an extreme reaction for partisans. They must be very displeased by their party before they would vote against it. While some may be so disgruntled, the displeasure of many more disadvantaged partisans is likely to stop short of defection. Partisan bias in the perceptions and evaluations made by disadvantaged partisans ought to blunt the impact of much of the campaign's bad news for the party. The bottom line is a lot of disadvantaged partisans upset enough not to vote in the presidential election but not so upset that they defect en mass.

Sources of the Surge

According to the revised theory of surge and decline, midterm losses by the president's party are to a large extent repercussions of that party's prior gains produced by a temporary surge of support in the presidential election year. A central question for the theory is where the temporary surge of support comes from? How do the presidential election year's short-term forces play themselves out?

The revised theory contends that there are two ways in which short-term forces favoring the winning presidential party are translated into a surge of votes for that party. *Short-term forces manifest themselves in the vote choices of independents and in the turnout of partisans.*

Independents are the most open of all voters to influence by the campaign. Their perception of the campaign—its candidates, issues and events—are likely to be less biased than others and these perceptions affect evaluations of the parties that are nearly neutral to begin with. In short, the campaign makes the difference between independents voting for Democrats or voting for Republicans.

While independents contribute to the presidential election surge by dividing their votes favorably for the winning presidential party, partisans contribute largely by turning out to vote at different rates. Within the general rise in turnout of the presidential election, there are systematic differences in the turnout of the two parties. Partisans of the advantaged party, the party winning the presidency, can be expected to turn out at a somewhat higher rate then they might otherwise because of the added enthusiasm of voting for a popular fellow partisan. Just the opposite should be true of the opposing party. Partisans of the disadvantaged or losing party in presidential elections should be expected to turn out at a lower rate than they usually would because of their greater likelihood of cross-pressures. The result is a partisan turnout gap. The winning presidential party wins, in part, because of an especially heavy turnout of its own partisans and a lighter than otherwise expected turnout among opposition partisans.

One important caveat is in order about the contribution of partisan defections to the presidential election surge and subsequent midterm decline. While the revised theory contends that the turnout of partisans is the most substantial means by which they contribute to the presidential election surge, partisan defections may also contribute (as the analysis in chapter 3 showed) and, on occasion, contribute significantly to the surge. Defections are likely to make the greatest difference in landslide presidential elections. The reason for partisan defections playing a role in landslide surges is that most partisans do not defect easily. Defection is an extreme response. Most partisans tend to give their party the benefit of the doubt. A certain amount of displeasure with their party can be tolerated or even avoided by not voting, but all partisans have a breaking point beyond which they are provoked to defection. When it becomes obvious to most that a party has put forward the inferior offering—as voters themselves judge to be the case of a party on the short side of a landslide—a significant number of its partisans may be driven past the point of mere abstention to outright defection (see Boyd 1969; DeVoursney 1977).

This caveat regarding defection may be understood with reference again to Sperlich's (1971) work on cross-pressures. Sperlich observed that the effects of cross-pressures should be proportional to their magnitude. Although this appears to be obvious, it has less obvious implications. The magnitude of cross-pressures is greater when the conflicting cues are equally clear in pointing to opposite decisions. As one cue weakens or strengthens relative to the other cue, the magnitude of cross-pressures diminishes. One of the cues can govern the decision. Figure 5.4 demonstrates how this logic applies to cross-pressures between partisanship and short-term evaluations. Three sections of the figure can be examined, at each point assuming partisanship is held constant. When short-term forces are judged to be only slightly unfavorable to a party (the first segment of the short-term evaluation dimension in figure 5.4), its partisans may tolerate their minor temporary differences and remain loyal to

Figure 5.4. Expected Turnout, Partisan Loyalty, and Extent of Party
Disaffection and Cross-Pressures

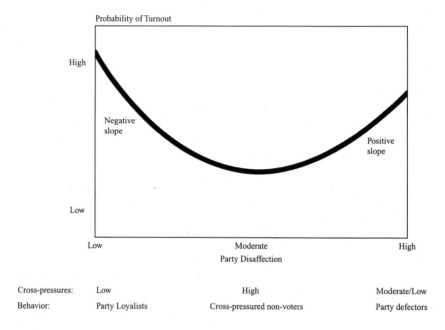

| Cross-pressures: | Low | High | Moderate/Low |
| Behavior: | Party Loyalists | Cross-pressured non-voters | Party defectors |

the party. Great displeasure with the party may increase cross-pressure
anxiety and diminish turnout. Even greater displeasure, however, may
diminish cross-pressures by pushing partisans to defection.

Variations in the Decline

At the midterm, with short-term forces diminished and less systematically advantageous to it, support for the president's party and its congressional candidates generally declines. The extent of this decline depends
in part on the extent of the prior surge of support for the party. The
independent vote advantage and the partisan turnout advantage are
greatest for the president's party in presidential elections in which short-
term forces are most strongly in its favor. It follows that the loss of both
temporary advantages—the vote of independents and the turnout of
partisans—would be most deeply felt by the president's party in midterms following these strong surge presidential elections.

The strength of the prior presidential election surge, however, is not
the only factor affecting the extent of the midterm decline for the president's party. Although the revised theory contends that national short-
term forces are somewhat weaker and less systematic with respect to the
president's party in midterm elections, national short-term forces in

Figure 5.5. The Revised Theory of Surge and Decline's Sequence

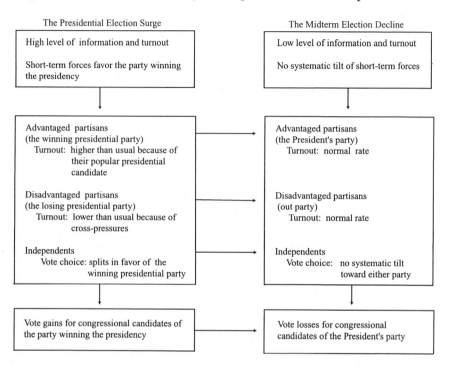

midterm elections are by no means inconsequential. As the review of research in chapter 4 concluded, midterm elections are in part referenda on the performance of the president. A popular president can shorten his party's midterm fall and an unpopular president can lengthen it. The president's party may lose less of its independent vote advantage and its partisan turnout differential advantage if the president is very popular at the midterm. Favorable short-term forces, in the midterm, presumably expressed as support for the president, may continue to attract independent votes, sustain enthusiasm among the president's partisans encouraging them to turn out, and maintain cross-pressures among the opposition's partisans discouraging them from turning out.

While the referenda aspect of the midterm affects the extent of midterm losses, even in the best of circumstances it does not turn potential losses into gains. A positive midterm referendum for the president's party means only that its losses are less than they otherwise would have been. The midterm referendum is unable to pull the president's party into the gain column because the effects of the midterm are circumscribed by the low-stimulus character of the nonpresidential campaign. Whether the president is very popular or very unpopular, he is not on the ballot and is not waging an aggressive midterm campaign. Midterm elections lack not only the intensity of presidential campaigns but the explicit focal point of presidential campaigns. As such, though the midterm is undoubtedly in part a referendum on the president, it is a muted referendum.

All of the elements of the revised theory of surge and decline have now been set forth. Figure 5.5 demonstrates how these various parts fit into a coherent whole. As the figure indicates, for each portion of the electorate—independents, advantaged partisans, and disadvantaged partisans—the president's party is generally better off in the presidential election year than in the midterm.

The Original and Revised Theories

The revised theory of surge and decline as set forth in the preceding pages can be set in perspective by comparing it to Angus Campbell's original formulation of the theory. In what respects is the revised theory in accord with the original? Where does it depart from the original?

The two theories of surge and decline are very much the same in their basic premises and propositions. In explaining both the consistency and variability of midterm losses, both theories focus on the prior presidential elections and the short-term political forces found in presidential elections. Although these short-term forces are by their very definition temporary or fleeting phenomena, both theories of surge and decline make three critical claims about presidential election year short-term forces. They both claim that: (1) The gross amount of campaign information circulating in presidential election years is substantial in magnitude, far exceeding that of midterm campaigns. (2) The presidential-year short-term forces have a substantial impact on the presidential and congressional vote choices, substantial enough to determine who wins the presidency. (3) The net effect of these short-term forces consistently favors the winning presidential party in the presidential election, even though the extent of these advantages may vary a great deal. Because of their shared perspective on presidential election year short-term forces, the two theories yield identical propositions at the aggregate level (propositions 1 and 2). Presidential election year gains and midterm losses for the president's party, according to both theories, should be proportional to the net advantage in short-term forces favoring the president's party in the presidential election. The two theories are also quite similar in their views of congressional vote fluctuations at the district level. As at the aggregate level, initial gains and subsequent losses for the president's party are supposed to be proportional to the short-term presidential year advantage of the party. The only difference between the theories at this level is in the original theory's contention that district turnout magnifies the effects of short-term forces.

One major point of difference between the two theories is in their views regarding the impact of midterm short-term forces. The original theory is exclusively a presidential election based theory, implicitly dismissing the political climate of the midterm. The revised theory, while concurring that short-term forces of the presidential election are most important, also recognizes that electoral change in the midterm is partially a consequence of the short-term forces at work in the midterm itself. Unlike the original theory, the revised theory contends that the public's midterm judgment of the president's party can add to or subtract from that party's midterm losses even though it cannot entirely prevent those losses.

Beyond recognizing the referendum component of the midterm pattern, the two theories of surge and decline differ at several points in specifying how the short-term forces of the presidential election affect different segments of the public. According to the original version of the theory, only the gross volume of short-term forces in presidential elections, and not their net partisan slant, affected turnout. Whether the news of the presidential campaign was beneficial to the Democrats or to the Republicans was of little consequence as far as turnout was concerned. The general surge of political information, regardless of which party is favored, brought out peripheral voters of both parties and especially the peripheral independents (proposition 8).

While the revised theory concurs that the information surge of the presidential campaign spurs turnout generally, it differs from the original theory in two respects. First, according to the revised theory, the information surge is not of particularly greater importance to the turnout of independents. The information surge stimulates the turnout of all potential voters whose self-motivation falls just short of the turnout threshold. Independents are not particularly more likely than partisans to fall into this near-voter category. Second, the revised theory argues that the net partisan slant of short-term forces, as well as their gross magnitude affects turnout. Among partisans, turnout can be influenced by the consistency or inconsistency of the prevailing political climate with their partisanship. Partisans finding the climate favorable to their party should turn out at higher rates than otherwise expected and cross-pressured partisans should turn out at lower rates than otherwise expected.[18]

The revised and original theories also differ on the contribution of partisan defection to the midterm pattern. While the original theory identifies partisan defection as the principal component of the presidential election surge (proposition 9), the revised theory claims that the surge does not depend solely on partisans of the losing party crossing over to vote for winning presidential party. Disaffected partisans can contribute to the presidential surge by opting not to vote rather than resort to the more extreme response of defecting.[19]

The revisions to the theory of surge and decline have accomplished two things. First, they preserve aspects of the original theory that are generally uncontradicted by previous research. The revised theory maintains the claim that the midterm pattern is largely a consequence of short-term forces in the presidential election affecting turnout and vote choices to the winning presidential party's advantage. Second, the revisions respond to the problems in the original theory revealed by previous research. By recognizing the referenda aspect of midterms, the revisions address the challenge posed to the original theory of surge and decline by the referenda explanations of midterm. The revisions also respond to challenges raised by previous analyses of turnout and partisan defections in presidential and midterm electorates. By incorporating the psychological theory of cross-pressures, the revised theory offers propositions concerning the composition and behavior of the electorates that differ in important respects from the original theory's propositions. As the review of the evidence in chapter 3 indicated, it is precisely with respect to these propositions regarding the electorate that the original theory has proven most vulnerable.

In the chapters to follow, the revised theory of surge and decline is examined in detail from a variety of angles. The first angle in this empirical analysis is a longitudinal examination at the national level of partisan seat and vote change between elections. However, before turning to this analysis, we briefly consider a variant of the theory involving the emergence of congressional candidates.

Surge and Decline for Strategic Politicians

The theory of surge and decline, in both its original and revised forms, is concerned exclusively with how presidential election short-term forces directly affect the turnout and vote choice decisions of the mass public. However, as Jacobson and Kernell (1981) have argued with respect to the referenda theory, prospective congressional candidates also make important decisions that may significantly influence election outcomes. It seems quite plausible that the same presidential election short-term forces that have been supposed to affect the general public might also affect prospective candidates and their decisions to seek office. While the revised theory of surge and decline proposed here is primarily a mass behavior theory of elections, it certainly could embrace the possibility that elite behavior, in the form of prospective candidates' decisions to run for office, may augment or reinforce the electoral effects of surge and decline in the electorate.

How would an elite version of surge and decline work as a companion to the mass version in helping to account for the pattern of midterm losses for the president's party? Suppose first that the pool of potential quality congressional candidates for a party in most districts is fairly well fixed over the cycle of a presidential and a midterm election. While there are a number of factors that might affect the decision to run for these potential candidates, one important consideration would be their assessment of whether the political climate of the particular election year was likely to make it easier or more difficult to win the election. If the political climate appears hostile, a prospective candidate may reasonably postpone his run for the seat for a couple of years until the climate might be more hospitable. Many of the factors most likely to affect the deliberations of a potential candidate are quite likely to be national factors, since many local conditions like the partisan composition of the district tend to be nearly constant from one election to the next. Presidential campaigns, unlike many local conditions, generate significant changes in the political climate. A prospective congressional candidate seeing an unpopular presidential candidate heading his party's ticket may well decide to sit out the race and run two years later at the midterm, when he doesn't have to bear the extra burden of a weak presidential candidate dragging down his candidacy. Conversely, a popular presidential candidate may well boost the confidence of prospective quality congressional candidates in his party. Some of these candidates, who might not otherwise have risked the run, may seize the opportunity to run when they can get help from the top of the ticket.

In the presidential election year, the short-term forces generally favoring the party winning the presidency encourage potential quality congressional candidates of the advantaged party and discourage serious potential candidates of the disadvantaged party. Given a fixed pool of candidates over this short period and the impact of short-term forces on the decisions to run for office, the advantaged party should be able to recruit its stronger field of congressional challengers in the presidential year whereas the disadvantaged party should put forward its stronger field in the following midterm election. The presidential election year incentives for prospective congressional candidates of the advantaged party should draw an unusual number of them into that race and deplete that party's pool of available viable challengers for the midterm. The party's candidates drawn into running in the presidential election year either were successful, in which case they are incumbents and cannot add to the party's holdings in the midterm, or were defeated, in which case they may be discouraged from running again or weakened as candidates

Figure 5.6. Surge and Decline for Strategic Politicians

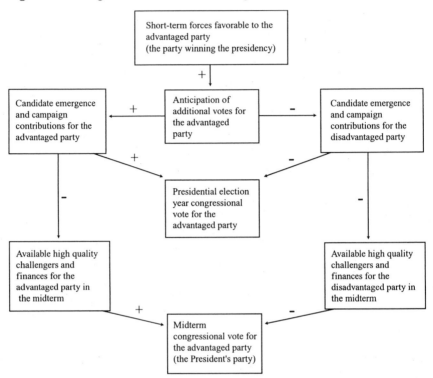

by their prior loss. Conversely, the disadvantaged party in the presidential election year is in a promising position at the midterm. With many of their attractive potential candidates postponing their run for office in the inhospitable presidential year, they have an unusual number of good challengers eager to run in the next midterm when conditions might be more favorable.

It is also quite possible that the political climate of the presidential campaign affects potential campaign contributors in a similar manner. Jacobson and Kernell's theory of strategic politicians encompasses potential campaign contributors as well as potential congressional candidates. Potential contributors may be more likely to give more money to candidates they think have a better chance of winning than to those less viable. As such, the revised theory of surge and decline might suppose that the advantaged party may have an easier time extracting more resources from potential givers in the presidential year while the party disadvantaged in the presidential year may have its relatively greater success in the midterm, as some of its givers, like its prospective candidates, wait out the inhospitable presidential year.

The basic structure of this strategic politician variant of surge and decline is outlined more formally in the causal model in figure 5.6. As I described, the effects of short-term forces on the fortunes of the president's party should be positive in the presidential election year but negative in the following midterm. Both compound paths to the vote for the advantaged party are positive and both compound paths to the midterm congressional vote for the president's party are negative. As the model indicates, the president's party should enjoy a relative advantage in candidate recruitment and financing going into the on-year election and a relative disadvantage in candidate recruitment and financing going into the midterm. In terms of the causal model, the key paths are between candidate recruitment and finances in the presidential election year and the availability of quality candidates and finances in the midterm. The expected negative effects reflect the suspected trade-off of expending the relatively fixed pool of candidate and financial resources between the on-year or midterm elections.

The bottom line is that short-term forces in the presidential election may well affect the decisions of potential congressional candidates to run for office and the decisions of potential campaign contributors to finance congressional campaigns, as well as the decisions of the public to turn out and to vote for particular candidates. Moreover, the consequences of short-term forces on elite behavior and voter behavior are most probably reinforcing.[20] Both may help to account for the pattern of midterm losses for the president's party.

6

Evidence from National Elections

To every action there is an equal and opposite reaction.
—Newton's third law of motion

Since the original purpose of the theory of surge and decline was to explain the national losses by the president's party in midterm elections, an appropriate starting point in examining the revised theory is to determine how well it explains the pattern of national electoral change. There are three parts to this analysis of national evidence. The first examines national evidence of the midterm decline. How well does the revised theory explain variation in both midterm seat and vote losses for the president's party? The second part examines evidence of the presidential surge in the prior presidential election. According to both versions of the theory, an initial presidential-year surge sets up the subsequent midterm-year decline. Evidence of the presidential surge is as important to the theory as evidence of the midterm decline. How well does the theory explain variation in partisan seat and vote changes in the prior presidential election years? The tracks of presidential election short-term forces, factors generally benefiting the winning presidential party, ought to be evident in the congressional election results of the prior presidential election year. The third part examines how both presidential surge and midterm decline effects may have changed over time. Have surge and decline effects weakened? Do they still exist in contemporary elections or are they only a matter of electoral history?

Of course, both theories of surge and decline claim to explain the consistency as well as the variation in presidential midterm losses. However, given that the basis of statistical analysis is the examination of variation rather than constants, the thrust of this analysis, like all others, is generally restricted to explaining the variation in rather than the consistency of midterm losses. Nevertheless, before proceeding to analyze this variability, we ought to make note of the obvious common thread running through all midterm seat and vote losses by the president's party—they happen to the president's party, the party winning the presidency in the prior election. The president's party may or may not be popular at the midterm and it may or may not have a healthy economy after two years in office, but it has always won the prior presidential election. This pattern of presidential victories followed quite consistently by congressional losses does not necessarily indicate the validity of surge and decline. However, it lends some additional credibility. Applying Occam's razor, a single theory offering an explanation of both the consistency and the variability of midterm losses is preferable to two separate theories, one to explain the consistency of midterm losses and a second to explain their variation. Of course, as Cervantes wrote, "the proof of the pudding is in the eating." How well does surge and decline stand up to the evidence? We turn first to national-level evidence of partisan seat and vote changes in midterms.

Explaining Midterm Losses

Both versions of surge and decline (and one might add Bean's more simple theory of coattails) suggest a common hypothesis regarding midterm seat and vote losses: they should be proportional to the short-term forces favoring the president's party in the prior presidential election (proposition 1 in chapter 3). They also suggest that, at least in normal times (without a critical realignment), the direction and force of short-term forces is measurable by the presidential vote (as discussed in chapter 2). In rough terms, evidence supporting this contention has already been offered (table 3.1). Midterm seat losses were shown to have been more substantial following presidential landslides. The following analysis examines this evidence of both midterm seat and vote losses at somewhat greater depth, with the greater precision and reliability offered by statistical techniques.

Before proceeding to the data, we should note that surge and decline in its revised form claims that while midterm losses are largely a function of the prior presidential surge; they are not solely a function of that surge. They are also affected by the public's evaluations of the in-party at the midterm itself. Midterms are in part referenda on the president's and his party's performance. While the analysis will take this referenda adjustment to the midterm decline into account, the analysis begins by examining only the midterm repercussions of the presidential election surge. This initially more restricted analysis permits an examination of a longer series of elections, since Gallup poll approval ratings of the president measuring the public's midterm evaluations have only been available since 1946.

We begin the analysis by examining the fundamental association between the short-term forces of the presidential election, as captured by the presidential vote, and the change in the number of seats and votes

Figure 6.1. Prior Presidential Vote and Midterm Congressional Vote
Change, 1902-1990

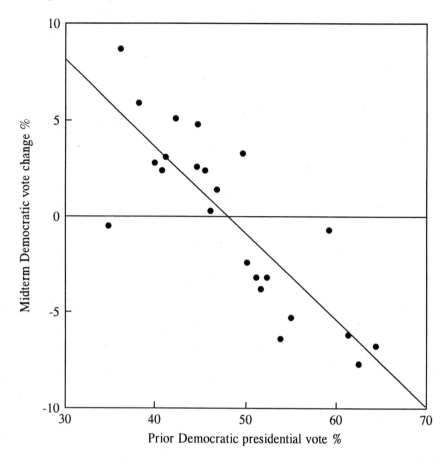

won by each party after the midterm election. Midterm changes in Democratic congressional votes are plotted against the prior Democratic share
of the two-party presidential vote in figure 6.1 for the twenty-three
midterms between 1900 and 1990. The Democratic share of the two-party
vote for elections until 1976 are the Stokes and Iversen series (Niemi and
Fett 1986,85). The congressional vote data since 1976 are calculated from
Ornstein, Mann, and Malbin (1990). Turning from votes to seats, figure
6.2 displays midterm Democratic seat gains or losses plotted against the
Democratic share of the two-party presidential vote in the prior presidential election. The number of seats held by the Democrats at each election
are calculated from the series in Ornstein, Mann, and Malbin (1990). For
the sake of comparability, the number of seats won or lost in the early

Figure 6.2. Prior Presidential Vote and Midterm Congressional Seat Change, 1902-1990

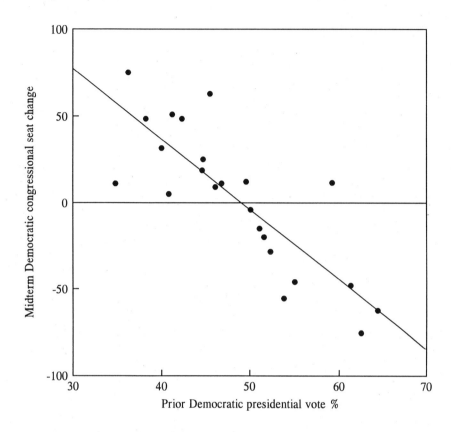

elections of this century are adjusted to reflect a House size of 435 members, as set in 1912. Seats held by third parties (primarily in elections early in the series) are equally divided between the two major parties, again for purposes of comparison.

As both figures suggest, a party's midterm fate is cast by how well it did in the prior presidential election. The plots indicate a strong negative association between a party's presidential vote and the change in its share of seats and votes in the subsequent midterm. This is anticipated by both versions of the theory of surge and decline.

Regression analysis offers a more rigorous assessment of the basic proposition of a negative association between the prior presidential vote and the following midterm loss of congressional votes and seats. There are two dependent variables. The first is the midterm change in the number of seats (adjusted to a constant House size of 435) held by Democrats. The second is the midterm change in the Democratic party's share of the congressional vote. Different regression analyses are performed on both of these dependent variables to ensure the reliability of the findings. In both the seat change and vote change regressions, the independent variable of principal interest is the Democratic presidential vote, a measure of the general direction and magnitude of short-term forces in the prior presidential election year. A parallel analysis with dependent and independent variables oriented in terms of the presidential party rather than the Democratic party is presented in appendix 1.[1] In addition to the standard OLS regression estimates, the data are also examined using a "least median squares" robust regression technique (Rousseeuw and Leroy 1987). These results are confined to appendix 2 since they confirm the OLS findings in all basic respects.

For both the seat change and vote change dependent variables, four separate regression analyses are conducted. The two sets of regressions, one with vote change as the dependent variable and one with seat change, are identical in all ways. The differences among these regressions are intended to take into account the idiosyncratic aspects of several of the elections and changes in electoral volatility or stability over time. The first regression of both sets examines all midterm elections from 1902 to 1990 (n = 23). This regression involves only a single independent variable, the prior Democratic presidential vote. The second regression is conducted on the same series of elections but includes a dummy variable for the New Deal realignment midterm of 1934 (1 in 1934 and 0 otherwise), a midterm that there is good reason to believe was quite atypical. This variable should, in an admittedly rough way, control for the jolt of the critical New Deal realignment.[2]

The third regression excludes four pairs of presidential and midterm elections in which nonmajor party presidential candidates received a significant vote. Presumably, a party's share of the two-party presidential vote would not as accurately reflect the tilt of short-term forces when there is a large third-party vote. The two-party presidential vote implicitly assumes that the popular sentiment behind third-party votes is proportionate to the vote division between the two major party candidates. However, in some cases, this may be an erroneous assumption. The error would be especially severe when most of the third-party vote would have gone to the losing major party presidential candidate and when the proportion of the total vote going to the minor parties is large. Given this potential source of error, presidential elections in which the Democrats and Republicans jointly received less than 93 percent of the total presidential vote were excluded from the third regression. This excludes 1912-14 because of Theodore Roosevelt's second-place finish in the popular vote; 1924-26 because of Robert La Follette's 17 percent of the vote; 1968-70 because of George Wallace's 14 percent; and 1980-82 largely

Table 6.1. The Presidential Vote's Effect on Midterm Change in the Democratic Congressional Vote, 1902-1990

Dependent variable: Change in the Democratic congressional vote from the presidential to the midterm election

Independent variables	All midterm elections included		3rd party elections excluded	
	1	2	3	4
Prior Democratic presidential vote	−.45 (6.77)	−.49 (7.39)	−.54 (8.83)	−.60 (12.69)
New Deal	—	4.94 (1.86)	—	6.34 (3.96)
Constant	21.73	23.19	25.66	28.37
Number of cases	23	23	19	19
R^2	.69	.73	.82	.91
Adjusted R^2	.67	.71	.81	.90
Std. error	2.63	2.49	2.00	1.47
Mean abs. error	1.98	1.75	1.51	1.17

NOTE: The Democratic presidential and congressional votes are the Democratic share of the two-party vote. The New Deal variable is a dummy taking on a value of 1 for 1934 and zero otherwise. The significant third-party elections excluded from regressions 3 and 4 are 1912, 1924, 1968, and 1980. The t-ratios are in parentheses.

because of John Anderson's 6.6 percent of the vote. After excluding these potentially confounding cases, the third regression with the single independent variable of the Democratic presidential vote is estimated on the remaining nineteen elections. The fourth regression examines these same major-party elections, but includes the New Deal dummy variable along with the Democratic presidential vote. The regression results for the seat change and vote change analyses are presented in tables 6.1 and 6.2, respectively.[3]

Both sets of national seat change and vote change regressions strongly support surge and decline's claims about midterm losses. All estimates of the midterm repercussions of the presidential vote consistently lead to the same conclusion: *a party's congressional midterm losses are proportional to its presidential vote in the previous presidential election.* The estimated effect of the presidential vote on the extent of midterm seat and vote losses remains strong under a variety of specifications and over the different series of examined elections. Whether or not all elections are included in the analysis and whether or not the New Deal realignment jolt is taken into account, a two percentage point gain in a party's presidential vote is associated with about a one percentage point loss in

Table 6.2. The Presidential Vote's Effect on Midterm Change in Democratic House Seats, 1902-1990

Dependent variable: Change in the Democratic congressional seats from the presidential to the midterm election

Independent variables	All midterm elections included		3rd party elections excluded	
	1	2	3	4
Prior Democratic	−4.06	−4.48	−4.63	−5.31
presidential vote	(6.58)	(7.86)	(6.45)	(8.81)
New Deal	—	59.72	—	68.35
		(2.61)		(3.35)
Constant	199.03	216.65	227.85	257.03
Number of cases	23	23	19	19
R^2	.67	.76	.71	.83
Adjusted R^2	.66	.73	.69	.81
Std. error	24.27	21.48	23.68	18.72
Mean abs. error	17.02	14.57	16.41	11.94

NOTE: The Democratic presidential vote is the Democratic share of the two-party vote. The number of seats have been adjusted to a constant House size of 435 seats. Seats held by third parties have been divided equally between the two major parties for comparability across years. The New Deal variable is a dummy taking on a value of 1 for 1934 and zero otherwise. The significant third-party elections excluded from regressions 3 and 4 are 1912, 1924, 1968, and 1980. The t-ratios are in parentheses.

its midterm congressional vote ($b = -.45$ to $-.60$). In terms of seats, a one percentage point increase in the presidential vote sets the party up to sustain a loss of four to five seats in the next midterm ($b = -4.06$ to -5.31). In all eight regressions over the century, the coefficient estimates are at least five times their standard errors (easily surpassing conventional significance tests) and, moreover, each regression estimated accounts for no less than two-thirds of the variance in the Democratic party's midterm change in votes or seats.

While multiple correlation coefficients provide a summary view of how well the surge and decline regressions fit the data (at least in terms of proportion of seat loss and vote loss variance), a more direct view of how well the equation performs comes from a comparison of expected and actual losses. The mean absolute errors of the regressions in tables 6.1 and 6.2 indicate that the expected seat and vote losses were fairly accurate. In these very parsimonious equations estimated over an extended history, the mean vote error was less than two percentage points and the mean seat error was anywhere from seventeen to twelve seats. Moreover, the equations correctly indicated which party would lose seats in all but a single case (1970) and that midterm followed an extremely close presidential election with a sizeable third-party presidential vote. It incorrectly predicted vote losses in only two elections. Both cases involved midterms following presidential elections with significant third-party votes, 1926 following the 1924 election with a sizable third-party presidential vote for LaFollette and again 1970.

As to specifics, the equations expected the big Democratic gains of 1974 following Nixon's 1972 landslide victory over McGovern, of 1930 following Hoover's 1928 landslide over Smith, and of 1922 following Harding's 1920 landslide over Cox. At the other extreme, the equations expected the big Republican gains of 1914 following Wilson's victory over a badly divided Republican party, of 1938 and 1942 following FDR's landslide over Landon and strong victory over Willkie, and of 1966 following Lyndon Johnson's landslide over Barry Goldwater. The equations also expected many of the more modest gains and losses. For instance, the modest Democratic gains of 1954 were expected, as were the minor Republican gains of 1962.

Not all of the equations' expectations were directly on target. The average error of the best fitting general regression (equation 4) was still plus or minus 1.2 percent of the vote and a dozen seats. Of course, some of this error can be traced to idiosyncracies (such as the extensive involvement of third-parties in the 1910 congressional elections). Other errors may be the result of the complications caused by third parties in presidential politics, but still other significant errors do not seem as easily attributable to problems in measuring presidential year short-term forces. For instance, the Democrats lost many more seats than expected in 1946. The equations in this case underestimated Democratic losses by about thirty seats. Even when the equation was relatively accurate, there is often a significant gap between actual and expected losses. For instance, in 1958 the equation correctly expected the Republicans to suffer extensive losses, but even the most accurate of the estimates still underestimated the extent of those losses by more than 1 percent of the vote and more than seven seats.

The examination of the actual and expected losses indicates that though the equations generally fit the data quite well, there is room for improvement. The improvement may come from introducing the public's midterm evaluations of administrations into the analysis. The revised theory of surge and decline argues that midterm changes are not entirely repercussions of the presidential surge, but are a result of both the withdrawal of the strong and positive short-term forces of the prior presidential election year and the public's midterm judgment of the administration's performance.

Much goes on in the midterm election itself that undoubtedly has national-level partisan ramifications. Sometimes the midterm climate hurts the president's party. For instance, it is hard to imagine that the Watergate scandal, President Nixon's resignation, and his subsequent pardon by President Ford within three months of the 1974 midterm failed to hurt Republican congressional candidates. In a more mundane crisis, it is a good bet that Democrats in 1946 were hurt by the public's displeasure with meat shortages caused by post-war price controls. *Newsweek* (October 21, 1946) reported that President Truman attempted to diffuse the issue by decontrolling meat prices just three weeks before the election, but the damage had already been done. In other midterms, the political climate is favorable to the president's party. For instance, it is difficult to believe that Democrats in 1962 were not helped greatly in November's election by President Kennedy's handling of October's Cuban missile crisis. Although each midterm does not have an issue of this intensity associated with it, the prevailing political climate of any midterm adds to or subtracts from the losses the president's party are positioned to sustain by the prior presidential election.

The fully specified midterm equation, incorporating the midterm referenda perspective into the analysis, includes three independent variables: the prior presidential vote, the public's approval rating of the president, and the annual change in real disposable income. The analysis of this full midterm equation is conducted on only the twelve midterms from 1946 to 1990 because the midterm approval ratings or presidential popularity measure, obtained from Gallup surveys, is only available since 1946. The variables in this portion of the analysis are oriented in terms of the presidential party rather than in terms of Democrats and Republicans in order to simplify the interpretation of the two variables measuring the referenda evaluations of the in-party. The full midterm equation is estimated for both the midterm congressional vote and seat change. Since significant negative autocorrelation was found in the initial OLS regressions, a companion regression was estimated after taking first differences of all variables with their lagged values.[4] The regression estimates are presented in table 6.3.

Several aspects of these results deserve note. First, consistent with the findings already discussed and the expectations of the revised theory, the presidential vote has the expected significant and negative effect on both midterm vote and seat changes after controlling for possible referenda effects. Every percentage point added to the presidential vote margin sets the stage for nearly two-tenths of a percentage point drop in the party's midterm congressional vote and a loss of about two seats.[5]

Second, consistent with both the midterm referenda research and the revised theory of surge and decline, presidential popularity has a signifi-

Table 6.3. The Presidential Vote and Midterm Referenda Effects on Midterm Change in Congressional Votes and Seats for the President's Party, 1946-1990

	Dependent variable			
	Vote change		Seat change	
Independent variable	OLS	First differences	OLS	First differences
Prior presidential vote	−.21 (2.02)	−.21 (4.93)	−2.26 (2.42)	−2.47 (5.71)
Midterm presidential popularity	.11 (2.79)	.10 (4.17)	1.11 (3.15)	1.15 (4.77)
Midterm economic change	.06 (.35)	.11 (1.67)	1.23 (.88)	1.20 (1.74)
Constant	2.04	.30	37.58	1.25
Number of cases	12	11	12	11
R^2	.63	.91	.71	.93
Adjusted R^2	.48	.88	.61	.90
Std. error of est.	1.36	.94	11.99	9.69
Mean absolute error	.86	.56	7.60	5.51

NOTE: The t-ratios are in parentheses. First difference estimates are based on taking the difference of each variable's value with its lagged value and using these differences in place of the simple variables.

cant positive effect on both midterm vote and seat changes for the president's party. That is, presidents popular in the midterm are able to cut their party's losses. A one percentage point increase in approval ratings cut congressional vote losses by about one-tenth of a percentage point and saved one seat from being lost.

The third finding from table 6.3 was not expected. Although the estimated effects of economic growth on midterm vote and seat changes were positive, as expected, in both cases they were not statistically significant (see Erikson 1990; Jacobson 1990), though they approached significance in the first difference equations. This does not mean that economics are irrelevant to midterm changes. There is substantial research to indicate that economic change matters. However, there is reason to believe that it matters somewhat less than some have supposed; that its effects occur earlier in the process, and these effects are more indirect in nature. Some evidence of earlier and more indirect economic effects has already been discussed in chapter 4. There is a good deal of other research to show that the health of the economy may influence midterm change by affecting presidential approval ratings and

Table 6.4. The Presidential Vote and Midterm Presidential Popularity
Effects on Midterm Change in Congressional Votes and Seats for the
President's Party, 1946-1990

| | Dependent variable | | | |
| | Vote change | | Seat change | |
Independent variable	OLS	First differences	OLS	First differences
Prior presidential vote	−.23 (2.35)	−.23 (5.40)	−2.51 (2.86)	−2.74 (6.11)
Midterm presidential popularity	.11 (3.02)	.10 (3.77)	1.17 (3.40)	1.15 (4.26)
Constant	2.62	.34	50.22	1.58
Number of cases	12	11	12	11
R^2	.62	.88	.69	.90
Adjusted R^2	.53	.85	.62	.88
Std. error of est.	1.30	1.04	11.83	10.85
Mean absolute error	.89	.73	8.02	8.64

NOTE: The t-ratios are in parentheses.

that this effect has some significant lag associated with it (Campbell
1985,1148; Norpoth and Yantek 1983; Jacobson and Kernell 1981; Monroe 1979). Presidents get credit for prosperity and take the blame for recession, but the public is not so attentive as to grant credit or place blame
immediately.

Two cases illustrate the point: 1946 and 1982. In both cases the
economy went into recession before the midterm. These recessions were
translated into political terms. The public assigned blame for the economic downturns to the incumbent administrations. Truman's approval
rating among the public sank to a mere 32 percent and Reagan's rating
dropped to just 42 percent. With the leaders of the parties in disrepute,
owing in no small part to the state of the economy, both parties suffered
substantially greater midterm losses.

Given the lack of significant direct economic effects in table 6.3, the
prior literature in support of this finding, and the small number of cases
considered in this portion of the analysis, the equation was reestimated
after dropping the economy variable. Table 6.4 presents estimates of the
trimmed equation for both midterm seat and vote losses. The trimmed
equation fits the data quite well. The prior presidential vote along with
the midterm referenda evaluation accounts for about one-half to two-
thirds of the variation in midterm vote and seat losses in the simple

equations and nearly 90 percent of the variance in the first differences equations.

As one might expect, the estimates of the effects of the prior presidential vote and midterm presidential popularity are not greatly changed by trimming the economic variable from the equation. As in the full equation in table 6.3, for every percentage point of the vote added to the winning presidential candidate's margin, his party can expect to lose about two-tenths of a percent of the congressional vote and about two to three more seats in the midterm. Also as indicated in the full equation, the trimmed equation confirms the significant referenda component of midterms. Presidential party midterm setbacks are not entirely predetermined. For every additional percentage point of approval, a popular president can reduce midterm vote losses by about one-tenth of a percentage point and seat losses by about one seat.

While it is now clear that midterm losses are a product of both the withdrawal of the prior presidential surge and the public's midterm referenda appraisal of the administration's performance, which matters more? This is not as easy a question to answer as it might seem. On the one hand, the effect of a one percentage point change in the prior presidential vote has two to three times as great as the effect of a one percentage point change in midterm presidential approval ratings. On the other hand, presidential approval ratings are more than twice as variable as the presidential vote margin. That is, a two percentage point change in presidential approval ratings is about as likely as a one percentage point change in the winning presidential vote margin.

While it might be tempting to conclude simply that the two effects are of approximately equal strength, we should remember that in orienting the analysis in terms of the president's party the variance of the presidential vote has been artificially restricted. Unlike either major party's presidential popular vote, the presidential vote of the winning presidential party effectively has a lower bound of 50 percent. This restricted variation is reflected in the standard deviations of the two votes. While a standard deviation the presidential vote of the winning party in this period was 4.1 percentage points of the vote, the standard deviation of the Democratic and Republican presidential votes was 6.4 percentage points. Moreover, this restricted variance attenuates the estimated effect of the presidential vote. This attenuation is evident in estimating the simple bivariate equations in table 6.1 and 6.2 both ways, orienting variables in terms of the Democratic and Republican parties and in terms of the winning and losing presidential parties. Both sets of regressions were estimated over the same set of postwar elections (1946-90). The estimated effects of the winning presidential candidates' vote were substantially greater ($-.60$ vs. $-.23$ in the vote change equations and -4.57 vs. -2.51 in the seat change equations) when variables were oriented in terms of the Democratic and Republican parties rather than the winning and losing presidential parties.

If we proceed on the premise that the earlier estimates of presidential vote effect (oriented by Democratic and Republican parties) are more appropriate in displaying the true variation in the presidential vote as well as more accurate (unattentuated compared to the later estimates), the presidential vote would appear to be more influential in midterm seat and vote changes than the midterm referendum is. The presidential year short-term forces, measured by the presidential vote, not only account for a party being in the midterm win or loss column, but greatly affect the size of the gains or losses. Dividing the question of midterm change into its two components, the consistency and variability of presidential party losses, it now seems clear that the president's party consistently loses in the midterm because of the prior presidential surge; its losses vary a good deal because the public's midterm judgments vary but also, at least as importantly, because the magnitude of the prior presidential surge varies.

Finding Prior Presidential Gains

Given the above findings of midterm decline effects, we ought to find the mirror-image surge effects in the previous presidential election years (proposition 2 in chapter 3). Both versions of surge and decline contend that congressional elections in on-years are affected by presidential coattails or, at least, by short-term causes that affect both presidential and congressional elections. As the initial examination of seat changes in landslide and non-landslide presidential election years suggests (table 3.2), it would appear that there is evidence of presidential coattails or something like them. The winning president's party is more likely to gain seats and gain more seats in landslide elections.

Figures 6.3 and 6.4 display plots of Democratic vote and seat changes in presidential election years against the Democratic share of the two-party presidential vote. The generally positive association between a party's presidential vote and the change in its congressional fortunes is suggested by both plots. Regression analysis, however, offers a more precise reading of this relationship.

As in the examination of midterm losses, the analysis of presidential election years considers four different regressions for both seat and vote changes. Two equations examine all elections in this century. Two equations exclude from this series those four elections in which there was a substantial third-party presidential vote. Like the midterm analysis, two of the equations also control for the relatively abrupt change in the partisan base caused by the New Deal realignment.

Figure 6.3. Presidential Vote and Congressional Vote Change,
1900-1988

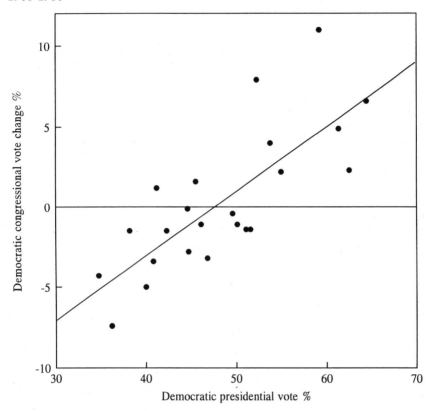

There is one difference in the presidential year equations other than
the expectation of a positive effect of the presidential vote. That difference
is the inclusion of the party's initial vote or seat share going into the
presidential election, its percentage of the congressional vote or number
of House seats held after the prior midterm election. The rationale for the
inclusion of a party's initial holdings is that it is more difficult to gain votes
or seats when a party already holds a large proportion of them. A party
cannot gain what it already has. At the extreme, it is impossible for a party
having previously won all votes and seats to do any better. Conversely at
the other extreme, it is impossible for a party without votes or seats to
lose. Between these extremes, a party holding a large majority of votes
and seats would do well just to hold that majority. It might do well and
still lose votes and seats if it just is not as popular as it had been. A party
with a minority of votes and seats doing just as well in its next election
ought to expect to register gains. Given this logic, a party's initial vote and
seat holdings ought to be *negatively* associated with vote and seat

Figure 6.4. Presidential Vote and Congressional Seat Change, 1900-1988

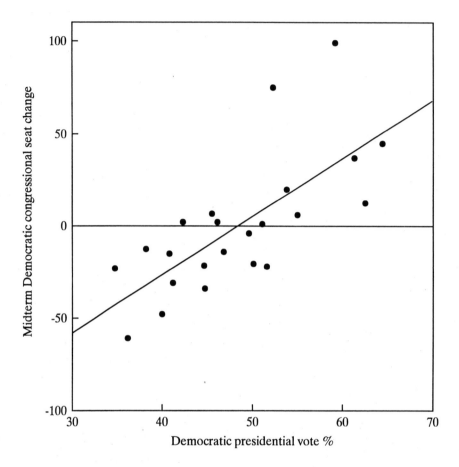

changes. This initial holding variable will be included in three of the regressions.[6]

Tables 6.5 and 6.6 present the presidential year regression results for congressional vote change and seat change. The single most important finding here is that regardless of the election series considered or the additional variables included in the analyses, *in presidential election years a party gains both seats and votes in proportion to its presidential vote*. The results are strong, consistent, statistically significant, and supportive of the theory of surge and decline in both of its versions. For every additional percentage point of the presidential vote, the party can expect typically to gain approximately two-fifths of a percentage point in the national congressional vote and better than three House seats. There are essentially no differences among estimates of the presidential vote coefficients in the

Table 6.5. The Presidential Vote's Effect on Presidential Year Change in the Democratic Congressional Vote, 1900-1988

Dependent variable: Change in the Democratic congressional vote from the prior midterm to the presidential election

Independent variables	All presidential elections included		3rd party elections excluded	
	1	2	3	4
Democratic	.40	.40	.41	.39
presidential vote	(5.61)	(6.70)	(4.40)	(4.86)
New Deal	—	5.15	—	5.15
		(2.13)		(1.85)
Prior Democratic	—	−.31	—	−.30
congressional vote		(2.71)		(2.30)
Constant	−19.16	−3.58	−19.47	−3.38
Number of cases	23	23	19	19
R^2	.60	.79	.53	.75
Adjusted R^2	.58	.76	.51	.70
Std. error	2.82	2.15	3.09	2.40
Mean abs. error	2.17	1.43	2.45	1.64

NOTE: The Democratic presidential and congressional votes are the Democratic share of the two-party vote. The New Deal variable is a dummy taking on a value of 1 for 1932 and zero otherwise. The significant third-party elections excluded from regressions 3 and 4 are 1912, 1924, 1968, and 1980. The prior Democratic congressional vote is the party's share of the vote in the previous midterm. The t-ratios are in parentheses.

vote change analysis and only very slight differences in the seat change analysis, a range of just one-quarter of a seat (b = 3.16 to 3.43). Moreover, the equations fit the data quite well, accounting for between about one-half and three-fourths of the variation in on-year seat and vote changes. The coefficients are nearly four to more than six times their standard errors and easily surpass conventional standards of statistical significance.

While not integral to the surge and decline proposition, the two "control" variables, the New Deal realignment variable and the prior congressional holdings variable, had their expected effects. As a result of the New Deal realignment, Democrats won an additional five percentage points of the congressional vote and about sixty-one or sixty-two more seats. Also, as expected, a party's initial seat and vote holdings reduced any expected gains it might have made. For every additional percentage point of the congressional vote it had won before the presidential year election, its expected vote gains were reduced by about one-third of a percentage point. Initial seat holdings also limited seat gains. Every four additional seats

Table 6.6. The Presidential Vote's Effect on Presidential Year Change in Democratic House Seats, 1990-1988

Dependent variable: Change in Democratic congressional seats from the prior midterm to the presidential election

Independent variables	All presidential elections included		3rd party elections excluded	
	1	2	3	4
Democratic presidential vote	3.16 (4.71)	3.18 (4.98)	3.43 (4.01)	3.30 (3.81)
New Deal	—	61.73 (2.62)	—	60.97 (2.28)
Prior Democratic House seats	—	− .24 (1.74)	—	− .22 (1.36)
Constant	− 152.82	− 98.23	− 164.81	− 109.10
Number of cases	23	23	19	19
R^2	.51	.72	.49	.69
Adjusted R^2	.49	.67	.46	.63
Std. error	26.38	21.13	28.20	23.22
Mean abs. error	19.51	14.71	21.04	16.22

NOTE: The Democratic presidential vote is the Democratic share of the two-party vote. The number of seats have been adjusted to a constant House size of 435 seats. Seats held by third parties have been divided equally between the two major parties for comparability across years. The New Deal variable is a dummy taking on a value of 1 for 1932 and zero otherwise. Significant third-party elections excluded from regressions 3 and 4 are 1912, 1924, 1968, and 1980. The number of prior Democratic seats are from the prevous midterm election. The t-ratios are in parentheses.

held prior to the election reduced potential seat gains by a one seat. While the inclusion of these "control" variables did not, as noted above, clarify or significantly alter estimates of the surge effects, they did contribute to more completely accounting for variation in both seat and vote changes.

As in the case of the expected midterm losses, the accuracy of the equations may be best assessed by directly comparing the actual to the expected presidential year seat and vote changes. The presidential surge regression equations, on the whole, perform quite well for very parsimonious equations extended over a lengthy stretch of history. The mean absolute error of the expected congressional vote change ranged from less than 2.5 percentage points to just 1.4 percentage points. The mean absolute error of the expected seat change ranged from twenty-one to fifteen seats.

The equations indicate that a number of elections fit theoretical expectations quite well. For instance, the big Democratic gains accompanying Wilson's election in 1912 and Johnson's landslide of 1964 are much as expected. Given the substantial initial Democratic vote and seat holdings going into the presidential election, the modest to moderate size Democratic gains following Franklin Roosevelt's 1936, 1940, and 1944 elections are also generally as expected. The equations also were fairly accurate in expecting healthy Republican gains in the elections of Teddy Roosevelt in 1904, Hoover in 1928, Eisenhower in 1952, and Reagan in 1980.

Despite a fairly good fit in most cases, there are several elections in which the equations were a good distance off the mark. In Woodrow Wilson's reelection of 1916, Democrats should have registered gains, but did not. In Truman's election of 1948, Democratic gains were expected, but the actual gains substantially exceeded the expected. Finally, Republicans in 1972 fell short of what they might have been expected to gain in the wake of Nixon's landslide victory over McGovern. This discrepancy between the expectations and the reality of the 1972 election is addressed below.

Surge and Decline over Time

While the analysis indicates that national electoral change in both presidential and midterm elections in the twentieth century has been generally consistent with the theories of surge and decline, the question remains of whether surge and decline structures electoral change in recent elections as it has in the past. Is the process of surge and decline a relic of the past— when parties were parties and congressmen hung on to presidential coattails for dear life?

To assess the possible change in surge and decline effects, the presidential and midterm change equations were reestimated on three subsets of presidential and midterm elections. These are: (1) the first eight pairs of presidential and midterm elections in this century up to the New Deal realignment (1900-30), (2) the seven pairs of elections following the New Deal realignment (1936-62) and (3) the most recent seven pairs of elections (1964-90). These regressions will help us determine how surge and decline effects may have changed over time.

Table 6.7 presents the midterm decline equations for the three subsets of elections. As in the first general equations of tables 6.1 and 6.2, the prior Democratic presidential vote is used to explain midterm congressional vote and seat change. There are three important findings: (1) The most notable finding is that the prior presidential vote has the expected significant negative effects in each series. In each series, including the most recent, the prior presidential vote coefficient is at least three times its standard error. (2) Although significant and strong in each era, midterm

Table 6.7. Trend in the Presidential Vote's Effect on Midterm Change in Democratic House Votes and Seats, 1902-1990

Dependent variables: Change in the Democratic congressional votes or seats from the presidential to the midterm election

Independent variables	Election series					
	1902-1930		1938-1962		1966-1990	
	Votes	Seats	Votes	Seats	Votes	Seats
Prior Dem.	−.39	−3.77	−.67	−6.25	−.50	−3.59
presidential vote	(3.20)	(3.20)	(6.73)	(7.99)	(3.85)	(4.62)
Constant	18.48	189.82	31.80	301.67	24.63	175.18
Number of cases	8	8	7	7	7	7
R^2	.63	.63	.90	.93	.75	.81
Adjusted R^2	.57	.57	.88	.91	.70	.77
Std. error	3.09	29.91	1.64	12.94	2.42	14.53
Mean abs. error	1.96	20.55	1.14	9.16	1.75	10.20

NOTE: The t-ratios are in parentheses.

Table 6.8. Trend in the Presidential Vote's Effect on Presidential Year Change in Democratic House Votes and Seats, 1900-1988

Dependent variable: Change in the Democratic congressional vote or seats from the prior midterm to the presidential election

Independent variables	Election series					
	1900-1928		1936-1960		1964-1988	
	Votes	Seats	Votes	Seats	Votes	Seats
Democratic	.55	3.48	.31	4.19	.29	2.34
presidential vote	(5.69)	(2.58)	(4.00)	(3.15)	(3.61)	(3.21)
Prior Dem.	−.83	−.32	−.67	−.72	−.31	−.39
congressional	(2.84)	(.58)	(5.23)	(3.60)	(1.20)	(1.05)
vote or seats						
Constant	13.06	−108.02	20.47	−26.12	2.41	−11.52
Number of cases	8	8	7	7	7	7
R^2	.87	.72	.90	.79	.81	.74
Adjusted R^2	.82	.60	.85	.68	.72	.61
Std. error	1.92	20.61	1.26	18.31	1.44	13.59
Mean abs. error	1.09	14.09	.83	12.75	.92	9.07

NOTE: The t-ratios are in parentheses.

decline effects are somewhat smaller in recent years than they were in mid-century. They declined by 25 percent in the case of vote change and 43 percent in the case of seat change. (3) The midterm decline effects are weaker now than they were from the late thirties through the early sixties, but they are not appreciably weaker than they were in the first elections of this century. Midterm effects on seat changes were slightly stronger in the earlier period, but midterm effects on vote changes were actually weaker in early elections. While recent midterm decline effects may compare favorably with effects early in the century because of complications from third-party elections, the comparison suggests that, though diminished, midterm decline effects remain potent by historical standards.

The analysis of surge effects in presidential election years in the three subsets of elections generally reinforces the midterm findings. These regressions are presented in table 6.8. Like midterm decline effects, presidential surge effects are significant and positive in all three eras, including the most recent elections. Also, as in the case of the midterm decline, presidential surge effects, though significant, are generally weaker now than in the past. There is very little difference in the effects of the presidential surge on vote change, but its effects on seat change are just more than one-half its previous magnitude.

The apparent weakening of surge and decline effects may reflect, in part, trends in voting behavior. Partisan dealignment may have weakened coattails (accounting for the drop in the presidential vote coefficients) and increased incumbency advantages may account for the reduced vote and seat changes (accounting for the increase effects of the initial vote and seat holdings). It is also likely that some portion of this apparent weakening of presidential coattails may be unrelated to voting behavior. Presidential coattails in several recent elections have been "wasted" by the absence of congressional candidates to ride them. In elections since the late 1960s (see the discussion of 1972 to follow), favorable Republican short-term forces in many Southern congressional districts have not helped Republican congressional candidates because there were no Republican candidates in these districts; Democratic congressional candidates went unchallenged.

Although I will return to the issue of the weakening of the presidential pulse and its possible causes in chapter 9, one point of the above analysis should be emphasized: presidential surge and decline effects on congressional elections remain substantial. Even in recent years, a party's success in presidential elections helps it to win more congressional votes and seats. As in the past, these are short-lived gains. As in the past, a party should reasonably expect to lose congressional votes and seats in midterms in proportion to how well its presidential candidate performed in the previous election.

Two Cases of Surge and Decline

A couple of cases may illustrate both the dynamics of surge and decline and some problems in estimating its effects at the aggregate level. I will first consider a fairly typical case: the cycle of the 1952 presidential and the 1954 midterm elections. The second case is less typical: the cycle of the 1972 presidential and the 1974 midterm elections. The 1972-74 set of presidential and midterm elections is very unusual and somewhat problematic case for several reasons that will be discussed.

A typical case: Eisenhower's 1952 election and the 1954 midterm. The election cycle of 1952 and 1954 reflects quite clearly the dynamics of surge and decline. In 1952 the Republican presidential candidate Dwight Eisenhower defeated Democratic candidate Adlai Stevenson by a margin of 55 percent to 45 percent of the two-party presidential vote. The only thing unusual in this was the victory of a Republican after twenty continuous years of Democratic control of the White House. But in factors potentially important to measuring surge forces or to translating them into congressional votes and seats, 1952 was unproblematic. The presidential vote was neither complicated by a significant third-party vote nor distributed regionally in way in which Republican congressional candidates could not take advantage of it (unlike the case of 1972, which we will address shortly).

Quite in keeping with the theory of surge and decline, the Eisenhower victory of 1952 had very visible and important effects on that year's congressional elections and the partisan composition of the House. Largely because of Eisenhower's solid defeat of Stevenson, Republicans gained twenty-two additional seats in the House, raising the number of Republican seats from 200 to 222. These gains were sufficient to reestablish a bare Republican majority in the House that had been lost following Truman's 1948 presidential victory. The popular press at the time attributed these gains to Eisenhower's coattails. In its report of the election returns *Time* magazine wrote: "The great Eisenhower landslide apparently carried with it a Republican majority into the House of Representatives. . . . The Eisenhower uprising dropped Republicans into some seats which have long been warmed by Democrats. Harry Truman's home district in Missouri (the Fourth) elected a Republican Representative for the first time in 22 years. Virginia, which had not elected a Republican Congressman since 1930, gave three of its ten House seats to the G.O.P. Arizona, which had never sent a Republican to the House, elected Republican John Rhodes over Democratic Incumbent John Murdock" (November 10, 1952).

The more systematic analysis of coattails over time concurs with

Time's assessment of the impact of Ike's coattails in this election. The Republican seat gains of 1952 are fairly close to those expected by the regression estimates in table 6.6.[7] Given the initial seat holdings of the Republicans from 1950 (200) and Eisenhower's share of the two-party vote (55 percent), Republicans should have gained between twelve to fourteen seats or about eight or ten fewer than they actually gained.

Eisenhower's 1952 coattails are of special significance because they undoubtedly contributed to Republicans gaining control of the House. If Eisenhower and Stevenson had finished in a dead heat, according to the historical evidence of surge effects, Republicans would not have won enough seats to replace the Democrats as the majority party controlling the House. Without Eisenhower's victory, Republicans would have captured anywhere from sixteen or seventeen fewer seats, leaving them twelve or thirteen seats short of a majority.

As the theory also maintains, the effects of the Eisenhower victory in 1952 were, by their withdrawal, felt in the midterm election of 1954. In the 1954 midterm, Republicans lost 2.6 percent of the national congressional vote and eighteen seats. Like the gains of two years before, these losses were critical. As a result of these lost seats, Republicans lost control of the House and forty years later they still have not regained it.

These losses are quite close to those expected from the withdrawal of Eisenhower's 1952 coattail help and the public's assessment of the first two years of his administration. Based on the 1952 Eisenhower vote of 55 percent and his high midterm approval rating of 65 percent, the seat and vote equations (table 6.4) indicate that Republicans should have lost about 1.5 percent of the vote (2.1 percent by the more recent series of table 6.7) and seventeen or eighteen seats in the 1954 midterm. Had Eisenhower evenly split the vote in 1952, Republicans not only would have gained fewer seats in that election but also lost significantly fewer seats in the following midterm. Of course, the general approval for Eisenhower's first two years also affected the extent of Republican losses. Eisenhower's popularity in 1954 obviously had its roots in his previous record of leadership in World War II but was also based on the performance of his administration. Despite the divisiveness generated by the impending censure vote of Sen. Joseph McCarthy, the first two years of the Eisenhower administration won widespread public approval for two achievements in particular. First, fulfilling his 1952 campaign pledge to "go to Korea," Eisenhower brought the Korean war to a cease-fire in 1953. Second, the Eisenhower administration was also credited, as *Newsweek* put it, with "one of the most prosperous peacetime years on record" (November 1, 1954). If the record were less favorable and Ike's approval rating had been only 50 percent, rather than 65 percent, Republicans probably would have lost about seventeen or eighteen more seats.

A complicated case: the Nixon surge and the Watergate decline. The cycle
of the 1972 presidential and 1974 midterm is an atypical one in several
respects. First, both the presidential year forces and conditions at the
midterm pointed to substantial losses for the president's party. Conditions in the presidential year were very good for the president's party, but
by the midterm election just about everything had gone wrong. Second,
there are good reasons to believe that both the presidential vote and the
midterm presidential approval ratings were somewhat misleading in
reflecting the national political climate in these two particular elections.

The year 1972 was a Republican year. The incumbent president,
Richard Nixon, who had only narrowly won election against a bitterly
divided Democratic party four years earlier, convincingly defeated Democratic candidate George McGovern in a landslide. Nixon carried every
state in the nation except Massachusetts (and the District of Columbia)
and won 62 percent of the popular vote.

On the basis of this landslide, Republicans should have registered
substantial gains. The regression estimates (equation 1 in tables 6.5 and
6.6) indicate that the 1972 landslide should have added about 3.8 percentage points of the vote and about thirty-two seats to the Republican
congressional totals. Even the more recent series (table 6.8) indicate that
Republicans should have gained about 3.3 percentage points of the vote
and about twenty-one seats. The press held similar expectations of substantial Republican gains in the wake of Nixon's victory. Yet Republican
gains fell far short of these expectations. As *Congressional Quarterly* reported, "While Nixon was overwhelming Democrat George McGovern,
. . . presidential coattails materialized for his fellow Republicans in only a
handful of other races" (November 11, 1972: 2947). The party gained only
1.5 percent of the congressional vote and only twelve additional seats.

Why did Republicans fail to register greater congressional gains
with Nixon's landslide? Were his coattails for some reason shorter than
other presidents who had won as decisively? One reason for the shortfall may be the rise of split-ticket voting as a result of weakened partisan
attachments and increased congressional incumbency advantages. This,
however, probably does not account for the full difference. The apparent shortfall is, at least in part, a result of the distribution of Nixon's
strength.

In 1972 Nixon pursued a "Southern Strategy." It was an obvious
success. Although he won just about everywhere, he did especially well
in Southern states. Seven of Nixon's ten strongest states were in the
South. He won more than 70 percent of the vote in four of these Southern
states. This presented a problem for Republicans. Republican congressional candidates were not recruited in many districts within Nixon's
strongest states. For instance, Nixon won more than 75 percent of the

vote in Georgia while six of the nine Democratic congressmen went entirely unchallenged. This was not uncommon. In Arkansas, Nixon received 69 percent of the vote but Democratic congressional candidates were uncontested in three of the state's four seats. In both Texas and Louisiana, Nixon won 66 percent of the vote, but Democrats won ten seats in Texas (of twenty-four) and six in Louisiana (of eight) without a challenge. Republicans left Democratic congressional candidates unchallenged in thirty-five southern congressional districts that their presidential candidate carried. Nixon's coattails weren't short, there just weren't enough congressional candidates available to ride them where they might have made a difference. Moreover, this problem was not limited to the failure to offer a challenge. Undoubtedly, in many longtime Democratic areas of the South, Republican challengers were not competitive candidates. Even when coattails are provided, a party needs local candidates who are serious enough to benefit from coattail help.[8] As Nixon told political chronicler Teddy White before the election: "part of our problem is that we have a lot of lousy candidates; the good ones will go up with me, the bad ones will go down" (White 1973, 403).

In short, Nixon's coattails were often wasted coattails. When that is taken into account, the effectiveness of his coattails in pulling added votes and seats to his party was much more like a candidate winning 52-55 percent of the vote instead of 62 percent.

Nevertheless, while most of the Republican potential of 1972 was not realized, some surge effects can be found. The party did register some modest gains in Nixon's reelection, which they might not have received had the candidates and issues of 1972 not been so favorable to the Republicans. Examining congressional district- and individual-level data, Jacobson (1976) reached the same conclusion.[9] In the district portion of his study, Jacobson examined the effect of the presidential vote on the congressional vote in 165 districts in twenty-five states, only two of which were Southern. He found the congressional deviation from the estimated normal vote to correlate quite strongly with the presidential deviation from the normal vote ($r = .53$). In his individual-level multivariate analysis of NES data, the single strongest effect on the 1972 congressional vote was the presidential vote. The presidential surge of 1972, even though largely wasted, did have some effects and should have had some repercussions in 1974.

The political climate of 1974 was substantially different from that of 1972. It is difficult to imagine a recent election year in which conditions favored the Democrats more than they did in 1974. About three months before the election, Nixon resigned as a result of the protracted scandal of Watergate. Following that, his appointed successor, Gerald Ford, granted Nixon a pardon that in itself stirred great controversy. The economy, following the boom of 1972, was slumping. Inflation was in double digits. The strife of Vietnam was still fresh.

Despite the Vietnam aftermath, the economic problems, the Watergate scandal, and the Nixon pardon, the last approval rating before the midterm for President Ford was, amazingly, a respectable 55 percent. Because of the unusual events surrounding the midterm election, the presidential popularity rating in this case would seem to have been less reliable than usual. Under the very peculiar conditions of his elevation to the presidency, the midterm approval rating in this instance undoubtedly reveals less about the public's reaction to the previous two years of the Republican administration than about its relief that the Watergate crisis had passed and its good wishes for the new president. Nixon's last approval rating before leaving office, again just three months before the midterm balloting, was an all-time low of 24 percent. An accurate picture of public midterm evaluations is probably somewhere between the two scores. The peculiarity of Ford's rating aside, 1974 was nothing short of a Republican catastrophe.

The election returns of 1974 showed the depths of this catastrophe. Republicans lost almost six percentage points of the national congressional vote and a total of forty-nine seats. Jacobson and Kernell (1981, 1986) conclude that a good deal of these losses were a result of strategic politicians anticipating the political climate of 1974. It did not take much of a political weatherman to forecast inclement weather for Republicans and sunshine for Democrats in 1974. The Watergate scandal broke early and both the Senate investigation and House impeachment hearings were being conducted before potential candidates reached their decision to run. Undoubtedly, many good and sensible Republican candidates must have decided to opt out of the 1974 campaign and some good Democratic candidates may have been gained greater encouragement to run. Uslaner and Conway (1985, 1986), on the other hand, interpret Republican losses as a straightforward midterm referendum rejecting the incumbent party. Undoubtedly, there is truth in this interpretation as well. Many voters must have held the Republican party accountable for the scandals and problems of the preceding two years.

While the referenda explanation would seem to account for much of the presidential party losses in 1974, there is also evidence that suggests that the withdrawal of Nixon's 1972 coattails also contributed to these losses. Although Nixon's coattails were often wasted, they did pick up some riders. Bauer and Hibbing (1989, 266) have observed that fourteen Republican seats won in 1972 with more than 60 percent of the vote, apparently safe Republican seats, were lost to Democrats in 1974. Compared to other recent election years, this was an unusually large number of such losses. These dramatic Republican losses are listed in table 6.9. In

Table 6.9. The Fourteen Districts in Which Republicans Appeared Safe in 1972 but Lost in 1974

State & district	1972 Republican candidate	1972 Nixon vote %	Republican congressional vote % 1972	1974
Calif. 18*	Mathias	52	66.4	48.1
Calif. 43*	Veysey	54	62.7	49.7
Colo. 2	Brotzman	65	66.3	48.0
Georgia 4	Blackburn	77	75.0	44.9
Illinois 3	Hanrahan	70	62.3	47.4
Indiana 6	Bray	74	64.8	47.6
Indiana 8	Zion	65	63.3	46.6
N.J. 2	Sandman	66	65.7	41.3
New York 2	Grover	72	65.7	44.7
New York 29	King	70	69.9	45.5
N.C. 5	Mizell	71	64.8	47.6
N.C. 8	Ruth	73	60.2	43.0
Oklahoma 6	Camp	79	72.7	44.4
Oregon 4	Dellenback	56	62.5	47.1

NOTE: The district numbers are those for 1972. An asterisk (*) indicates redistricting between 1972 and 1974. The congressional votes are the actual, not two-party, percentages. The two California districts were numbered 17 and 35 in 1974.

examining these fourteen unusual cases, there is evidence of a sharp decline from a prior substantial presidential election surge. Many of the fourteen districts appeared to be safely in Republican hands because the 1972 Republican congressional vote had been temporarily boosted by Nixon's coattails. Not surprisingly, given the landslide proportions of Nixon's national victory, he won a majority of the vote in each of these districts. More impressively, Nixon received 65 percent or more of the vote in eleven of the fourteen districts and won 70 percent or more of the vote in eight of them. While redistricting between 1970 and 1972 complicates matters considerably, it also appears that in each of these districts (or areas that comprised the 1972 districts) the Republican congressional vote was greater with coattails in 1972 than without them in the 1970 midterm. In those districts not radically redistricted between 1970 and 1972 (nine of the fourteen), Republican congressional candidates gained between 3 percent and 14 percent of the vote in 1972, an average of 7 percent. The conditions of 1974, their effects on candidates as well as voters, no doubt played a role in these losses, but it would appear that the decline of the 1972 Nixon surge also contributed.[10]

7
Evidence in Congressional Districts

Surge and decline effects should be evident at the level of individual elections in congressional districts as well as at the nationally aggregated level. While aggregated data generally offer the benefit of reducing both measurement error and highly idiosyncratic variation (Kramer 1983), it is possible that inferences drawn from such data, like changes in the national distribution of votes and seats, may be erroneous. There is always the risk of drawing fallacious ecological inferences (Robinson 1950; Langbein and Lichtman 1978). Moreover, since the theory of surge and decline makes claims about national, district, and individual voter behavior, the positive evidence at the national level only goes part of the way in testing the theory. We now take the next step to examine less-aggregated evidence, the individual elections held in the congressional districts.

There are four parts to the analysis of congressional district level evidence. First, congressional elections held in presidential election years are examined. The theory contends (proposition 4 in chapter 3) that short-term forces of the presidential election year affect the fortunes of congressional candidates. Since short-term forces are not uniform across the nation, they may actually help some congressional candidates of the losing presidential party. However, in most instances, they will favor candidates running on the same ticket as the winning presidential candidate. The net effect, as demonstrated by the aggregate analysis in chapter 6, should be a boost to the incoming presidential party. The second part of this analysis examines the midterm repercussions of the events of the presidential election year. As the surge declines, those who benefited from it may then suffer proportionately by its withdrawal (proposition 3). The third part of the analysis examines the overlap districts registering presidential year seat gains followed by midterm seat losses. Finally, the process of surge and decline is illustrated by case studies of elections in two congressional districts.

Two Pairs of Elections

In examining surge and decline effects at the district level, data are drawn from congressional district elections held in two sets of presidential and midterm years—1976-78 and 1984-86. Two sets of elections are examined to ensure that findings are not peculiar to a single set of elections. The 1976-78 and 1984-86 elections in particular are chosen for their recency, the availability of data (especially district-level presidential votes, past votes that are needed to construct a district normal vote, and amounts of candidate campaign spending), and the maintenance of district boundaries extending back at least to the prior midterm election. The data throughout are coded so that positive values are in terms of the president's party (Democratic in 1976-78 and Republican in 1984-86).

Districts with uncontested elections are dropped from the analysis. Without the opportunity to choose between candidates, possible coattail effects may not be expressed at the polls. While uncontested seats may be interesting from the standpoint of candidate recruitment, they are of little value in revealing influences on the voters' thinking. For similar reasons, districts are also dropped if a candidate faced only token opposition. Since the study does not include a direct measure of candidate quality, a minimal actual vote criterion may distinguish cases of a serious opponent from just nominal opposition so that possible surge and decline effects, as well as other effects, might be more clearly detected. Operationally, token candidacies are those in which a candidate received 10 percent or less of the vote.

Confining the analysis to seriously contested seats leaves 384 districts in the analysis of the 1976 vote, 339 districts in 1978 vote change analysis, 371 districts in 1984, and 330 districts in 1986.

The principal variables. For the congressional vote, three different variables are examined as dependent variables in this analysis. The first two variables concern the congressional vote in the presidential election year. The first of these is simply the percentage of the two-party congressional vote in the presidential year received by the congressional candidate of the party winning the presidency. The second is the change in the congressional vote from the prior midterm election to the presidential year. These dependent variables are examined to test the proposition of presidential election year surge effects. The third congressional vote dependent variable addresses the midterm decline question. This variable is the change in the congressional vote from the presidential election to the midterm. The congressional vote data are taken from CQ's *Guide to U.S. Elections* (1985) and its report of the 1986 returns (March 14, 1987: 486-93).[1]

The presidential vote is the principal independent variable in the analysis. This is the percentage of the district's popular vote for the presidential candidate winning nationally. That vote should reflect the direction and extent of short-term forces, coattail as well as short-term common causes of the votes, in the congressional district.[2] The presidential vote is specified as having a direct and positive effect on the congressional vote in presidential years. In midterms, its effect is specified as indirect and negative. The presidential vote, in the midterm analysis, is an antecedent variable having a mediated effect on midterm losses. It is the starting point of a simple causal chain. The presidential vote generates congressional vote gains in the on-year that, in turn, set the stage for congressional vote losses in the midterm.

Beyond their additive effects, both direct and indirect, two interactive effects involving the presidential vote will also be examined. First, surge and decline contends, in at least its original form, that turnout fluctuations magnify the effects of short-term forces. If short-term forces are strong enough to boost turnout substantially above what it had been, then they may also be strong enough to swing more votes to the party favored by the political climate. In the midterm, the reverse should occur. The greater the decline in turnout, the greater the withdrawal of presidential help to the party's candidates. Second, it may be that local conditions play somewhat less of a role in open seat contests. Without a congressional incumbent as a focal point, "national" factors may come forward. Thus surge and decline effects may also be more pronounced or positively interact with the open seat status of the district.

By examining the ratios of those voting in the different elections, the measurement of the surge and decline in turnout avoids problems of calculating the number of voting age eligibles in each district. Both the turnout surge and decline measures are based on the total number of voters casting ballots in a district's House races for each of three elections: the prior midterm, the presidential election, and the subsequent midterm. The turnout surge is calculated as the ratio of the presidential election year turnout to the prior midterm turnout. The turnout decline is similarly computed as the ratio of the presidential election turnout to the subsequent midterm turnout. High values on the two indexes indicate a greater surge and a greater decline.

The control variables. Former House Speaker Tip O'Neil is often quoted as having claimed that "All politics is local." Although undoubtedly an exaggeration and while it is not always easy to distinguish local from national effects, much of what affects congressional races would seem to be local in character. A good deal of congressional research in recent years concurs with O'Neil's sentiments that congressional elections depend heavily on local conditions (e.g., Mann 1978). Obviously these local factors, both the long-term partisan complexion of the district as well as conditions specific to the congressional campaign, must be taken into account in order to estimate accurately both surge and decline effects.

In controlling for district political conditions that are not directly related to surge and decline, three "local" or district conditions are taken into account. This will permit surge and decline effects to be more clearly and accurately estimated. These three district "control" variables are the normal partisan vote of the district, the incumbency status of the district, and the relative campaign spending of the congressional candidates.

The normal partisan vote of the district is the first local condition taken into account. In order to isolate and estimate the effects of presidential election year short-term forces it is necessary to determine the effects of long-term partisan forces in the district. Obviously, the presidential and congressional votes in districts may be positively associated because they are cast by the same partisan electorate as well as because of the particular appeal of a presidential candidate. All things being equal, predominantly Democratic districts can be expected to vote for Democratic congressional candidates as well as Democratic presidential candidates. Similarly, both Republican presidential and congressional candidates should expect to do well in traditionally Republican districts. Only by taking the long-term influence of the normal vote on the congressional vote into account can the separate influence of the presidential vote, undoubtedly influenced partially by the normal party vote as well, be accurately estimated.

While the normal vote of a party is expected to have a positive influence on that party's congressional vote, its effect on the change in that vote should be negative. The reason for this suspected negative influence of the normal vote on congressional vote change can best be explained with pair of hypothetical district situations. District A is a strongly Democratic district in which the normal vote is 75 percent Democratic. District B is a strongly Republican district in which the normal vote is 25 percent Democratic. If the presidential vote in both districts is 50 percent Democratic, it is reasonable to assume that the short-term forces responsible for change in the congressional vote are more strongly pro-Democratic in District B. Since the presidential vote is some composite of long-term (normal vote) and short-term forces and given the stipulated difference in long-term forces between the two districts, the short-term forces in district B logically had to be more strongly pro-Democratic for the two presidential votes to be equal. From a different angle, a 90 percent Republican presidential vote is much more impressive in a traditionally Democratic district than in a traditionally Republican district. Put more generally, for any presidential vote, the normal vote is inversely related to the magnitude of short-term forces favoring a party.

Although inclusion of the normal vote is very important to the proper estimation of short-term influences, there are a variety of problems associated with measuring the normal partisan vote in congressional districts (see Goldenberg and Traugott 1981; Goldenberg and Traugott 1984, appendix). Because of data limitations it is simply not feasible to estimate district normal votes with survey data as Converse (1966b) originally estimated the national normal vote or as it might be adjusted in light of Achen's (1979) criticism of the original estimation method or Petrocik's (1989) revised method. Instead, we must construct estimates of the normal vote at the district level from past votes as others have done at the national level (see for example Tufte 1978, Abramowitz, Cover, and Norpoth 1986).

Normal partisan district votes are computed using prior votes in each district. These prior votes are combined using principal components factor analysis. The normal Democratic district vote in the 1976-78 analysis is based on four prior votes: the 1974 Democratic congressional vote, the 1972 Democratic congressional vote, the 1972 Democratic presidential vote, and the 1968 Democratic presidential vote. The 1968 Democratic presidential vote was computed as the vote for Democratic nominee Hubert Humphrey plus half of those cast for Alabama Democratic Governor George Wallace, who ran as a third-party presidential candidate. All four of these votes are taken from *The Almanac of American Politics 1976* (Barone, Ujifusa, and Matthews 1975). The normal Republican district vote in the 1984-86 analysis is based on three prior votes: the 1982 Republican congressional vote, the 1980 Republican presidential vote, and the 1976 Republican presidential vote. Congressional Quarterly's *Politics in America* (Ehrenhalt 1985, 1987) reconstructed the 1980 and 1976 presidential votes for the post-1980 redistricted boundaries.

In both sets of elections a strong normal vote factor emerged from the principal components factor analysis.[3] Both factor analyses produced a single strong factor with nearly equal weighting of the previous district votes. In the 1976-78 factor analysis, the four variables produce only one factor with an eigenvalue over one (2.66). This factor accounts for 67 percent of the common variance. All four votes load heavily on this factor. The loadings range from .74 for the 1972 presidential vote to .90 for the 1968 presidential vote. The factor score coefficients are also not far from equal. The three prior votes in the 1984-86 analysis produce even stronger results. The single factor has an eigenvalue of 2.39, explaining 80 percent of the common variance. Moreover, like the 1976-78 analysis, all of the prior votes load strongly on this factor and contribute nearly equally to its composition. The loadings are .82 for the 1982 congressional vote; .92 for the 1980 presidential vote; and .94 for the 1976 presidential vote.

There is an abundant literature on the advantages of incumbency in House elections (e.g., Erikson 1971; Hinckley 1981, chap. 3). While the reasons why incumbency benefits candidates are unsettled, there is no dispute that incumbency is a distinct advantage to a candidate. Given the wide variety of advantages and resources available to incumbents, the congressional vote for the winning presidential party should be greater in seats defended by its incumbents and lower in seats defended by opposition party incumbents. As operationalized here, the incumbency status of the district indicates whether the seat is being defended by an incumbent of the winning presidential party, an incumbent of the opposing party, or is contested by two nonincumbent candidates. The incumbency variable takes on a value of $+1$ when an incumbent of the winning presidential party (Democrats in 1976-78 and Republicans in 1984-86) is seeking reelection, -1 when an incumbent of the opposing party is seeking reelection, and zero in open seat contests.

There is no doubt that campaign spending by congressional candidates also influences how well they do at the polls. While raw campaign expenditures by the individual candidates are entered separately into most analyses (and sometimes transformed by a nonlinear function to take into account diminishing returns for higher levels of spending), an alternative measurement is used here. The relative campaign spending advantage is measured as the difference between the expenditures by the candidate of the winning presidential party (Democrats in 1976-78 and Republicans in 1984-86) and the expenditures by the opposing party's congressional candidate as a proportion of the total campaign spending by both major party candidates. Values of this measure range from $+1$, when all spending is by the presidential party's candidate, to -1, when all spending is by the opposing presidential candidate.

This campaign spending advantage measure has several virtues. First, it directly compares one candidate's spending to his opponent's. The absolute value of a dollar spent in behalf of a candidate is presumed to be the same as a dollar spent in opposition to that candidate. Second, it also implicitly controls for the varying expense of campaigns in different districts and under different circumstances. Running an effective campaign in some districts may be a good deal more expensive than running in other districts. For instance, candidates can more cost-efficiently use the mass media in their campaigns when running in districts whose boundaries more nearly correspond to those of the media market (Campbell, Alford, and Henry 1984). The problem is determining the price of comparable campaigns in different district situations. The total spending of the two candidates, the index's denominator, should take this difference (at least partially) into account. Third, since the index uses current dollars in both the numerator and denominator, there is no need to make any adjustment for inflation. The index has the same value whether nominal or constant dollars are used. Fourth, it also incorporates the notion of diminishing returns (Jacobson 1980, 40), without resorting to various curvilinear functions (e.g., natural logarithms, squared terms, etc.) that are less readily interpretable. As total spending increases, the impact of each additional dollar of spending in either candidate's campaign should make less of a difference, and this logic is reflected in the campaign spending advantage index.[4]

The comparative campaign spending advantage is specified as having both an additive and an interactive effect. Although the extent of the difference has been challenged (Green and Krasno 1988), a good deal of research on campaign spending in House elections indicates that campaign finances are more important to challengers than to incumbents (see Jacobson 1980). Money is more important to challengers, presumably, because they must compensate for many advantages (e.g., voter recognition) that incumbents enjoy by virtue of having previously sought, won, and served in office. To allow for this possibility, an interaction term of the incumbency status variable and the campaign spending advantage variable will be included in the analysis.

When the dependent variable is the congressional vote change, both the incumbency and campaign spending variables will also be computed as their change from one election to the next. In addition, a variable indicating the open seat status of the district was also included in the vote change analyses. The variable is +1 when the open seat is being vacated by a representative from the president's party and −1 when the open seat is being vacated by a member of the opposition party. For seats contested by the incumbent, the variable is coded zero. Given that a positive value indicates the lost incumbency advantage, a negative effect is expected for this variable.

Locating the Gains for the President's Party

Before proceeding to the multivariate analysis, the amount and direction of simple district vote changes in these particular elections and the bivariate associations between the presidential vote and the congressional vote might be examined. In 1984 the president's party made substantial congressional vote gains; however, this was not true of 1976. In 1984, as expected, given Reagan's near landslide victory, Republican congressional candidates received nontrivial vote gains (more than two percentage points) in 181 districts examined (58 percent) and gained four percentage points over 1982 in the median district. Democratic vote gains in 1976 were not so common. Given Carter's bare majority of the presidential vote and the strong Democratic showing in the 1974 post-Watergate midterm, Democratic congressional candidates won nontrivial vote gains in just ninety-six of the districts examined (30 percent) and actually lost two percentage points of the vote in the median district.

The bivariate associations also present a somewhat mixed picture. On the one hand, the congressional and presidential votes are positively associated, as expected. The associations are also quite strong in both years (1976: $b = 1.16$, $r = .66$; 1984: $b = 1.14$, $r = .70$). On the other hand, from a simple bivariate perspective, the presidential vote is not strongly and consistently associated with the change in the congressional vote. While there is a slight association in 1984 ($b = .17$ and $r = .19$), the 1976 presidential vote and the change in the congressional vote from 1974 to 1976 appear unrelated ($b = .02$ and $r = .02$). The conflicting evidence may mean one of two things. Either there is no real effect of the presidential vote and the apparent association is only a result of both votes coming from a common partisan electorate, or there is a real effect of the presidential vote that is masked in the congressional vote change correlation by the negative effects of the normal vote on congressional vote change. In either case, the bivariate appearances may be deceiving. An accurate estimate of the effects of short-term forces can come only from the multivariate analyses.

The multivariate regressions of the congressional vote are presented in table 7.1 and the comparable regressions on congressional vote changes are presented in table 7.2. In these tables the regression analyses have been conducted for 1976 and 1984 both with and without the two interaction terms with the district presidential vote. In most important respects, the eight separate regressions (with and without presidential vote interactions for 1976 and 1984, and with the simple congressional vote as well as its change from the prior midterm) yield quite consistent results. All equations explain a respectable amount of variance in the dependent variables. The fit of those regressions examining the simple congressional vote (table 7.1) are especially impressive, accounting for between 85 percent and 92 percent of the variance. As expected, the normal partisan vote had significant positive effects in the simple congressional vote equations (table 7.1) and significant negative effects in the congressional vote change regressions (table 7.2). Also as expected, incumbency and the candidates' relative campaign expenditures were strong influences on the congressional vote. The standardized regression coefficients (in equations 2 and 4) ranged from .24 to .37 for the incumbency variables and .42 to .53 for the campaign spending variables. However, there is no evidence supporting the suspected negative interaction between incumbency and campaign spending advantages.

Table 7.1. The Presidential Vote's Effect on the Congressional Vote of the Winning Presidential Party in the Presidential Election Year, 1976 and 1984

Dependent variable: Congressional vote for the candidate of the winning presidential party

Independent variables	1976		1984	
	1	2	3	4
Incumbency advantage	7.72	6.98	5.89	5.72
	(13.21)	(12.63)	(10.11)	(9.81)
Campaign spending advantage	11.64	12.67	12.74	13.10
	(11.70)	(13.27)	(14.18)	(14.56)
Interaction of incumbency & campaign spending	.03	−1.73	2.20	2.40
	(.03)	(1.94)	(2.59)	(3.02)
Normal vote	2.11	2.34	3.10	2.92
	(3.11)	(3.42)	(4.78)	(4.49)
Presidential vote	.31	.32	.21	.28
	(4.99)	(5.60)	(3.82)	(6.21)
Interaction of pres. vote with:				
Turnout surge	−.01	—	.04	—
	(.29)		(2.46)	
Open seat	.08	—	−.01	—
	(3.40)		(.31)	
Constant	37.42	38.11	34.26	33.36
Number of cases	380	384	366	371
R^2	.86	.85	.92	.92
Adjusted R^2	.85	.85	.92	.92
Std. error	6.60	6.72	5.26	5.40

NOTE: The winning presidential party was the Democratic party in 1976 and the Republican party in 1984. All variables are oriented so that positive values are favorable to the winning presidential party's congressional candidate. The t-ratios are in parentheses.

Table 7.2. The Presidential Vote's Effect on Change in the Congressional Vote of the Winning Presidential Party in the Presidential Election Year, 1976 and 1984

Dependent variable: Congressional vote for the candidate of the winning presidential party

Independent variables	1976		1984	
	1	2	3	4
Change in incumb. advantage	4.16	3.97	2.92	2.96
	(9.01)	(8.28)	(5.50)	(5.54)
Change in spending advantage	9.02	9.30	10.34	10.33
	(12.53)	(12.33)	(12.75)	(12.68)
Open seat of pres. party	−1.17	−.46	−2.12	−2.29
	(1.04)	(.40)	(1.50)	(1.66)
Normal vote	−2.37	−2.50	−2.08	−2.60
	(3.92)	(3.95)	(3.03)	(3.90)
Presidential vote	.31	.25	.20	.31
	(4.60)	(4.26)	(2.81)	(5.68)
Interaction of pres. vote with:				
Turnout surge	−.04	—	.06	—
	(2.11)		(2.46)	
Open seat	.12	.—	−.04	—
	(5.59)		(1.72)	
Constant	−15.68	−15.14	−11.02	−13.12
Number of cases	340	340	324	326
R^2	.56	.51	.54	.53
Adjusted R^2	.55	.50	.53	.52
Std. error	6.13	6.45	5.72	5.77

NOTE: The winning presidential party was the Democratic party in 1976 and the Republican party in 1984. All variables are oriented so that positive values are favorable to the winning presidential party's congressional candidate. The t-ratios are in parentheses.

The most important finding is that the presidential vote has a signifi-cant influence on the congressional vote in each of the regressions. Approximately 30 percent of the presidential vote in a district carries over to the congressional vote. The typical congressional candidate gains roughly an additional 3 percent of the vote for every additional 10 percent increase in the party's presidential vote in the district. In the equations without the complicating interaction terms, the effect of the presidential vote ranged from .25 to .32.

While the main effects of the presidential vote are consistently signifi-cant, their interaction terms are not. The regressions fail to provide consistent evidence that presidential short-term forces are greater in open seat districts or in districts with a greater turnout surge. The effects of the presidential vote are significantly greater in open seats in the 1976 analy-sis but not in 1984. Similarly, two of the four turnout surge interaction coefficients were positive and statistically significant. The lack of turnout amplifying effects fails to support, in part, the contention of original theory of surge and decline (proposition 4). However, it is not inconsis-tent with the revised theory. For the revised theory, the turnout of different partisans matters, but the overall increase in turnout does not. The revised theory does not necessitate an unusual rise in turnout, since the turnout boost to advantaged partisans can be offset by the depressed turnout of cross-pressured disadvantaged partisans.

As the discussion of strategic politicians in chapter 5 suggests, the effect of the presidential surge may not be limited to the direct effects on the voter. The presidential vote may also indirectly affect the congres-sional vote by influencing both the recruitment of stronger congressional candidates and the level of campaign contributions. The causal model displayed as figure 7.1 shows the indirect effects of the presidential vote through the relative campaign spending of the congressional candidates. Although the analysis does not include an explicit candidate quality measure, a second aspect of the strategic politician thesis, Green and Krasno (1988) have shown that the ability to attract campaign financing is positively associated with the relative experience of the candidates, one measure of candidate quality. The campaign spending measure, there-fore, may also be a partial measure of the effects of any difference in candidate quality. As the coefficients in figure 7.1 indicate, the presiden-tial vote, as expected, had a significant positive effect on relative cam-paign spending in both 1976 and 1984. It may be inferred that in anticipation of assistance from the top of the ticket, congressional candi-dates of the president's party may find fundraising somewhat easier than it might have been, and perhaps the anticipation of a favorable political climate causes some stronger candidates to jump into the race who might have otherwise sat on the sidelines. The unstandardized effect of the

Figure 7.1. A Causal Model of the Congressional Vote in Presidential
Election Years, 1976 and 1984

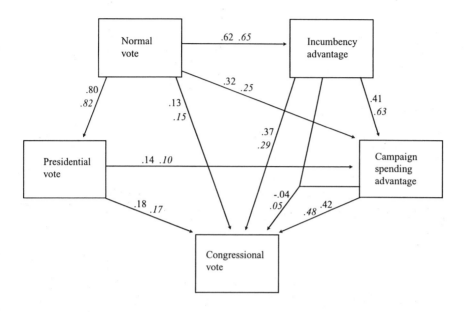

Note: The coefficients are standardized regression coefficients. The first or top
coefficient is for 1976. The second or bottom coefficient in italics is for 1984.

presidential vote on the spending advantage index is .008 (t = 2.58) in
1976 and .006 (t = 2.11) in 1984. Given the direct effects of campaign
spending advantages, adjusted by the interaction term (b = 12.26 in 1976
and b = 12.72 in 1984), this translates into an indirect effect of the
presidential vote on the congressional vote of approximately .10 in 1976
and .08 in 1984, almost one-third of the magnitude of the direct surge
effects.

Combining the direct and indirect effects of the presidential vote on
the congressional vote indicates a total effect of about .42 in 1976 and .36
in 1984. In more tangible terms, the vote for the congressional candidate
of the winning presidential party is boosted by approximately four percentage points for every ten percentage point increase of the party's presidential vote in the district. The total effect of the presidential vote, in the
vicinity of 40 percent of the presidential vote, corresponds quite closely to
other estimates of presidential vote effects. It is quite close to the national
estimates of chapter 6 (tables 6.6 and 6.8). It also corresponds quite closely
to the earlier estimates of Born (1984) and to Ferejohn and Fiorina (1985).

How much of a difference do these presidential short-term forces
actually make to the congressional vote? Part of the answer to this

Table 7.3. Presidential Surge Seats in 1976

State and district	Winning candidate & party	Dem. pres. vote %	Est. Dem. coattail effect %	Dem. cong. vote %	Pres. party gain?
Ariz. 4	Rudd (R)	37	−5.40	50	R-Held (O)
Calif. 4	Leggett (D)	55	+2.08	50	D-Held
Ga. 6	Flynt (D)	68	+7.47	52	D-Held
Ga. 7	McDonald (D)	64	+5.81	55	D-Held
Idaho 2	Hansen (R)	35	−6.23	49	R-Held
Ill. 15	Corcoran (R)	40	−4.15	46	D-Loss
Mass. 4	Drinan (D)	58	+3.32	52	D-Held
Mich. 2	Purcell (R)	45	−2.08	50	R-Held (O)
Mich. 3	Brown (R)	39	−4.57	49	D-Loss
Mich. 5	Sawyer (R)	32	−7.47	47	D-Loss
N.J. 14	Guarini (D)	57	+2.91	53	D-Held (O)
N.C. 11	Gudger (D)	54	+1.66	52	D-Held (O)
Ohio 12	Devine (R)	43	−2.91	50	R-Held
Ohio 19	Carney (D)	60	+4.15	51	D-Held
Okla. 5	Edwards (R)	41	−3.74	49	D-Loss (O)
S.C. 5	Holland (D)	60	+4.15	52	D-Held

NOTE: The estimated coattail effect is based on the total effect of the presidential vote. It is computed as .415∗ (Democratic presidential vote −50). An "O" in the last column indicates an open seat.

question depends on the magnitude of the presidential vote total (direct and indirect) effects, but it also depends in part on the variability of the presidential vote and the baseline from which the variation is measured. The natural baseline for the two-party presidential vote, given the inclusion in the model of controls for the normal partisan district vote, is the 50 percent mark. Presidential candidates who win more than 50 percent of a district's two-party presidential vote can help their party's congressional candidate. In the elections examined here, the mean absolute presidential vote deviation from an even split of the vote was 7.2 percent in 1976 and 12.4 percent in 1984. Using the total effects coefficients for the presidential vote (.42 in 1976 and .36 in 1984), this translates into a mean absolute coattail effect of 3 percent of the 1976 congressional vote and 4.5 percent of the 1984 congressional vote. An impact of plus or minus three to five percentage points, while not of enormous impact, is not something to be dismissed.

The surge seats of 1976 and 1984. Of course, the ultimate difference is in affecting election outcomes. By the above estimates of presidential ef-

Table 7.4. Presidential Surge Seats in 1984

State and district	Winning candidate & party	Repub. pres. vote %	Est. Repub. coattail effect %	Repub. cong. vote %	Pres. party gain?
Ala. 1	Callahan (R)	64	+4.99	51	R-Held (O)
Ariz. 5	Kolbe (R)	62	+4.28	52	R-Gain
Calif. 38	Dornan (R)	69	+6.77	54	R-Gain
Conn. 5	Rowland (R)	67	+6.06	54	R-Gain
Ga. 4	Swindall (R)	66	+5.70	53	R-Gain
Ind. 3	Hiller (R)	62	+4.28	53	R-Held
Ind. 8*	McIntyre (R)	61	+3.92	50	R-Gain
Iowa 5	Lightfoot (R)	58	+2.85	51	R-Gain (O)
Ky. 4	Rogers (R)	69	+6.77	54	R-Held
Md. 2	Bentley (R)	66	+5.70	51	R-Gain
Mich. 10	Schuette (R)	67	+6.06	51	R-Gain
N.J. 11	Gallo (R)	69	+6.77	56	R-Gain
N.Y. 1	Carney (R)	66	+5.70	53	R-Held
N.Y. 20	DioGuardi (R)	56	+2.14	51	R-Gain (O)
N.Y. 30	Eckert (R)	63	+4.63	55	R-Held (O)
N.C. 4	Cobey (R)	60	+3.56	51	R-Gain
N.C. 6	Coble (R)	65	+5.35	51	R-Gain
N.C. 9	McMillan (R)	65	+5.35	50	R-Held (O)
N.C. 11	Hendon (R)	63	+4.63	51	R-Gain
Pa. 23	Clinger (R)	63	+4.63	52	R-Held
Tex. 13	Boulter (R)	75	+8.91	53	R-Gain
Tex. 14	Sweeney (R)	67	+6.06	51	R-Gain
Tex. 19	Combest (R)	75	+8.91	58	R-Held (O)
Tex. 26	Armey (R)	77	+9.62	51	R-Gain
Utah 2	Monson (R)	68	+6.41	50	R-Held (O)

NOTE: The estimated coattail effect is based on the total effect of the presidential vote. It is computed as .3563* (Republican presidential vote − 50). An "O" in the last column indicates an open seat.

* Indiana's District 8 was awarded in a controversial vote of the House to the Democratic candidate, McCloskey. The data source used in this study, Congressional Quarterly's *Guide to U.S. Elections,* indicates Republican McIntyre won a plurality in this district.

fects, they apparently made the difference between winning and losing in sixteen of the 1976 districts (4 percent of the total) and twenty-five of the 1984 districts (7 percent of the total). In these districts the winning candidate's margin of victory was less than the help he or she apparently received from presidential coattails. These districts, the winning candidates and parties, the estimated presidential vote or coattail effects, and the congressional vote for the presidential party are presented for 1976 in table 7.3 and for 1984 in table 7.4.

Since the 1976 presidential contest was quite close, the number of districts in which Democratic candidates benefited from Carter heading their ticket was offset by districts in which Republican candidates were helped by Ford carrying their district. The net result was a Democratic gain of only one seat. Given the near balance of short-term partisan forces in 1976, it should not be too surprising that the regression estimates indicate that the presidential vote helped an equal number of Democrats and Republicans win office (see table 7.3). Eight Democrats and eight Republicans owed their election to help from the top of their respective tickets. In half of these cases, the presidential vote helped incumbents hold on to seats that they otherwise would have lost and in three other cases helped a party hold a seat that became open. Four seats were identified as coattail losses for the Democrats; however, two of these seats were in Michigan, the home state of Republican President Ford.

The circumstances of 1984 were quite different and produced a very definite partisan change. With short-term forces more universally favorable to 1984's winning presidential party, as evidenced in Reagan's landslide in both popular and electoral votes, Republican congressional candidates in most districts (334 of 384) benefited from Reagan's candidacy. Moreover, when presidential coattails were critical to an election's outcome in 1984, they worked consistently to the advantage of Republican congressional candidates (see table 7.4). Most of these coattail seats were real gains. Of the twenty-five Republicans boosted to victory with Reagan's help, only four were incumbents and five were Republican candidates who held onto previously Republican seats. Republicans won previously Democratic seats in the remaining sixteen districts by defeating Democratic incumbents (fourteen) and winning open seats that had previously been Democratic (two). It is interesting to note that the sixteen expected Republican seat gains in the district analysis closely corresponds to the actual Republican gain of fifteen seats in 1984.[5]

Locating the Presidential Party's Midterm Losses

As one might expect, the president's party in both the 1978 and 1986 midterms lost votes in a majority of districts. The Democrats in 1978 suffered nontrivial losses (more than two percentage points) in 176 districts (52 percent of the 339 examined). They lost eight percentage points or more in almost one-quarter of the districts (24 percent). Similarly, Republicans in 1986 suffered congressional vote losses of two percentage points or more in 193 districts (58 percent of the 330 examined) and losses of eight percentage points or more in over one-quarter of the districts (28 percent).

Like the initial bivariate analysis of presidential gains in presidential election years, the bivariate analysis of midterm vote losses in the districts offers mixed results. In simple bivariate regressions, the prior presidential vote is not negatively associated at a significant level with the extent of congressional vote change in the midterm for the president's party in either 1978 or 1986 (b = .01, t = .23 in 1978 and b = − .02, t = .41 in 1986).[6] However, in both midterms, there is a significant association between the prior congressional vote gains and the subsequent congressional vote losses in the midterm. At least in the bivariate analysis, the more votes gained in the presidential year, the more votes lost in following midterm (b = − .19, t = 3.22 in 1978 and b = − .10, t = 2.03 in 1986).[7]

Of course, as the presidential year analysis demonstrates, simple bivariate analysis may not present an accurate view of a relationship. Before moving to the multivariate analysis of midterm losses in the districts, we must observe a serious problem that complicates that analysis, the lack of one crucial piece of data: midterm presidential popularity in the district. Unfortunately there is no available district-level measurement of the president's midterm approval rating such as that routinely measured for a national sample. The specification error created by the unavailability of a midterm presidential popularity variable has two probable consequences. First, without one of the significant influences on the extent of midterm losses, the explanation of midterm losses is undoubtedly less complete than it would have been had there been a district measure of the public's midterm judgment of the president's performance. Without that district measure, it is impossible to say whether a particularly popular president in a district is reducing midterm vote losses for his party's congressional candidate or whether an especially unpopular president is adding to that congressional candidate's midterm burden.

The second and more serious problem raised by the lack of a midterm district referenda variable concerns the bias its omission introduces into the estimation of the withdrawal of the prior presidential surge. If the president's midterm popularity in districts were not associated with the prior presidential vote, then the effects of the withdrawal of the presidential surge could be estimated accurately in the midterm, even if the midterm presidential popularity rating were not included in the analysis.

Figure 7.2. Causal Relationships among the Presidential Vote, Midterm Presidential Popularity, and Midterm Congressional Vote Losses in the Districts

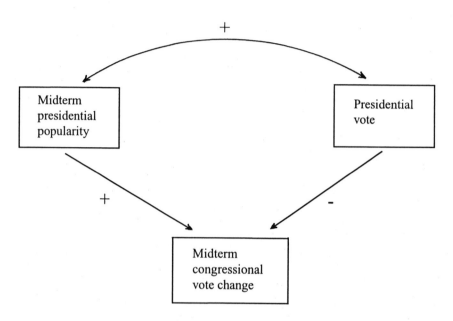

However, this is not a realistic assumption. Most probably, district presidential votes and midterm presidential popularity ratings are positively related. Most districts that were positively disposed to a presidential candidate in the presidential election year are probably positively disposed toward that president two years later in the midterm. Conversely, a president will probably receive less than average support at the midterm from the same districts he received a below average share of the vote in the presidential election.

What is the consequence of this unfortunate, but unavoidable, misspecification for the estimate of the midterm decline effects? The consequence is to bias the effects of the presidential vote so that it appears more weakly negative than it truly is. The problem is illustrated in figure 7.2. If presidential popularity is not included in the analysis, some part of its positive effects on midterm congressional vote change for the president's party will be wrongly attributed to the prior presidential vote, given that the prior presidential vote and midterm presidential popularity are positively correlated. That is, if districts with strongly positive short-term forces in the presidential election (portending greater midterm vote losses) are also those most favorable in evaluating the president at the midterm (tending to reduce midterm vote losses), then the specifi-

Figure 7.3. Surrogate Measure of Midterm Popularity in Congressional Districts, 1978 and 1986

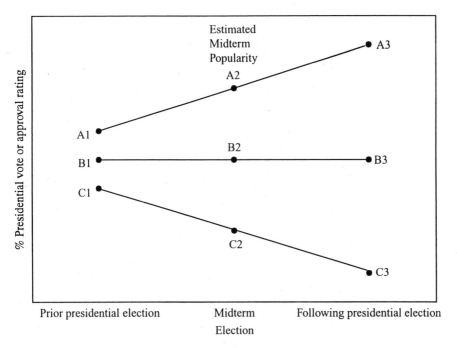

Note: The prior presidential elections are 1976 and 1984. The midterms are 1974 and 1986. The following presidential elections are 1980 and 1988.

cation error of omitting midterm presidential evaluations should cause an underestimation of surge and decline effects. The bottom line is that the estimated effects of the prior presidential vote will be a mix of its actual negative effects on midterm congressional vote change and the misattributed positive effects of presidential popularity.

Lacking a direct measure, it is necessary to create a surrogate measure of midterm presidential popularity in the districts. This will permit the repercussions from the prior presidential surge to be estimated accurately and the variation in midterm losses to be explained more fully, as suggested by the revised theory's incorporation of the midterm referendum perspective. A plausible surrogate for presidential popularity in a district is the average of the district's presidential votes two years before and two years after the midterm. The logic of this surrogate is depicted in figure 7.3. Presumably, if a president gained support in a district from one election to the next (district A in figure 7.3), it is a good guess that he rose in public esteem halfway between the two elections. Conversely, if a president lost votes in a district from one election to the next (district C), it seems likely that his popularity in that district would have slipped by the time of the midterm. Adding to the plausibility of this strategy is the fact that the same Democratic presidential candidate, Jimmy Carter, ran in both 1976 and 1980.[8] While Republican presidential candidates differed in 1984 (Reagan) and 1988 (Bush), George Bush's eight-year service as Reagan's vice-president and loyalty to the Reagan record both before and during the 1988 campaign makes the Bush vote a useful second point by which to estimate Reagan's midterm popularity. Of course, it is quite possible that a president's popularity in a district may not change at a constant rate (making the surrogate measure less than ideal). Events may change public evaluations of a president's performance quite quickly and it is possible that midterm evaluations may either exceed or fall short of presidential votes both before and after the midterm.[9] Nevertheless, without a direct measure, the average of the two presidential votes is a reasonable estimate of midterm presidential popularity and can be included in a more fully specified multivariate analysis of midterm congressional vote change.

Before examining the multivariate results, a couple of differences from the previous multivariate district analysis should be noted. First, as indicated above, the key independent variable in the examination of midterm vote change is the congressional vote change in the prior presidential election. Second, since these prior vote gains already incorporate the effects of the presidential surge, the normal vote is unnecessary in these regressions. However, since the decline may be more precipitous in districts in which the president's party originally held more votes (there are more votes for the presidential party to lose), the congressional base vote for the party at the prior midterm election is included. One final difference: while estimating the regressions for all districts, the analysis of midterm losses also examines just those seats held by the president's party going into the midterm.

Table 7.5 presents the multivariate regressions of the change in the midterm congressional vote. These estimates generally confirm expectations: (1) The "local" influences of changes in incumbency status and campaign spending advantage, as expected, strongly affect midterm vote changes. (2) The surrogate measure of midterm presidential popularity had a significant positive effect in 1978 but not in 1986. The lack of significant positive coefficients in 1986 undoubtedly says more about the difficulty of constructing a good data for district-level popularity than about the actual effects of public reactions to the administration at the midterm. (3) The base vote was, as anticipated, consistently significant and negative in 1978. However, it was not in 1986.[10] (4) The prior vote gain interaction terms with turnout decline and with the absence of an incumbent in the race do not receive consistent support, just as in the

Table 7.5. The Effect of the Prior Congressional Vote Gain on Midterm Change in the Congressional Vote of the President's Party, 1978 and 1986

Dependent variable: Midterm change in the congressional vote for the presidential party

Independent variables	1978 All districts		1978 Pres. districts		1986 All districts		1986 Pres. districts	
	1	2	3	4	5	6	7	8
Change in incumb. adv.	3.49	3.57	1.80	1.74	3.12	3.05	.86	1.44
	(3.96)	(3.96)	(1.47)	(1.36)	(4.71)	(4.63)	(.96)	(1.58)
Open seat of pres. party	−2.25	−1.62	−5.63	−3.56	−3.05	−2.70	−4.23	−2.75
	(1.39)	(.99)	(2.48)	(1.58)	(2.37)	(2.14)	(2.28)	(1.56)
Change in spending adv.	9.12	9.36	8.00	8.30	11.25	11.33	11.50	11.08
	(8.70)	(8.89)	(6.57)	(6.73)	(12.49)	(12.63)	(8.49)	(7.90)
Presidential popularity	.21	.22	.30	.32	−.04	−.04	.03	−.01
	(3.41)	(3.50)	(4.58)	(4.63)	(.93)	(.94)	(.37)	(.18)
Base vote (1974, 1982)	−.18	−.19	−.37	−.39	.03	.03	−.13	−.08
	(4.30)	(4.53)	(4.99)	(5.15)	(1.07)	(1.06)	(1.95)	(1.20)
Prior congress. vote gain	−.21	−.25	−.40	−.43	−.09	−.07	−.57	−.14
	(.78)	(4.84)	(1.47)	(5.51)	(.49)	(1.66)	(2.79)	(1.92)
Interaction with:								
Turnout decline	.02	—	.05	—	.01	—	.27	—
	(.12)		(.25)		(.09)		(1.99)	
Open seat	−.30	—	−.32	—	.19	—	.04	—
	(3.03)		(2.97)		(1.36)		(.25)	
Constant	−1.20	−.91	8.00	8.80	−2.30	−2.23	5.07	4.30
Number of cases	337	339	214	216	323	325	158	160
R²	.42	.40	.46	.42	.50	.50	.54	.49
Adjusted R²	.41	.39	.43	.40	.49	.49	.51	.47
Std. error	8.49	8.69	7.55	7.87	6.02	6.01	5.24	5.46

NOTE: The presidential party is the Democratic party in 1978 and the Republican party in 1986. "Pres. districts" were those held by the presidential party going into the midterm. All variables have positive values when favorable to congressional candidates of the president's party. The t-ratios are in parentheses.

analysis of the presidential year. Again, while the lack of significant turnout amplification contradicts the original theory of surge and decline, it is not inconsistent with the revised version.

The most important finding is that in the midterm the president's party loses some of the votes it had gained in the prior presidential election. The effects of the prior congressional vote gain in each additive equation (even-numbered equations in table 7.5), as expected, are negative and statistically significant. Given the difficulty with the estimation of midterm presidential popularity, the estimates of the midterm decline coefficients unfortunately vary a good deal. Anywhere from 10 percent to 40 percent of congressional vote gains won in the prior presidential election—many a result of the presidential surge—are lost in the subsequent midterm. However, including all districts in the analysis, those not seriously contested as well as those that were, produces estimates that are both stronger and more consistent.[11] From these estimates and the addition of indirect effects of the prior presidential surge, it appears that about one-quarter to one-third of presidential year gains are lost in the midterm.[12]

The sequence is now complete. As demonstrated in the first section of this chapter, in presidential election years congressional candidates of the winning presidential party gain votes proportionate to the relative appeal of their party's presidential candidate in their districts. In the midterm, there is a decline. As is evident in table 7.5, these candidates lose a significant portion of the votes that they had temporarily gained in the presidential year.

The lost seats of the 1978 and 1986 midterms. The previous analysis demonstrates that the presidential surge has repercussions for the decline in midterm support; however, it does not speak to their effects on midterm seat losses. Were the seats lost by the president's party in the 1978 and 1986 midterms attributable to the decline from the prior presidential surge? Each of the twenty-two districts lost by the president's party in 1978 and the thirteen lost in 1986 may be examined to determine whether its loss was a consequence of the midterm decline. The vote percentages and normal vote for each district are presented in table 7.6 for the 1978 losses and table 7.7 for the 1986 losses.

It is important to bear in mind in examining these districts that the theory of surge and decline does not contend that all midterm losses are a consequence of the prior presidential surge. It claims that the repercussions of prior presidential coattails contribute to the systematic losses in midterms; but also acknowledges that a variety of other factors, including both midterm reactions to presidential performance and many local conditions, also affect the outcomes in many midterm elections.

Table 7.6. Midterm Seat Losses for the President's Party in 1978

State and district	Congressman of President's party	Prior presidential election year ('76)			Midterm year ('78)		Normal vote factor score
		% Dem. congress. vote	% Change from prior cong. vote	% Dem. pres. vote	% Dem. congress. vote	% Change from prior cong. vote	
Arkansas 2	Tucker	86*	+27	68	49*	−37	+.45
Calif. 14	McFall	73	−2	49	45	−28	+.57
Calif. 17	Krebs	66	+14	46	46	−20	−.42
Calif. 34	Hannaford	51	+1	42	45	−6	−.38
Georgia 6	Flynt	52	0	68	46*	−6	−.22
Illinois 22	Shipley	61	+1	48	46*	−15	−.29
Indiana 8	Cornwell	51*	−2	50	48	−3	−.62
Iowa 2	Blouin	50	−1	49	47	−3	−.08
Kansas 2	Keys	52	−4	44	48	−4	−.52
Kentucky 6	Breckinridge	90	+15	52	47	−43	+.01
N.J. 13	Meyner	51	−6	41	48	−3	−.73
New York 1	Pike	68	−1	45	43	−25	−.50
New York 29	Pattison	51	−3	39	46	−5	−.94
Ohio 19	Carney	51	−22	60	49	−2	+.86
Penn. 4	Eilberg	68	−3	56	44	−24	+.60
Penn. 15	Rooney	65	−25	52	47	−18	+.69
Penn. 23	Ammerman	56	+9	45	46	−10	−.71
S.C. 4	Mann	74	+12	51	47	−27	−.61
Texas 21	Krueger	72	+18	40	43	−29	−.71
Texas 22	Gammage	50	−21	49	49	−1	+.22
Wisconsin 8	Cornell	52	−2	47	42	−10	−.53
Wyoming AL	Roncalio	56	+1	40	41	−15	−.61

NOTE: * indicates an open seat. Positive normal vote scores indicate Democratic orientation.

An examination of presidential party seats lost in the 1978 midterm indicates that only a few might be traced to the withdrawal of presidential coattails.[13] Only eight of the twenty-two lost Democratic seats had registered vote gains in the 1976 presidential election year, and Democratic presidential candidate Jimmy Carter had been able to carry only eight of these districts. Nevertheless, though coattails may not have been the sole reason for a number of 1976 Democratic victories, they appear to have extended substantial help in at least a few districts. The clearest cases in which the withdrawal of surge effects may have cost Democrats seats are in Arkansas (2d), Georgia (6th), and Ohio (19th).

The finding of few 1978 midterm "decline" districts is consistent with the relatively small net loss to the president's party that year (sixteen seats) and the fact that the prior presidential surge was minimal (as evidenced by majority party candidate Carter's very narrow margin over Ford). In addition, few Democratic seats registered vote gains in the prior

Table 7.7. Midterm Seat Losses for the President's Party in 1986

State and district	Congressman of President's party	Prior presidential election year ('84)			Midterm year ('86)		Normal vote factor score
		Repub. congress. vote	Change from prior cong. vote	Repub. pres. vote	Repub. congress. vote	Change from prior cong. vote	
Colorado 3	Strong	58*	+12	63	48	−10	+.55
Indiana 5	Hillis	68	+7	69	48*	−20	+1.19
Iowa 3	Evans	61	+6	52	45*	−16	+.22
Maine 1	McKernan	63	+13	60	45*	−18	−.02
Maryland 4	Holt	66	+5	59	50*	−16	+.39
Michigan 2	Franklin	70	+3	64	59	−11	+.84
New York 1	Carney	53	−11	66	45*	−8	+.86
New York 30	Eckhert	55*	−16	63	49	−6	+.58
N.C. 4	Cobey	51	+3	60	44	−7	−.07
N.C. 11	Hendon	51	+2	63	49	−2	+.02
S.C. 4	Campbell	64	+2	70	48*	−17	+.44
Utah 2	Monson	50*	−4	68	44*	−6	+1.30
Virginia 2	Whitehurst	90	0	63	45	−44	+.82

NOTE: * indicates an open seat. Positive normal vote values indicate Republican orientation.

presidential election since the president's party (the Democrats) had been unusually advantaged in the 1974 Watergate midterm.

While there had barely been a surge to decline from in 1976-78, the presidential landslide of 1984 provided a substantial surge and set the stage for what might have been a very steep decline, had it not been for the president's popularity at the midterm. Even so, the decline following the 1984 surge appears to have played a role in each of the thirteen districts lost by the Republicans in 1986. As presented in table 7.7, Reagan carried each of the thirteen districts lost in the next midterm and in most of these districts (nine of thirteen) the Republican congressional candidate picked up more votes in the presidential year. Reagan won 60 percent or more of the district's presidential vote in ten of these thirteen districts. In accord with the regression results, seat losses were especially likely in districts in which the president's party not only lost the advantage of the presidential surge but also the advantage of incumbency. Open seat contests are fairly uncommon, only about one-tenth of all House races; however, more than one-half of the seats lost to the president's party in 1986 were open seats.[14]

Matching Presidential Gains and Midterm Losses

From a comparison of previous tables (tables 7.3 and 7.6, tables 7.4 and 7.7), it is clear that few seats gained in the presidential surge are lost in the midterm decline and few seats lost in the midterm had been won through coattail help in the presidential year. In most cases, presidential election "surge" seats and midterm "decline" seats are not the same, though some such cases exist. From 1972 to 1986, nineteen seats were gained by the president's party in the presidential year and subsequently lost in the next midterm (three in 1972, one in 1976, twelve in 1980, and three in 1984). These are presented in table 7.8. The presidential candidate winning nationally carried fifteen of the nineteen districts (79 percent) and received more than 60 percent of the two-party presidential vote in seven of the nineteen districts. While most of these cases appear to fit the surge and decline profile, they are still only a small minority of all seats gained by the president's party in presidential years or lost in midterms.

Is the lack of overlap among the two sets of seats indicative of a weakness in the theory of surge and decline? Absolutely not. The theory does not require that the midterm seats lost be the same as those previously gained. First, as demonstrated earlier, a number of seats kept in the presidential year because of coattails do not count as "gains" because the seats were already held by the presidential party going into the presidential election. Second, a district's approval of the president's performance may prevent a seat gain from turning into a midterm loss. Third, there are numerous "local" reasons in on-year and off-year congressional elections that in individual cases may overwhelm the impact of surge and decline. For instance, a presidential surge may not be decisive in a district with a well-financed incumbent of the president's party; however, if the incumbent decides to retire and the opposition recruits a strong candidate, the decline from the prior surge may be decisive to the midterm outcome. Conversely, a district won or kept because of a presidential surge might not be lost in the midterm if the incumbent exploits his advantages or if the opposition cannot recruit a good challenger.

Two Case Studies

While this analysis has provided evidence of a general pattern of surge and decline within congressional districts, the effects of surge and decline can be best illustrated by examining a couple of specific districts more closely.[15] Two districts in the 1984-86 pair of elections quite clearly display the effects of a presidential surge and a midterm decline. They are the second district in Nevada and the fourth district of Texas.[16] Although neither district incurred the midterm seat turnover associated with the midterm decline, they both exhibited substantial changes in the midterm vote and only the strength of the incumbency advantage may have prevented seat changes. These districts are not necessarily typical. They were selected because they depict, more clearly than other districts, the

Table 7.8. Seats Won in the Presidential Surge and Then Lost in the Midterm Decline, 1972-1990

Election series	State and district	Candidate of President's party in on-year	Prior midterm Congress. vote	Presidential election year Congress. vote	Vote change	Pres. vote	Midterm election year Congress. vote	Vote change
1970-74	IN 11	Hudnut	41.7	51.2	+9.5	63	47.5	−3.7
1970-74	NY 3	Roncallo	38.1	53.1	+15.0	67	46.1	−7.0
1970-74	SC 6	Young	34.9	54.4	+19.5	68	48.0	−6.4
1974-78	PA 23	Ammerman	47.3	56.5	+9.2	45	45.7	−10.8
1978-82	CA 21*	Fielder	35.9	48.7	+12.8	57	40.4	−8.3
1978-82	CA 42*	Hunter	26.3	53.3	+27.0	53	31.8	−21.5
1978-82	CT 3	Denardis	40.0	52.3	+12.3	57	49.0	−3.3
1978-82	MI 6	Dunn	43.3	50.6	+7.3	57	47.5	−3.1
1978-82	NY 3	Carman	47.9	50.1	+.2	62	46.0	−4.1
1978-82	NC 6	Johnston	49.6	51.1	+1.5	56	45.6	−5.5
1978-82	NC 11	Hendon	46.6	53.5	+8.9	52	49.2	−4.3
1978-82	OH 9	Weber	30.3	56.2	+25.9	51	39.3	−16.9
1978-82	PA 11	Nelligan	46.7	51.9	+5.2	54	46.2	−5.7
1978-82	SC 6	Napier	0.0	51.7	+51.7	46	47.5	−4.2
1978-82	WV 2	Benedict	44.7	55.9	+11.2	50	36.0	−19.9
1978-82	WV 3	Staton	40.8	52.7	+11.9	48	4.6	−48.1
1982-86	CO 3	Strang	44.8	57.1	+12.3	63	48.1	−9.0
1982-86	NC 4	Cobey	47.4	50.6	+3.2	60	44.3	−6.3
1982-86	NC 11	Hendon	49.2	51.0	+1.8	63	49.3	−1.7

NOTE: The district numbers are those in the presidential election year. Some changed in redistricting (1980's CA 21 became CA 26 in 1982, CA 42 became CA 44).

vote swings associated with surge and decline. As simple case studies, they are also not intended to be regarded as evidence generally supporting the theory, only as examples of how the theory may manifest itself in particular cases.

The case of Nevada's second district. The decennial reallocation of seats to the House of Representatives in 1980 added a second seat to the state of Nevada's delegation. The newly apportioned second district was drawn to cover a small portion of Las Vegas and most of the remainder of the state's territory, including the city of Reno. The first representative elected from this district was Republican candidate Barbara Vucanovich, a long-time supporter of Nevada's conservative Senator Paul Laxalt. In the 1982 open seat contest, Vucanovich received 8 percent of the two-party vote and defeated Mary Gojak, a liberal former state senator who two years earlier had been defeated in a bid for a U.S. Senate seat.

In her 1984 reelection, Vocanovich increased her vote margin considerably. The Republican congressional vote share rose from 58 percent in 1982 to 73 percent in 1984. Not coincidentally, from the standpoint of surge and decline, the district also strongly backed President Reagan's reelection.[17] Reagan won 70 percent of the district's 1984 presidential vote. While the district is a bit more Republican than the typical district (by the factor analysis generated normal vote the district is one-half standard deviation more Republican than average) and had supported both Ford (55 percent) in 1976 and Reagan (65 percent) in his initial 1980 victory over Carter (24 percent), the particularly strong showing for Reagan in 1984 reflects substantial short-term forces favoring Republicans. This Republican presidential surge seems to have been responsible, at least in part, for boosting Vucanovich's vote the additional fifteen percentage points above her 1982 totals.

Vucanovich's 1986 reelection vote, though sufficient to win a third term, suggests the temporary nature of the benefit obtained from the presidential surge. As one might expect, without a popular Republican presidential candidate again heading the ticket, her 1986 vote margin declined sharply from its impressive 1984 mark. In fact, the Vucanovich vote in the 1986 midterm fell back exactly to its 1982 presurge level of 58 percent.[18] The votes in this election sequence are displayed in figure 7.4.

The case of Texas' fourth district. Even though the fourth district in Texas elected the same Democratic congressmen in the 1982, 1984, and 1986 elections, as in Nevada's second district, the fingerprints of surge and decline are clearly in evidence. The fourth congressional district of Texas is located in northeastern Texas. It encompasses the outskirts of Dallas and the cities of Tyler and Longview. Although the district had long been

Figure 7.4. The Presidential and Congressional Votes in Nevada's Second District, 1982-86

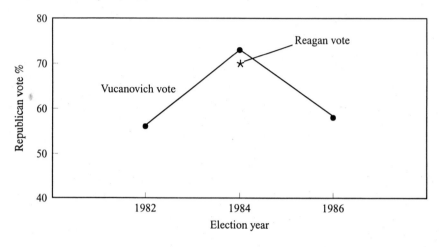

Figure 7.5. The Presidential and Congressional Votes in Texas' Fourth District, 1980-1988

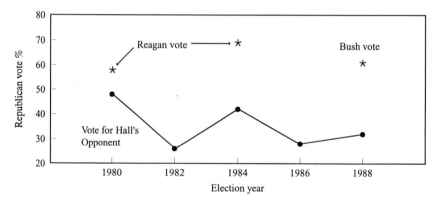

Democratic and had been the home district of Democratic Speaker Sam Rayburn, in recent years it changed a good deal. Although some Democratic strongholds in the district remain, the conservative constituency cannot be taken for granted any longer by the Democrats. Its normal vote factor score, based on recent elections, indicates that the district is right at the national average of Democratic partisanship. Given the Democrats are still the majority party, this score suggests that Democrats have a small edge in the district.

In 1980 the district elected conservative Democratic businessman Ralph Hall to succeed the retiring Democratic nine-term incumbent Ray Roberts. Hall barely survived his first election to the House, with his Republican opponent receiving a substantial boost from Reagan's defeat of Jimmy Carter in the 1980 election. In this Democratic-leaning district, Reagan won 58 percent of the 1980 presidential vote. As *Politics in America* (Ehrenhalt 1983, 1452) put it: "Because of Ronald Reagan's popularity among 4th District voters, Hall's November contest with Republican John H. Wright turned out to be closer than expected. Though Wright, a Tyler business manager, was well-known only in the eastern part of the 4th, Reagan's 30,000-vote margin in districtwide presidential voting helped Wright pull 48 percent of the vote against Hall." In 1982, without Reagan on the ticket to help the Republican, Hall easily won reelection. He convincingly defeated the Republican challenger, Pete Collumb, by a three-to-one margin.

The 1984 election was similar to the 1980 contest. Again Hall's Republican challenger (this time, Thomas Blow) was helped by a popular presidential candidate heading the ticket. While Reagan ran strong in most parts of the country in 1984, he ran especially well in the fourth district, carrying 69 percent presidential vote. Although Reagan's coattails failed to boost the Republican House candidate over the 50 percent threshold to unseat Hall, they were able to boost the Republican vote well above its 1982 level. With the 1984 Republican presidential surge, the district's Republican congressional vote rose seventeen percentage points to 42 percent of the vote.

The 1986 election was a rematch of Democratic incumbent Hall and Republican challenger Blow. The major difference from 1984 was the absence of the presidential contest and the votes that it had provided to the Republican challenger. Without that help Hall easily defeated his Republican opponent. The Republican challenger's vote declined in the midterm to just 28 percent of the vote.

The district's Republican swing held again in 1988. While popular Democratic Sen. Lloyd Bentsen running as the Democratic vice-presidential candidate as well as for reelection to his Senate seat and Hall's service of eight years as an incumbent undoubtedly dampened the extent of the

Republican surge, George Bush carried the district and Hall's Republican challenger won four percent more of the vote than in 1986.

The votes of the fourth District over this election sequence are charted in figure 7.5. This clearly displays the surge and decline roller-coaster ride of the district's congressional candidates. Republican candidates did well in presidential elections with a popular Republican presidential candidate, though not well enough to win given the Democratic disposition of the district and Hall's incumbency advantages. In the midterms, without the advantage of a conservative Republican presidential candidate to attract the fourth district's voters and without a liberal Democratic presidential candidate to discourage many of the fourth's conservative Democrats from turning out, the Republican candidates posed no serious threat to the Democratic incumbent's reelection.

8

Evidence in the Electorate

The electoral pulse of surge and decline depends ultimately upon the behavior of voters and potential voters. Their actions create the swings in the interelection seat and vote distributions observed at the national level over time in chapter 6 and at the congressional district level in chapter 7. At the root, any complete theory of midterm elections must draw the connection between individual voting behavior and the pattern of election results.

The full case for an electoral theory includes demonstrating the validity of its claims about the voter as well as its claims about the aggregate results arising from voters' behavior. This is particularly true with respect to the theory of surge and decline. As we have already seen, the original theory of surge and decline has been fairly well supported by aggregate election results. Where it fell short was in its claims about the composition and behavior of the presidential and midterm electorates. This too is where the differences between the original and revised theories of surge and decline are most pronounced. Thus we now turn to an examination of the turnout and vote choice decisions of the presidential and midterm electorates. The revised theory of surge and decline makes claims about the behavior of both independents and partisans. We turn first to the independents.

The Tilt of the Independent Vote

Like the original theory, the revised theory claims that independents are especially likely to respond to the prevailing short-term forces of the presidential election year and vote for the winning presidential candidate and his party's congressional candidates. The vote choice of independents over time, examined in chapter 3 (proposition 10), supports this claim. The aggregated vote choices of independents is further examined in equation 1 of table 8.1. As the estimates indicate, independents vote for the winning presidential candidate in proportion to prevailing short-term forces (as measured by the overall vote for that candidate). In fact, the steep slope in equation 1 indicates that independents have been especially sensitive to short-term forces in their presidential voting. More important for the theory, the response of independents to short-term

Table 8.1. The Surge and Decline of the Independent Vote, 1952-1988

Independent variables	Dependent variables (*Democratic* votes)				Midterm elections
	Presidential Elections				
	Independent vote			National congressional vote	Change in independent congressional vote
	Presidential	Congressional			
	1	2	3	4	5
Presidential year short-term Dem. forces	2.28 (4.22)	—	.70 (1.13)	—	−.86 (1.65)
Independent congressional vote for Dem.	—	—	—	.16 (3.57)	—
Independent presidential vote for Dem.	—	.49 (2.81)	—	—	—
Constant	−72.82	33.15	16.77	45.04	40.69
Number of cases	10	10	10	10	8
R^2	.69	.50	.14	.61	.31
Adjusted R^2	.65	.43	.03	.57	.20

NOTE: Short-term forces are measured as the Democratic share of the national presidential vote. The t-ratios are in parentheses. The presidential vote of independents is drawn from Asher (1992, 88). Equation 5 includes midterms from 1958 to 1986.

forces carries over to the congressional vote (equation 2). When independents vote for a party's presidential candidate, they are quite likely also to vote for that party's congressional candidates. As equation 3 suggests, the independent vote for congressional candidates of the winning presidential party is proportionate to the size of the presidential victory.[1] Moreover, though pure independents are relatively small in numbers, the analysis in equation 4 of table 8.1 suggests that the independent congressional vote is significantly related to the general congressional vote.

The independent vote for congressional candidates of the president's party ought to decline in the midterm following its temporary tilt in favor of the president's party in the presidential election year. It does. The midterm change in the Democratic share of the congressional vote of independents is inversely related to the presidential campaign's short-term forces, as measured by the Democratic presidential vote (equation 5 in table 8.1). Once again, the decline follows the surge.

Partisan Cross-Pressures and Turnout

Although the independent vote is an important component of the surge, independents remain only a small portion of the voting public. Even at the zenith of partisan dealignment, pure independents never constituted as much as 10 percent of the active congressional electorate (Ornstein, Mann, and Malbin 1990, 65). By their numbers alone, partisans should play a substantial role in the presidential election surge. There are only two ways in which partisans can contribute to the presidential surge. They can contribute either by changes in their vote choice or by changes in their turnout. As you may recall, the original theory of surge and decline suspected partisans to contribute to the surge through their vote choice, disadvantaged peripheral partisans would defect to the winning presidential party. However, the evidence, as presented in chapter 3, did not find a consistent pattern of greater partisan defections from the losing presidential party in presidential election years.

The revised theory hypothesizes that partisans contribute to the presidential surge primarily through their turnout. It contends that partisan turnout is significantly affected by short-term forces. While a presidential campaign naturally attracts more voters across the board, embedded within this general increase are important partisan differences. Partisans of the party advantaged by short-term forces are invigorated to turn out, while many partisans of the disadvantaged party are upset enough with their party's candidate to feel cross-pressured in their vote choice. As a result of these cross-pressures, disadvantaged partisans turn out at lower than expected levels and congressional candidates of their party are denied these votes. Although the midterm has a political climate of its own, without the strong and systematic tilt of the presidential campaign's short-term forces, midterm partisan turnout rates return nearly to normal.

The logic of the partisan hypothesis may be stated as a pair of simple syllogisms. First, concerning the behavior of disadvantaged partisans: *(1) Short-term forces in presidential elections increase cross-pressures for partisans of the losing presidential party (disadvantaged partisans). (2) Cross-pressured partisans are less inclined to turn out. (3) Therefore, disadvantaged partisans are less likely than usual to turn out in presidential elections.* If cross-pressured partisans stay away from the presidential election, the support they might have given their party's congressional candidate is lost. Moreover, these effects are proportional: stronger short-term forces create cross-pressures in more partisans, which further diminishes turnout to the greater advantage of the advantaged party.

The second syllogism concerns partisans of the winning presidential party: *(1) Short-term forces in presidential elections decrease cross-pressures for partisans of the winning presidential party (advantaged partisans). (2) Cross-pressured partisans are less inclined to turn out. (3) Therefore, advantaged partisans are more likely than usual to turn out in presidential elections.* With their party's standard-bearer cast in a favorable light, advantaged partisans may feel more comfortable in turning out to vote, and once at the polls, they are more likely than not to vote also for their party's congressional candidate. As with the earlier logic, the effects of short-term forces on advantaged partisans should also be proportional to how strongly short-term forces favor the winning presidential party.

At the midterm, short-term forces are neither so strong nor systematically to the disadvantage of the president's party. As a result, the relative turnout of partisans returns to its usual levels, thus contributing to midterm losses for the president's party.

Each point of the above scenario is subject to test. First, are partisans of the disadvantaged or losing presidential party more disaffected than usual from their party's presidential candidate? Conversely, are advantaged partisans less cross-pressured in their vote choice than usual? Second, are these cross-pressured partisans less likely to turn out in presidential elections? Conversely, are the advantaged partisans finding short-term evaluations consistent with their partisanship more likely to turn out to vote in presidential elections? Third, over time, has the partisan composition of electorates in presidential years reflected the prevailing short-term forces of presidential campaigns?

Short-Term forces and partisan cross-pressures. The first step in examining the revised partisan proposition is to establish whether partisans of the party disadvantaged by the short-term forces of the presidential campaign are, in fact, more likely to be disaffected from or dissatisfied with their party's presidential candidate. If so, we can conclude that they are, thereby, more cross-pressured in their presidential vote choice. *Dissatisfaction of a partisan with his party's presidential candidate reveals the presence of cross-pressures.* In the absence of cross-pressures, partisans should prefer their party's candidate. A weakening of this preference suggests that something is in conflict with the partisan's predisposition, placing him in a cross-pressured condition. For example, a Democratic party identifier is presumed to be cross-pressured to the extent that he thinks that his party's presidential candidate compares less favorably to the Republican candidate. Party disaffection, however, is indicative of cross-pressures only up to a point. Beyond a point, cross-pressures are relieved by rejection of the standing party identification cue in favor of short-term evaluations.

The party dissatisfaction or disaffection measure indicates the overall impression of the presidential candidate of the partisan's party compared to the opposition's candidate. It is constructed to indicate the extent of a partisan's dissatisfaction with that candidate. As such, it is party-specific in that the measures used for Democratic identifiers indicate their relative dissatisfaction with the Democratic candidate and those used for Republican identifiers' indicate their relative dissatisfaction with the Republican candidate.

The party disaffection index uses the number of positive and negative comments made about the two presidential candidates. The calculation is essentially that used by Stokes, Campbell, and Miller (1958) and Kelley and Mirer (1974), except that only responses to the questions regarding the candidates (as opposed to including responses about the parties) were used. This index of a partisan's relative displeasure with his or her own party's presidential candidate (or cross-pressures when used among partisans of the same party) is calculated by equation 1:

DISAFFECT = (#Pos. Other + #Neg. Own) − (#Pos. Own + #Neg. Other) [1]

The index indicates net dissatisfaction with the presidential candidate of the respondent's party.[2] The first two terms, the number of positive comments about the opposing party's candidate (#Pos. Other) and negative comments about the presidential candidate of the respondent's own party (#Neg. Own), indicate impressions pushing the respondent away from his or her own party's candidate or pulling him or her toward support for the opposition's candidate. This is contrasted to the final two terms, the number of positive comments about the respondent's party standard-bearer (#Pos. Own) and the number of negatives attributed to his or her opponent (#Neg. Other), both of which support party loyalty. Since respondents were allowed five responses to each of the likes/ dislikes questions (except in 1972 when only three responses were allowed), the index's values can conceivably range from − 10 to + 10. More positive values indicate greater relative disaffection with the candidate of the respondent's own party. Greater disaffection, at least up to a point, raises the possibility that the partisan feels cross-pressured. Respondents failing to say anything about either candidate were assumed to be apolitical or unresponsive to the survey rather than purely neutral and were omitted from the analysis.

Before addressing the effects of short-term forces on partisan disaffection, we should take note that the disaffection index indicates that generally partisans are restrained in their disapproval of their own party. The mean partisan disaffection scores for both Democrats and Republicans in the nine elections from 1952 to 1984 was always supportive of their party (a negative disaffection index average). Disaffection scores among

Table 8.2. The Effects of Presidential Short-Term Forces on Partisan
Disaffection, 1952-1984

	Dependent variable	
Independent variable	Mean Democratic disaffection	Mean Republican disaffection
Short-term forces	−.10	+.09
(Democratic pres. vote)	(2.39)	(2.86)
Constant	+2.97	−6.99
Number of cases	9	9
R^2	.45	.54
Adjusted R^2	.37	.47
Std. error	.81	.61

NOTE: The t-ratios are in parentheses.

Democrats ranged from −3.5 (1964) to −0.2 (1972). Among Republicans, the average disaffection score ranged from −3.7 (1956) to −0.9 (1964). This may be considered testimony to the influence of partisanship on voter perceptions and evaluations. More important for the theory, it also suggests that partisan disaffection much more commonly extends to the point of cross-pressures rather than to the point of estrangement.

Based on the disaffection index, are partisans of the disadvantaged party more dissatisfied with their party's presidential candidate than usual and, thereby, cross-pressured in their presidential vote? There is no surprise here; the answer is yes. Partisan dissatisfaction is inversely proportionate to the short-term forces favoring their party, as measured by the party's presidential vote.

Table 8.2 reports the regression of the average disaffection index values of Democrats against the Democratic presidential vote (the measure of short-term forces) for the nine presidential elections from 1952 to 1984. As expected, Democrats as a group generally responded to Democratic presidential candidates the same way the general voting public responded. Democratic disaffection rose when short-term forces, as judged by the electorate, ran against their party and fell when short-term forces were more favorable for the party. This is reflected in the estimated negative and statistically significant (p ⟨.03) effects of short-term forces of the mean disaffection score of Democrats.

Also as expected, the direction of short-term forces in the presidential campaign also affects the extent of Republican disaffection. The regression results in table 8.2 indicate that the mean disaffection of Republicans rose significantly (p ⟨.02) when short-term forces were generally more favorable to the Democrats. These results confirm the first premise of the partisan turnout argument: short-term forces in presidential elections increase cross-pressures among disadvantaged partisans.

The effect of cross-pressures on partisan turnout. Do these cross-pressures make a difference? What are the consequences of partisans of the disadvantaged or losing presidential party more often being cross-pressured? The theory contends that while some may be driven to defection, they are more commonly driven to abstention. For the disaffected partisan, nonvoting may be a middle course between a strained vote of loyalty and an unpleasant defection. As illustrated in figure 5.4, short-term partisan dissatisfaction should have a curvilinear relationship with turnout. The suspected relationships between disaffection and cross-pressures and between cross-pressures and turnout are portrayed with a restructured dependent variable in figure 8.1. The dependent variable is a three-category ordinal variable constructed from the reported vote, partisanship, and turnout. The first category are partisans who voted for their party's presidential candidate. The middle category consists of partisans who claimed that they did not vote. The third category are partisan defectors, those partisans who voted for the opposing party's candidate. The thesis expects progressively greater disaffection in each category. Some disatisfaction should detract from loyal partisan votes and depress turnout. Greater disaffection should push partisans beyond abstention to defection.

The mean disaffection scores for partisan loyalists, nonvoters, and party defectors in presidential elections from 1952 to 1984 are plotted in figure 8.2. These mean disaffection scores provide strong evidence for the party disaffection hypothesis.[3] In every case, nonvoting partisans were on average more disaffected than loyal partisans and less disaffected than those driven to defection. This is true, without exception, for each of the nine presidential elections examined. Moreover, there was no overlap among the three categories in their ranges of average disaffection scores. The average disaffection scores for loyal partisans ranged from -4.2 to -2.7. Average disaffection scores for non-voters ranged from -2.3 to -1.1 and for partisan defectors from $+.08$ to $+2.5$.

These findings are confirmed by both multinomial logit and regression analyses within each election sample.[4] The more straightforward, interpretable regression analyses are presented in table 8.3.[5] The results are quite consistent across elections. As expected, partisan disaffection is negatively and significantly related to the partisan loyalty variable in each election. Disaffection drives partisans from loyalty to abstention and from abstention to defection. Both the simple correlation and the unstandardized effect are very stable. The correlation ranged from $-.45$ to $-.59$. The

Figure 8.1. The Expected Relationship between the Presidential Vote, Turnout, and the Extent of Party Disaffection

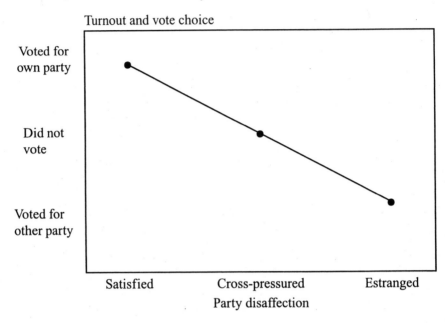

Figure 8.2. The Relationship between the Presidential Vote, Turnout, and the Extent of Party Disaffection

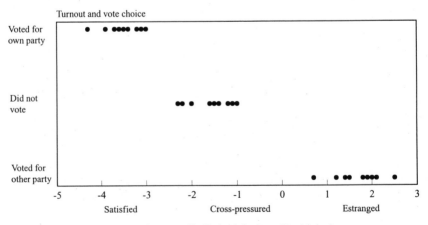

Note: Each point is a mean party disaffection score of respondents in a given vote choice-turnout category in a presidential election year (1952-84).

Table 8.3. The Effects of Partisan Disaffection on Partisan Loyalty, Turnout, and Defection in Presidential Elections, 1952-1984

Dependent variable: Partisan defector (− 1), non-voter (0) and loyal partisan voter (+1) in presidential voting

Independent variable: Partisan disaffection index (positive scores indicate greater disaffection)

Election	Constant	b	t	beta	R²	N
1984	.27	− .10	22.49	− .49	.24	1569
1980	.24	− .12	20.05	− .53	.29	1010
1976	.33	− .10	19.50	− .45	.21	1472
1972	.15	− .15	22.15	− .59	.35	924
1968	.30	− .09	18.85	− .49	.24	1141
1964	.28	− .10	23.91	− .53	.28	1485
1960	.34	− .11	15.41	− .46	.21	886
1956	.32	− .10	19.65	− .46	.21	1450
1952	.27	− .12	21.54	− .50	.25	1365

slope estimates ranged from − .09 to − .15. This suggests that one additional mention of partisan disapproval on the likes/dislikes questions is indicative of about a 10 percent drop in the likelihood of a loyal vote rather than abstention or a 10 percent drop in the likelihood of abstention rather than defection.

This analysis clearly supports the second premise of the partisan turnout argument: cross-pressures reduce turnout. The fact that nonvoting partisans typically indicate slight support for their own party's candidate (relatively low negative means) suggests that cross-pressures may depress turnout by raising uncertainty in the potential voter's decision as well as by creating indifference to the choice. Moreover, partisans need not be perfectly indifferent to the candidates, just indifferent enough for it not to be worth the effort to vote.

Before examining how the combination of the first two premises affects the distribution of partisans in the electorates, we need to establish that the effects of presidential election cross-pressures do not carry over to the midterm. The revised theory contends that partisans discouraged from turning out in the presidential election by cross-pressures are unaffected by those cross-pressures in the midterm. Presidential election year cross-pressures should be irrelevant in deciding whether and how to vote in the midterm.

The NES 1956-58 and 1972-74 panel studies allow a test of the irrelevance of presidential cross-pressures to the midterm vote. The party disaffection index, derived from the respondent's likes and dislikes of the

Table 8.4. The Effects of Party Disaffection in Presidential Elections on Party Loyalty, Turnout, and Defection in Presidential and Midterm Elections, 1956-58 and 1972-74

Dependent variable: Partisan defector (−1), non-voter (0) or loyal partisan voter (+1)

Independent variable	1956-58			1972-74		
	1956 on-year		1958 midterm	1972 on-year		1974 midterm
	Presidential voting	Congress. voting	Congress. voting	Presidential voting	Congress. voting	Congress. voting
Party disaffection index	−.10 (19.65)	−.05 (6.57)	−.03 (3.25)	−.15 (22.15)	−.02 (1.83)	.02 (wd)
Constant	.32	.69	.69	.15	.57	.69
N	1450	655	587	924	415	361
R^2	.21	.07	.02	.35	.01	.01

NOTE: The "wd" indicates that the sign of the coefficient was contrary to that hypothesized (in the wrong direction), thus making tests of statistical significance superfluous.

presidential candidates in the presidential election year, is examined for its effect on the congressional vote in both the presidential and midterm elections. In each election the congressional vote of partisans is scored $+1$ if they loyally voted for their party's congressional candidate, 0 if they did not vote, and -1 if they defected and voted for the opposition party's congressional candidate. The theory suggests that the disaffection of partisans with their party's presidential candidate should differ in the presidential and midterm elections. Party disaffection should have a negative effect on voter loyalty that is greater (more negative) in the presidential election year in which the disaffection is triggered. The effects of cross-pressures should be most firmly felt when the objects of the cross-pressures, the presidential candidates, are present.

The regression results of partisan disaffection's influence on partisan loyalties in congressional voting are presented in table 8.4 along with the pertinent on-year regressions involving partisan loyalty in presidential voting from table 8.3. Although the differences are not large, the coefficients tend to support the thesis.[6] In both panels, the disaffection index was more negatively related to the loyalty index in the presidential election year than in the midterm. While partisan disaffection with the presidential choice affects loyalties in the presidential year congressional vote, it does not have the same effect in the midterm. Thus disaffected partisans opting not to vote in the presidential year are not kept away in the midterm. Since these disaffected partisans are predominantly from the losing presidential party, that party's congressional candidates are denied their support in the presidential election year but regain it in the midterm.

The one-sided partisan turnout surge. Given that disadvantaged partisans are more cross-pressured than their advantaged counterparts and that cross-pressures depress turnout, a party's presence in presidential electorates ought to be proportionate to the hospitality of short-term forces after taking the party's raw size into account. Of course, a party's presence in any electorate is also determined by the party's size, whether majority or minority. However, regardless of size, the voting ranks of a party should swell in a favorable climate and contract in a hostile climate.

As the theory contends, short-term forces of presidential campaigns affect the turnout of partisans. Partisans encouraged by the slant of short-term forces turn out in greater numbers than usual, and partisans discouraged by the slant of short-term forces turn out in fewer numbers than usual. Table 8.5 presents regression results for the presence of Democrats and Republicans in presidential electorates from 1952 to 1988. The partisan compositions of congressional electorates were obtained from NES studies corrected for the known national congressional vote.[7] The par-

Table 8.5. The Effects of Presidential Election Short-Term Forces on the Partisan Composition of Presidential and Midterm Electorates, 1952-1988

Independent variables	Presidential electorates		Midterm electorates		Change in midterm electorates	
	Percent Democrats	Percent Republicans	Percent Democrats	Percent Republicans	Percent Democrats	Percent Republicans
Year counter variable for trend for trend	−.18 (3.75)	+.17 (3.39)	+.06 (.72)	−.11 (1.09)	+.14 (1.62)	−.22 (2.59)
Democratic presidential vote vote	+.32 (3.68)	−.23 (2.48)	−.05 (.45)	−.03 (.21)	−.42 (3.75)	+.21 (1.91)
Constant	+47.85	+41.14	+50.81	+49.45	+12.21	+3.94
N of cases	10	10	8	8	8	8
R^2	.83	.75	.17	.20	.82	.75
Adjusted R^2	.78	.68	.00	.00	.75	.65
Std. error	1.68	1.76	2.05	2.49	2.07	2.06

NOTE: The t-ratios are in parentheses. The year counter variable is the last two digits of the election year (e.g., 1956-56). The dependent variables are the percent Democrats (Republicans), including "independent leaners," of those who had reported having voted.

tisan composition of these electorates is explained by the partisan division of the two-party presidential vote and a simple variable of the election year included to control for any possible long-term partisan trend that might confound short-term effects.[8]

As the regression indicates, when short-term forces favor the Democrats, peripheral Democrats flock to the polls.[9] For the ten presidential elections examined from 1952 to 1988, prevailing short-term forces, as indicated by the Democratic presidential vote, strongly affect the percentage of the presidential electorate made up of Democratic partisans (b = .32, p 〈 .01).[10] The greatest Democratic presence in a presidential electorate was in the election most favorable to Democrats, Johnson's landslide defeat of Goldwater. Nearly 56 percent of that 1964 congressional electorate was Democratic. The least Democratic congressional electorates in on-years were in Reagan's 1984 reelection over Mondale (46.4 percent Democratic) and in Bush's 1988 victory over Dukakis (45.7 percent Democratic). The composition of the 1972 electorate, the election in which Nixon defeated McGovern in a landslide, also was composed of a relatively low proportion of Democratic partisans (47.1 percent Democratic).

The pattern of Republican turnout, of course, is quite similar. Republican participation swells when conditions favor their party and shrinks when conditions favor the Democrats. The Democratic presidential vote, as expected, has a negative effect on the percentage of the presidential electorate made up of Republicans (b = − .23, p 〈 .01). The Republican presence in the presidential electorate ranged from 45 percent to 48 percent in the elections most favorable to Republicans (1972, 1984, and 1988) to less than 40 percent in three elections (1964, 1968, and 1976). Two of these three were elections in which short-term forces were not very favorable for Republicans (1964 and 1976). A five- to six-percentage point drop may at first sound meager, yet recall that it is accompanied by gains in the opposing party. Recall also that the largest congressional vote change between a presidential and midterm election since 1950 was just over six percentage points, and the mean interelection vote change in this period (1950-1990) was only 2.7 percentage points.

These findings support the conclusion of the partisan turnout syllogism: disadvantaged partisans are less likely than usual to turn out in the presidential election. The turnout surge of advantaged partisans in presidential elections, holding constant defection rates, accounts for a large portion of the presidential surge in the congressional vote. When short-term forces are strongly to a party's advantage, as indicated by a strong presidential vote, the party's peripheral voters are stimulated to turn out. This one-sided partisan turnout surge helps the party's congressional candidates. They may be helped somewhat less by this turnout surge than presidential candidates because of the many confounding district-level factors that blunt the effect, but they are helped never-theless.

The final link in this connection of partisanship and turnout is found in the midterm election. The one-sided partisan turnout surge would fail as an explanation of midterm losses unless the partisan turnout in the midterm were unrelated to the short-term forces in presidential election years. Put differently, the midterm change in the partisan composition of the electorate should be inversely related to the short-term forces of the prior presidential election. The turnout effects of the presidential elec-tion's short-term forces should be only temporary. The party benefiting from the turnout surge of its partisans should register a proportionate turnout decline in the midterm. Conversely, the cross-pressure de-pressed turnout in the disadvantaged party should rebound in the mid-term. This is exactly what happens.

As expected, the partisan composition of the midterm electorate is unrelated to the short-term forces of the prior presidential campaign. As indicated in table 8.5, there was no significant association of the prior Democratic presidential vote with the presence of either Democrats (b = −.05) or Republicans (b = −.03) in midterm electorates. Given the previously noted association of the presidential vote with partisan turn-out in the presidential election year, the lack of a similar association in the midterm sets up the presidential party for a decline in its presence in the midterm electorate. The final two regressions reported in table 8.5 dem-onstrate the turnout repercussion effect. The change in the partisan composition of the midterm electorates is inversely related to the short-term forces of the presidential campaign. Midterm electorates are less Democratic following presidential elections in which Democratic turnout is boosted by a favorable presidential year climate. Conversely, they are more Democratic following presidential elections in which Democratic turnout is depressed. In midterms from 1958 to 1982, the Democratic presidential vote, the indicator of short-term forces, was negatively asso-ciated with the midterm change in the Democratic presence in the electo-rates (b = −.42, p < .01) and was positively associated with the midterm change in the Republican presence (b = +.21, p < .06).[11]

Trends in Partisan Defection and Turnout

Before leaving the analysis of the electorate, it may be worth taking one final look at the sole alternative to the partisan turnout contribution to the presidential surge: contributions through partisan defections. Recall that the original theory suspected that disadvantaged partisans would defect in the presidential election and return to the fold in the midterm. While the analysis of chapter 3 found only weak evidence of the expected

Table 8.6. Trends in Partisan Defection in the Congressional Vote and the Partisan Composition of the Electorate, 1952-1988

Dependent variables	Constant	Coefficient for trend, year counter*	Adjusted R^2
Democratic defection rate	−1.45	+.23 (2.77)	.28
Republican defection rate	−16.48	+.50 (8.74)	.82
Democratic % of electorate	58.73	−.10 (1.54)	.07
Republican % of electorate	35.64	+.08 (1.25)	.03

NOTE: (N=18) The year counter variable is the last two digits in the election year (e.g., 1952 = 52, 1956 = 56). Partisan defection if the percentage of partisans reported having voted for the opposing party's congressional candidate. The composition of the electorate variables are the percentages of all reported voters claiming an attachment to the particular party. "Independent leaners" are counted as partisans.

Table 8.7. The Effects of the Presidential Surge and the Trend of Partisan Dealignment on Partisan Defection Rates in Voting for Congress in Presidential Election Years, 1952-1988

Independent variables	Dependent variable	
	% Democratic defection on congressional vote	% Republican defection on congressional vote
Year counter trend variable	+.18 (1.43)	+.52 (8.65)
Democratic presidential vote %	−.04 (.16)	+.13 (1.20)
Constant	+7.14	−23.65
Number of cases	10	10
R^2	.24	.92
Adjusted R^2	.02	.89
Standard error	4.44	2.15

NOTE: The t-ratios are in parentheses. The Democratic presidential vote percentage and defection rates are based on the two-party vote.

partisan defection differences, it remains a possibility that short-term changes in partisan defections could be obscured by long-term partisan trends. Specifically, there is considerable evidence that the parties' hold over partisans has weakened since the 1950s. It is possible that this long-term trend of partisan dealignment may have hidden the partisan defections resulting from short-term presidential forces.

The regressions reported in table 8.6 examine possible trends in partisan defection, as well as partisan realignment, for both presidential and midterm elections from 1952 to 1988. As these regressions indicate, while there is no evidence of a significant realignment throughout this period, there is evidence of partisan decomposition or dealignment.[12] Partisan defection rates in congressional voting rose in both parties over this period. The regressions indicate that partisan defection in congressional voting became much more common in recent years. The growth in defection rates over time is especially great for Republicans. Defection rates among Democrats rose from the general range of 10 percent to 12 percent in the 1950s and early 1960s to the low-20 percent range in the 1980s. Republican defection rates grew from about 10 percent in the 1950s to the mid-20 percent range in the 1980s.

Is it possible that short-term surge-induced changes in partisan defections, changes expected by the original theory of surge and decline, have been hidden by the longer term trend? The regressions reported in table 8.7 provide mixed results. While Republican defection rates in presidential years rise a bit when short-term forces favor the Democrats (b = +.13), Democratic defection rates are essentially unaffected by the prevailing short-term forces. On balance, it would appear that the driving mechanism of the presidential surge does not depend on differences in partisan defection rates. Given that the presidential surge must logically be a result of partisan defection rates or turnout, these findings lend support to the turnout interpretation of the revised theory. In sum, the revised theory is supported by both the negative evidence regarding a defection-based presidential surge and the positive evidence of a turnout-based presidential surge.

9

Surge and Decline in Subpresidential Elections

The theory of surge and decline, as noted initially in the first chapter, is a theory of interelection change. While designed to explain swings in elections to the House, the theory is not exclusively about electoral change in the House. It applies to elections to other offices as well. Any subpresidential election synchronized with and then held apart from presidential elections should be subject to surge and decline effects. To determine whether the theory remains valid beyond elections to the House, we now examine interelection change for two different offices, the lower chamber of state legislatures and the U.S. Senate.

Surge and Decline in State Legislative Elections

Voters generally pay little attention to elections to the House; but they usually pay even less attention to state legislative elections. Most voters know very little about state legislative candidates and their issue positions. Because of this, state legislative elections may be even more dependent than congressional elections on short-term forces generated outside their own particular campaigns, such as those generated by the presidential campaign. Informed evaluations of presidential candidates may fill the information void of the state legislative decision. Voters may transfer informed evaluations of the presidential candidates to the parties' candidates who are not so well known. In addition, like congressional races, state legislative races may be affected by the presence or absence of partisans of either party. Discouraged partisans absent from the presidential vote are just as absent for the state legislative vote as they are for the congressional vote.

The aggregate evidence of surge and decline effects in state legislative elections was first observed by Bibby (1983a). He found that the president's party consistently suffers a net loss in control of the lower chamber of state legislatures in midterm elections. In examining the proportion of seats held by the president's party, I find a similar pattern of midterm decline as well as a prior pattern of presidential election year gains (Campbell 1986c). Figures 9.1 and 9.2 present the distribution of presi-

Figure 9.1. Net Change in the Percentage of State Legislative Seats for the Winning Presidential Party Following Presidential Elections, 1944-1984

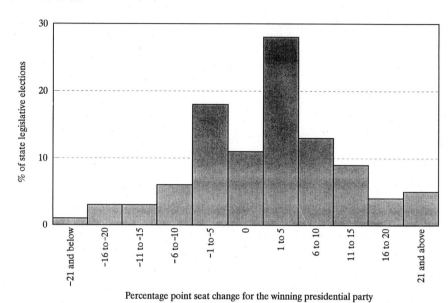

Percentage point seat change for the winning presidential party

Note: N=443

Figure 9.2. Net Change in the Percentage of State Legislative Seats for the President's Party Following Midterm Elections, 1946-1982

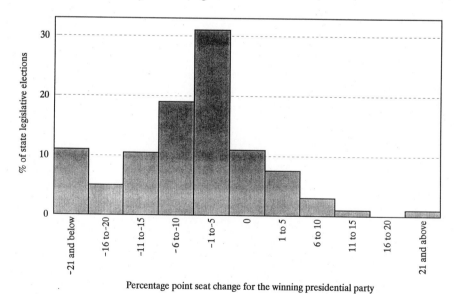

Percentage point seat change for the winning presidential party

Note: N=402

dential year and midterm seat changes (in terms of the net percentage of seats) for the president's party in the state legislative elections of forty-one states held between 1944 and 1984. As figure 9.1 shows, the party winning the presidency gains seats in most state legislatures. As we might expect, the winning presidential party gained at least 1 percent more of state legislative seats in 58 percent of the state elections in this period and lost seats in only 31 percent of these elections. The presidential surge pulls in state legislative candidates of the winning party. As we might expect, the distribution tilts the opposite way in the decline of the midterm. The president's party lost ground in 77 percent of state legislatures following midterm elections and gained ground in only 13 percent. Of course, presidential election year short-term forces are not uniform across the nation, and the party winning nationally does not win in every state. As we also have noted, all surges are not equal. What is required is a state-level examination of statewide legislative seat change and the statewide presidential vote over time.

The state-level examination of state legislative elections more clearly demonstrates the effects of surge and decline. The state-level analysis was conducted over time (1944 to 1984) on the forty-one states that conducted partisan elections throughout this period, scheduled elections in concert with national elections, and had two-year terms for the lower chamber of their state legislatures (Campbell 1986c). The full analysis is too lengthy to report here, but the essence of the findings is presented in table 9.1 which summarizes the forty-one state regressions conducted separately for presidential and midterm election years from 1944 to 1984. As in the case of House elections, state legislative seat gains for a party in presidential election years were generally proportionate to the party's statewide presidential vote, after controlling for its initial seat holdings and any trend in partisanship. The median effect of a one percentage point increase in the state's presidential vote for a party was about one-half of a percentage gain in the party's state legislative seat holdings. More importantly, positive surge effects were found in thirty-nine of the forty-one state regressions.[1] The evidence of a midterm decline is just as consistent. The median coefficient is, as expected, negative and of similar magnitude. Again, the midterm repercussions of the prior presidential surge are found in thirty-nine of the forty-one states.

While the results are statistically significant in just over one-half of the regressions, possibly owing to the limited number of elections examined, they nevertheless appear to be robust. As one might expect, both presidential surge effects and midterm decline effects across states are strongly correlated ($r = -.80$). Both effects, again as might be expected, tend to be stronger in competitive states and states having a straight party vote option on their ballots. Finally, estimates of both presidential surge

Table 9.1. Summary of Regression Analyses of Surge and Decline in State
Legislative Elections, 1944-1984

Independent variables	Median coefficients of 41 state regressions Dependent variables	
	% State legislative seat change for Democrats in the presidential year	% State legislative seat change for Democrats in the midterm election
Democratic presidential vote	+ .49	− .67
Initial Democratic base	− .57	− .06
Constant	− .11	+ .36
Median R²	.63	.49
% Presidential coefficient in expected direction	95% (39 of 41) Positive	95% (39 of 41) Negative
% Significant at p ⟨ .05	54% (22 of 41)	51% (21 of 41)

SOURCE: Campbell 1986c, tables 1 and 2. Note: The above summary is based on separate presidential and midterm regressions over time in 41 states. Except for newly admitted states, N = 11 in the presidential year equations and N = 10 in the midterm equations. A trend variable was included in some states where trends were noted but is not included in this summary table. The initial base variable is the percentage of seats held by Democrats prior to the presidential election.

and midterm decline effects are largely unaffected by the inclusion of possible gubernatorial coattails.

The evidence seems persuasive that the surge and decline pulse extends beyond the House to state legislative elections. Having established that surge and decline affects partisan elections for offices of apparently marginal interest to voters, we might also ask whether it influences elections to offices of greater salience than a seat in the House? We examine now whether the pulse of surge and decline appears in the much more intensely fought and more highly visible elections to the U.S. Senate?

Senate Midterm Elections

Senate elections, like state legislative elections in most states and elections to the House, are held both concurrently with presidential elections and subsequently in midterm election years. As such, they may be subject to surge and decline effects—a surge for the president's party followed by a decline in the midterm when the Senate candidates must run without help from the top of the ticket.

The six-year rather than two-year election cycle of Senate seats presents an interesting opportunity to compare once again the presidential and referenda theories of midterms. Purely presidential theories, such as the original theory of surge and decline, suggest that the president's party will lose seats when the class of Senate seats helped by the president are next up for election—six years following the presidential election. Senators elected with the help of strong short-term presidential forces in their party's favor, like their colleagues in the House, should suffer when they must next stand for reelection without the help of the presidential surge. The logic of the midterm referenda theories suggests that the president's party, whether because of diminished presidential popularity or negative voting, should sustain losses in the very next midterm—two years following the presidential election. In essence, though midterm Senate losses are expected by both the presidential theories and referenda theories, they are expected in different midterms. Incorporating the arguments of both theories, the revised theory of surge and decline expects midterm losses in both types of midterms, all things being equal.

Although there has been no explicit examination of Senate midterms, previous related research offers support to both theories. In examining 150 on-year Senate elections from 1972 to 1988, in a study with Sumners (1990) I found evidence of presidential coattails. Although they were only about one-half as long as those in the House (perhaps as a result of examining more recent elections), they nevertheless were significant and appeared to have been large enough to have affected the outcome in about a dozen elections (8 percent of those examined).[2] Abramowitz and Segal (1986) and Lewis-Beck and Rice (1985) indirectly suggest support for the surge and decline Senate elections. In examining aggregate Senate election outcomes, both studies found that the president's party lost seats in proportion to the number of seats they held going into the election. Parties with more seats at stake tended to suffer greater losses. Presumably, if presidential coattails helped a party gain more seats in the presidential year, they would have more seats to lose going into the midterm six years down the road.

The referenda theory also finds support in prior research. Like studies of elections to the House, aggregate studies of Senate outcomes (Abramowitz and Segal 1986; Lewis-Beck and Rice 1985) have found seat changes to be proportionate to the president's popularity and economic conditions. In addition, in his multivariate study of individual Senate elections from 1974 to 1986, Abramowitz (1988) found that the president's party lost anywhere from 1.1 to 1.9 percentage points of the Senate vote in midterms, depending on whether or not the incumbent was running for reelection.

While there is good reason to suspect that the salience and high visibility of Senate elections would attenuate the effects of national forces in either presidential or midterm elections, two complications may further attenuate the impact of national forces on Senate outcomes across the country.[3] First, because Senate seats are staggered into three classes so that one-third of the seats are up for election every two years, one-third of the states do not hold Senate elections in any particular election year. However, these states not holding Senate elections vote for president and, therefore, are included in assessments of the direction and magnitude of national presidential short-term forces. As a consequence, there may be a gap between short-term forces nationally and short-term forces in the two-thirds of the states holding Senate elections. Second, unlike House elections, Senate elections involve electoral units of vastly different constituency sizes. If short-term forces favoring a party are concentrated in large population states, the party's possible coattails may extend to fewer Senate candidates than if this same amount of support had been in more states with smaller populations. In short, both of these complications may mean that short-term forces prevailing nationally may not be prevailing in a majority of states holding Senate elections. These complications generally should weaken the *apparent* effects of national forces on Senate elections.[4]

Despite these complications, we can examine midterm seat losses in the Senate. Midterm seat changes two years and six years following presidential elections from 1860 to 1984 are presented in table 9.2. The table is divided between the 1912 and 1916 presidential elections to reflect the adoption of the Seventeenth Amendment to the Constitution, instituting the popular election of senators. Prior to the Seventeenth Amendment, state legislatures chose senators. While surge and decline or referenda effects may be felt indirectly in this earlier mode of election, they should be more clearly evident since the advent direct election.

As is evident from the table, the president's party generally loses Senate seats in *both* midterm years, in the midterm immediately following the presidential election, and also in the midterm six years following the presidential election in which the same Senate seats are again up for election. This is especially true since the adoption of the Seventeenth Amendment.

As the referenda theory suggests, the president's party suffered seat losses (or failed to gain seats) in two out of three elections. Since the popular election of senators, the president's party has lost seats in fifteen

Table 9.2. U.S. Senate Seat Change for the President's Party in Midterms Two Years and Six Years after the Presidential Election, 1860-1990

Presidential election and winning party	Midterm senate seat change	
	2 years later (referenda theory)	6 years later (surge & decline)
1860 Republican	1862 +8R X	1866 0
1864 Republican	1866 0	1870 −4R
1868 Republican	1870 −4R	1874 −8R
1872 Republican	1874 −8R	1878 −6R
1876 Republican	1878 −6R	1882 +3R X
1880 Republican	1882 +3R X	1886 −3R
1884 Democratic	1886 +3D X	1890 0
1888 Republican	1890 0	1894 +5R X
1892 Democratic	1894 −5D	1898 −7D
1896 Republican	1898 +7R X	1902 +2R X
1900 Republican	1902 +2R X	1906 +3R X
1904 Republican	1906 +3R X	1910 −10R
1908 Republican	1910 −10R	1914 −5R
1912 Democratic	1914 +5D X	1918 −6D
****Popular Election of Senators: 17th Amendment****		
1916 Democratic	1918 −6D	1922 +8D X
1920 Republican	1922 −8R	1926 −6R
1924 Republican	1926 −6R	1930 −8R
1928 Republican	1930 −8R	1934 −10R
1932 Democratic	1934 +10D X	1938 −6D
1936 Democratic	1938 −6D	1942 −9D
1940 Democratic	1942 −9D	1946 −12D
1944 Democratic	1946 −12D	1950 −6D
1948 Democratic	1950 −6D	1954 +1D X
1952 Republican	1954 −1R	1958 −13R
1956 Republican	1958 −13R	1962 −3R
1960 Democratic	1962 +3D X	1966 −4D
1964 Democratic	1966 −4D	1970 −2D
1968 Republican	1970 +2R X	1974 −5R
1972 Republican	1974 −5R	1978 +3R X
1976 Democratic	1978 −3D	1982 −1D
1980 Republican	1982 +1R X	1986 −8R
1984 Republican	1986 −8R	1990 −1R
1988 Republican	1990 −1R	1994 ?
Correct before 17th Amendment	5 of 12 (42%)	8 of 12 (67%)
Correct after 17th Amendment	15 of 19 (79%)	15 of 18 (83%)

NOTE: The X indicates a case contrary to the expectations of the referenda or the surge and decline theory. Elections with no net change were not counted in computing the number of correct predictions. R: Seat changes for Republicans; D: seat changes for Democrats.

of the nineteen midterms (79 percent) immediately following the presidential election.

The record of midterm losses six years following a presidential election is just as clear, as presidential election theories of midterms contend. For the entire series since the Civil War, the president's party sustained losses (or registered no gains) in more than three out of four midterms six years after the presidential election. Again, losses are more consistent in elections since the Seventeenth Amendment. Since the ratification of the Seventeenth Amendment, the president's party has lost seats in fifteen of the eighteen midterms held six years later (83 percent). This pattern strongly suggests a surge and decline in Senate elections. This might account for the large Democratic seat losses in the 1942 (-9 seats) and 1946 (-12 seats) midterms six years after the strong Democratic presidential victories of 1936 and 1940, respectively. It might also account for the substantial Republican seat losses in the 1958 (-12 seats) and 1986 (-8 seats) six years after the solid Republican presidential victories of 1952 and 1980, respectively.

Depending on whether or not the president's party wins reelection, the presidential and referenda theories may differ in their expectations about a midterm's outcome. If the president's party wins reelection, both theories would expect that party to lose Senate seats in the next midterm. The referenda theory would expect losses based on the last presidential victory, whereas surge and decline would expect losses because of the presidential surge favoring the same party six years earlier. However, if the opposing party wins the presidency, the referenda and presidential election theories would expect different parties to lose seats. For example, in the 1970 midterm, the referenda theory would expect Republican losses following Nixon's 1968 election. However, presidential election focused theories would expect Democratic losses when Democratic candidates helped by Johnson's 1964 landslide must run six years later without that help. How do the two theories fare? Between the adoption of the Seventeenth Amendment and 1990 there have been eighteen pairs of midterms (two years after and six years after a presidential election). Both theories expected the same party to lose seats in eleven of these midterms and differ in the remaining seven. The party expected to lose Senate seats actually suffered losses in each of the eleven midterms in which the theories were in accord. In the seven cases where the expectations of the theories differed, the presidential theories were correct in four cases (1934, 1962, 1970, and 1982) and the referenda theories were correct in three instances (1922, 1958, and 1978). It would seem that there is merit to both the presidential and referenda theories, as the revised theory of surge and decline contends.

The Case for a Revised Theory of Surge and Decline

This completes the case for the revised theory of surge and decline. The above analysis along with that of the three previous chapters in every respect supports the theory as described in chapter 5. There is a presidential pulse to congressional elections. The presidential surge is a temporary boost to congressional candidates of the winning party. Without that boost, the fortunes of those congressional candidates decline in the midterm. The case for the revised theory of surge and decline is summarized in table 9.3. It is worth reviewing.

First, at all three levels of analysis, the evidence is consistent: there is a presidential election year surge generally benefiting congressional candidates of the winning presidential party. Chapter 6 presented the national-level evidence of the presidential surge. National partisan swings in congressional elections throughout this century clearly reflect the presidential surge. This is true regardless of whether seat or vote changes are examined, the estimation method used, or the control variables included. A party's presidential vote, reflecting prevailing short-term forces, has a substantial influence on the change in its share of congressional votes and seats. Moreover, as noted earlier in this chapter, the aggregate evidence of the presidential surge is not limited to elections for the House. The effects of the presidential surge are also evident in state legislative and Senate elections. In a presidential election year, a party gains or loses state legislative seats and Senate seats in proportion to its statewide presidential vote.

Presidential surge effects were also found at the district level in chapter 7. The multivariate analyses of the congressional vote in both 1976 and 1984 found evidence of the presidential surge. Support for congressional candidates was influenced by support in their districts for the top of their party's ticket. As other studies have found (Born 1984, 71-72; Ferejohn and Fiorina 1985, 107), about 35 percent to 40 percent of the presidential vote carried over to the congressional vote. This was enough to make the difference between winning and losing in a number of districts, especially in 1984. Together with the aggregate findings we may conclude, to adapt an old saying: as a presidential candidate goes, so goes his party.

The basis of the presidential surge in individual voting behavior was examined in chapter 8. As expected, in addition to the sway of the independent vote to the winning presidential party, a good part of the presidential surge results from cross-pressured partisans of the losing presidential party staying home while partisans of the winning presidential party turn out to vote. Since straight ticket voting is still more preva-

Table 9.3. Evidence Supporting the Revised Theory of Surge and Decline

---

Presidential Surge Effects

1. The winning presidential party gains votes and seats in the presidential election year in proportion to the national presidential vote (chap. 6, tables 6.5, 6 and 8).
2. Congressional candidates gain votes in the presidential election year in proportion to the district presidential vote for their party's presidential candidate (chap. 7, tables 7.1, 2 and figure 7.1).
3. The vote choice of independents is affected by the prevailing presidential election year's short-term forces favoring the winning presidential party (chap. 8, table 8.1).
4. Partisans of the disadvantaged party more likely to be cross-pressured and therefore less likely to turn out to vote (chap. 8, table 8.2, 3 and figure 8.2).
5. A party gains or loses state legislative seats in presidential election years in proportion to its presidential vote in the state (chap. 9, table 9.1).

Midterm Decline Effects

1. The presidential party loses votes and seats in midterms in proportion to the previous national presidential vote (chap. 6, tables 6.1, 2, 3, 4, and 7).
2. Congressional candidates lose votes in the midterm in proportion to their vote gains in the prior presidential election (chap. 7, table 7.5).
3. Unlike presidential elections, the vote choice of Independents is not affected by the prevailing short-term forces that favored the presidential party in the presidential year (chap. 8, table 8.1).
4. Unlike presidential elections, partisans of the "out" or non-presidential party are not more likely to be cross-pressured and, therefore, turn out to vote at normal rates (chap. 8, table 8.2, 3, and 6).
5. A party gains or loses state legislative seats in midterm elections inversely proportional to the previous presidential vote in the state (chap. 9, table 9.1).
6. The Presidents's party regularly loses U.S. Senate seats in the midterm six years following the presidential election (chap. 9, table 9.2).

---

lent than ticket-splitting, the congressional candidates of the winning presidential party enjoy the benefit of this short-term effect on partisan turnout.

There is also clear evidence of the midterm decline. Chapter 6 presented the national evidence. National partisan swings in midterm congressional elections throughout this century clearly reflect the midterm decline. Like the presidential surge, this is true regardless of whether seat or vote changes are examined, the estimation method used, or the control variables included. While midterm losses are in part a referendum on the administration, they are also a repercussion of the prior presidential election year surge. The benefit of favorable presidential year short-term forces for the president's party are just that, short-term. Candidates of the president's party do not enjoy in the midterm election the strong and favorable political climate they enjoyed in the prior election. The result is consistent midterm losses. These losses vary inversely with the direction of the prior presidential surge. Candidates who gained more from the presidential surge have more to lose in the midterm decline. Moreover, like the presidential surge, the aggregate evidence of the presidential surge is not limited to elections for the House. As noted earlier in this chapter, the effects of the midterm decline are also evident in both state legislative elections and in Senate elections.

Chapter 7 presents evidence of the midterm decline in congressional districts in the 1978 and 1986 midterm elections. While the evidence is complicated by the difficulty of measuring midterm presidential popularity in the districts, the midterm decline from the prior surge is evident. According to the multivariate analysis, congressional candidates lose votes in the midterm in proportion to the vote gains they had made in the prior election. As in the aggregate national analysis, congressional candidates of the president's party lose a significant portion of the vote shares that they won as a consequence of the presidential surge of the previous election.

Chapter 8 offered evidence of the individual basis of the midterm decline for the president's party. Basically, this evidence entailed demonstrating the lack of effects. That is, the short-term forces influencing the vote choice of independents and the turnout of partisans in the presidential election were absent in the midterm. The absence of these effects in the midterm accounts for the midterm losses for the president's party.

A Weakened Presidential Pulse?

One final issue remains to be addressed: the weakening of surge and decline effects in recent elections. Is the presidential pulse of congressional elections a weakened pulse? There is considerable evidence that it is. The most obvious evidence of weakened state of surge and decline is the frequency of divided government. Divided government was once a fairly uncommon occurrence, especially following a presidential election. Of the twenty-five presidential elections from 1868 to 1964, only three (12 percent) resulted in divided government (1876, 1884, and 1956). In stark contrast, divided government has become the rule of recent elections. Of the seven presidential elections from 1968 to 1992, five (71 percent) resulted in divided government.

The more systematic analysis of the preceding chapters confirms impressions of a weakened presidential surge. As the analysis of chapter 6 makes clear, whether you examine congressional vote or seat gains, the presidential surge is smaller in recent elections. Elsewhere, I have estimated that surge and decline effects are anywhere from three-quarters to one-half their pre-1970s strength (Campbell 1991b, 1992). Fiorina's (1990, 125) individual-level analysis also finds the presidential surge to have declined to roughly one-half of its prior strength.

The weakening of surge and decline effects is apparently an immediate consequence of the rise in split-ticket voting to about twice its prior level (discussed in chapter 2). As a result, the partisan turnout advantage is now worth less to congressional candidates of the winning presidential party. Whereas congressional candidates could once count on receiving about nine out of ten votes cast for the head of their ticket, they now receive only three out of four of these votes. Although still a distinct advantage for the winning presidential party, the one-sided partisan turnout surge is not as big an advantage as it once was. The somewhat smaller impact of the presidential surge, of course, means a smaller midterm decline. Nevertheless, even if attenuated, the analysis of the preceding chapters indicates that surge and decline effects remain potent influences in congressional elections.

What has caused the increase in split-ticket voting and the resulting weakening of surge and decline effects? There are three plausible explanations: the decline in partisanship, the increased incumbency advantages, and the wasting of presidential coattail support in uncontested congressional districts.

First, the increase in ticket-splitting can be explained as a manifestation of the weakening of the public's partisanship, one aspect of partisan dealignment in the 1960s (Burnham 1970). Although most Americans remain partisan-minded, there is little doubt that partisanship does not mean quite as much to as many as it did before the 1960s. Since partisanship is a less important concept to organizing politics in the minds of many voters, they may be less inclined to associate evaluations and votes for presidential and congressional candidates of the same party and more inclined to split their tickets, thus muting the presidential pulse.

Second, the rise in ticket-splitting may also be a result of the increased advantage of incumbency (Erikson 1971; Mayhew 1974; Bauer and Hibbing 1989). By both exploiting the perquisites of office and obtaining a substantial campaign financing advantage over their challengers, incumbents have been able to win reelection even more consistently and by larger vote margins than they have in the past. In essence, they have been able to fight their elections on more local terms and are more insulated from, though by no means immune to, the effects of national short-term forces. Thus many voters may split their tickets to vote for a presidential candidate of one party and the incumbent congressman of the opposing party, thus weakening the presidential pulse.

Figure 9.3. Illustration of Uncontested Districts and the Relationship between the Congressional and Presidential Votes

(A.) Uncontested districts carried by Democratic presidential candidate

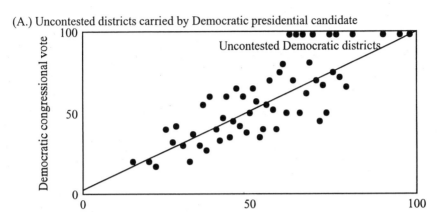

(B.) Uncontested districts carried by Republican presidential candidate

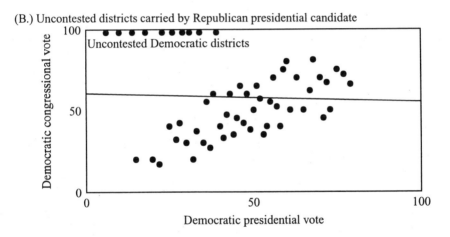

A third explanation for weakened surge and decline effects is that the weakening is a consequence of *wasted coattails*. Republicans since the 1960s have made substantial inroads in the South in presidential voting. There is now a substantial body of research documenting a secular realignment in the South favoring the Republicans.[5] Yet, despite these southern presidential gains, Republicans have been slow to develop a party infrastructure and a pool of serious candidates for local offices within many Southern states. All too often, the Republicans have not been able to mount even token opposition to the Southern congressional Democrats. As a consequence, many Republican presidential voters in the South, if they choose to vote for Congress at all, are forced to split their tickets since they have no option of voting for a Republican congressional candidate. In the aggregate, this would appear as though coattails were shorter. In fact, they were simply wasted.[6]

The logic of the wasted coattails argument can best be illustrated by the plots of hypothetical congressional and presidential district votes in figure 9.3. Plot A reflects the circumstances of the pre-realignment South in which Democratic presidential candidates regularly carried the uncontested Democratic congressional districts (the cases in the upper-right-hand corner). The effect of these uncontested districts, geometrically speaking, is to pull the regression line upwards. Estimates of surge effects are greater than they would be if the analysis had been limited to contested districts. Plot B reflects the wasted coattail situation in which the uncontested Democratic seats are now being won by Republican rather Democratic presidential candidates (the cases in the upper-left-hand corner). These uncontested seats have exactly the opposite effects on estimates of the presidential surge. Estimates of the presidential surge that include these districts may underestimate the impact of the surge in contested races.

There is considerable evidence for the wasted coattails explanation. As discussed in chapter 6, Nixon carried thirty-five Southern congressional districts in 1972, many by wide margins, in which Democrats won the House seat without even token Republican opposition. Presumably, Nixon could have offered Republican congressional candidates help in these districts but there were no Republican candidates to ride these coattails. Moreover, 1972 was not an isolated instance of Republicans wasting coattails in the traditionally solid Democratic South. The congressional situation for Republicans in the South has not improved much since 1972. In 1984 Reagan carried thirty-three Southern districts that Democrats won without Republican opposition, and in 1988 Bush carried twenty-four Southern districts in which there were no Republican candidates available to ride his coattails.

One more systematic test of the wasted coattail explanation is offered by the regressions reported in table 9.4. The first step in testing the thesis was to determine how many uncontested Democratic seats were carried by Democratic presidential candidates and how many were carried by Republican presidential candidates in each presidential election year since 1952 (when the presidential vote in each congressional district first became available). As figure 9.3 suggests, uncontested Democratic seats carried by the Democratic presidential candidate should inflate estimates of the presidential surge. Conversely, those carried by Republican candidates, the wasted coattail districts, should deflate estimates of the surge. The predominant effect of uncontested seats can be roughly measured by taking the difference in the number of these two types of districts (those carried by Democratic presidential candidate minus those carried by the

Table 9.4. The Effects of Uncontested Democratic Districts Carried by Democratic or Republican Presidential Candidates on the Presidential Surge, 1952-1988.

Dependent variable: Democratic seat change in presidential election year.

Independent variables	1	2
Democratic presidential	2.26	2.68
vote margin	[.76]	[.91]
	(3.01)	(3.94)
Wasted coattails in		− .32
uncontested seats	—	[− .42]
		(1.89)
Prior Democratic	− .36	− .37
House seats	[− .36]	[− .37]
	(1.42)	(1.71)
Constant	93.74	100.28
Number of cases	10	10
R^2	.58	.74
Adjusted R^2	.46	.60
Std. error	14.30	12.24
Durbin-Watson	2.67	2.72

NOTE: Standardized coefficients are in brackets. The t-ratios are in parentheses. The wasted coattails in uncontested seat variable is the number of uncontested Democratic congressional seats carried by the Democratic presidential candidate minus the number of uncontested Democratic congressional seats carried by the Republican presidential candidate (ranged: + 39 in 1960 to − 34 in 1984). This analysis does not include the effects of the uncontested Republican districts which are few in number (never more than 20) and which were rarely carried by Democratic presidential candidates. An analysis including these districts reconfirms the above analysis.

Republican presidential candidate, the uncontested seat variable in table 9.4). Positive values indicate that Democratic presidential candidates carried more of these uncontested districts while negative values indicate that Republican presidential candidates carried more of these districts and, in so doing, wasted their potential coattails. The index ranged from thirty-nine in 1960 to minus thirty-four in 1984.[7] If the wasted coattail thesis is correct, we should expect the index to have a significant negative coefficient (since wasted Republican coattail districts are scored as a negative value in the index).[8]

The regressions in table 9.4 bear out the wasted coattail thesis. Equation 1 estimates surge effects without taking the nature of uncontested districts into account. The presidential surge coefficient indicates that a party can expect to gain 2.26 seats for every additional percentage point of its presidential vote. Equation 2 estimates the presidential surge while taking into account the effects of uncontested districts. As expected, the coefficient for the uncontested seats term is negative and statistically significant. To illustrate the effects of wasted coattails in the equation, there would be an expected ten-seat difference between a Republican presidential candidate winning without wasted coattails and a net uncontested seat difference of 30 seats ($-.32 \times -30 = +10$ Democratic seats). Moreover, as a result of including the uncontested seat variable, the effects of the presidential surge appear modestly stronger than the earlier estimate of the first equation. Given the admittedly rough measure of wasted coattails used here, it would appear that some weakening of the presidential pulse is, in fact, attributable to the recent wasting of Republican coattails in uncontested districts.

The wasted coattail explanation of the weakened presidential pulse sets that trend in a new light. To the extent that the weakening of surge and decline effects can be explained by wasted coattails, it is a phenomenon that might best be regarded as regional (Southern) rather than national, elite (a candidate recruitment issue) rather than mass, and quite likely, transitory (a phase of realignment) rather than permanent.[9]

Each of the three explanations of the weakened presidential pulse appears to have merit. To some degree, the weakening is a consequence of partisan dealignment, of increased incumbency advantages, and of wasted coattails resulting from the secular partisan realignment, a very gradual growth of the Republican party in the South. Yet, whatever the mix of causes, we should not lose sight of the larger point: the cycle of surge and decline continues to shape electoral change in subpresidential elections.

With the revised theory of surge and decline now empirically established, even if perhaps in a slightly weakened condition, we turn in the final chapter to its implications. What are the consequences of surge and decline?

10
Reflections on the Presidential Pulse

The presidential pulse in support for congressional candidates of the president's party has possible consequences for a variety of different issues in American politics. In the following sections I discuss the possible implications of the pulse or the cycle of surge and decline in six areas: the interpretations of electoral change, the utility of elections as instruments promoting popular government, the quality of the electorate, the potency of political parties, the roll-call behavior of legislators, and the relationship between the executive and legislative branches of government. Finally, in light of the various probable effects of the presidential pulse, I examine the case for and against the constitutional restructuring of terms to eliminate midterm elections.

Interpreting Electoral Change

The process of surge and decline has its most obvious implications for the interpretation of any change occurring between congressional elections. As noted at the outset of this book as well as in the district analysis of chapter 7, local factors such as incumbency and district partisanship undoubtedly play a great role in congressional elections. In most cases, however, these factors are constants from one election to the next and, thus, cannot account for interelection change. There is generally great continuity in incumbency and in the partisan complexion of the district. Although evaluations of the presidential candidates in presidential election years, as well as evaluations of the incumbent president in midterms may not have the same impact as local factors in any particular election, they are much more variable between elections and have a substantial impact on interelection change.

The impact of presidential evaluations on congressional elections, however, is not always obvious. As the preceding analysis suggests, presidential effects are not always clear from the simple bivariate viewpoint and systematic effects may seem chaotic or very erratic. As the analysis in chapter 6 demonstrates, the change in a party's votes and seats in a presidential year is affected by its initial share of votes and number of seats as well as by coattail effects. Given this, it is quite possible that the coattail gains of a party winning the presidency may be masked by its preelection or precoattail strength. In this situation, coattails might be judged wrongly to be short or even entirely absent, unless the presidential surge or coattails are examined in their proper multivariate context.

Given that the midterm decline is a consequence of the surge two years prior, the journalistic tendency to explain events by the most proximate variable and the democratic tendency to read policy-oriented behavior directly into all electoral behavior, electoral change in midterms is even more susceptible to misinterpretation without the theory of surge and decline. Unless the decline from the prior surge is understood, electoral change in midterms may be consistently misread as public repudiations of the president. Moreover, quite perversely, presidents who win election most convincingly will be judged to be the most thoroughly repudiated, since their midterm losses will be greater and wrongly interpreted as reflecting the public's midterm assessment. If Neustadt (1964) is correct in his claim that the president's power to persuade Congress depends on its perception of his standing with the public, the short-term consequence of this misinterpretation of midterms may be a weakening of presidential influence in Congress. It may also have long-term consequences for the public's evaluation of government. To the extent that midterm declines simply read as presidential failures, the public may come to think that none of its politicians can master the presidency. Although midterm results are just one of many potential influences on evaluations of specific political leaders and the general political system, they would seem to have the effect of weakening political support and fostering cynicism if not rightly interpreted as a simple swing back from the prior presidential surge.

Electoral Accountability

In evaluating the effects of surge and decline on the electoral process, it is important to keep in mind the ultimate objective of that process: to hold government accountable to the public. Various ideological perspectives differ over what it means for the public to hold the government accountable. A common modern perception of elections is that they ought to make leaders responsive to public concerns as they arise. Walter Lippmann offered a more elementary (though perhaps also more sophisticated) and realistic view of elections. According to Lippmann, "To support the Ins when things are going well; to support the Outs when they seem to be going badly, this, in spite of all that has been said about tweedledum and tweedledee, is the essence of popular government" (1925,126). Despite these differences, all agree that elections are supposed to permit at least

Figure 10.1. The Suspected Effects of Election Synchronization on Unified Party Government, the Strength of Political Parties, and Electoral Accountability

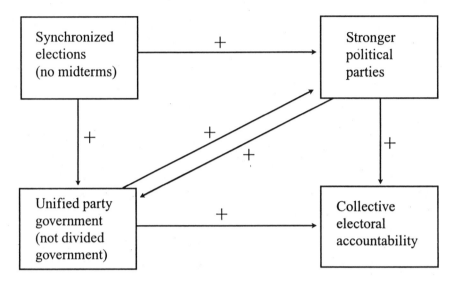

the public to make collective retrospective judgments about the performance of those in office in order to guide future decisions by the government. The question is: do surge and decline effects promote or impede the electoral process in holding government accountable?

The effects of the presidential surge would appear to increase the prospect of accountable popular government. The suspected effects of synchronizing presidential and congressional elections—holding only surge elections—are depicted in Figure 10.1. The presidential surge increases the likelihood that the separate branches of the government will be controlled by the same political party.[1] This is an important precondition for accountable government. Government can be held accountable to the public only if it is clear who controls the government. Government in a democracy is a collective enterprise, and accountability, therefore, must also be collective, if it is to be at all. Government populated by a mishmash of different political perspectives is not only government without anyone clearly in control but also government that is not easily controllable. That is, in a divided government, it is unclear to the public who to vote out if things go wrong and who to keep in if things go right. Who is to be held accountable? As has been thoroughly argued elsewhere (Schattschneider 1942; Ranney 1962), without clear partisan control of the government, the effectiveness of elections as instruments for popular control of the government is diminished. The presidential surge clarifies partisan control and thereby promotes responsible party government. In this, the effects of the presidential surge or coattails are very much like the effects of strong party voting: both provide coherence within government and coherence in the public's choice about whether and how government ought to be changed.

Actually, governments formed in the presidential surge may be more responsible than those formed by strict party identification voting. As is well documented, party identification is fairly well fixed, at the individual level and even more so in the aggregate. Thus party governments based on party identification voting are thus very secure governments, having little to fear of being thrown out of office. While this may provide a great deal of independence from the public in pursuing long-range policies, it may also make them too insensitive to the public. Party government based on ample presidential coattails provides both the responsibility of a coherent partisan government and a greater responsiveness to the public will—if unsuccessful, the Ins might easily be Outs after the next presidential surge.

The effects of the midterm decline would seem to be largely to the contrary. From one standpoint, the midterm election provides the public with an opportunity to judge the performance of the president's party midway through the president's term—the referendum component of the midterm election. To the extent that midterms are referenda of presidential performance, they serve an accountability function similar to the "vote of confidence" provision of a parliamentary system of government. However, as has been shown in the preceding chapters, the midterm election is not merely a referendum on the president. The midterm also withdraws support from the president's party that had been won with the presidential election. The uncoupling of the fates of presidential and congressional candidates makes party government less likely. The systematic weakening of the presidential party by the midterm decline obscures who controls the government and, consequently, makes it more difficult for voters in the next election to hold government responsible.

This analysis carries with it a clear normative implication. Given that the presidential surge tends to make elections more useful in holding government accountable and that the midterm decline has the opposite effect, if greater accountability in government is desired, then midterm elections ought to be eliminated. I will return to the possibility of eliminating the midterm later in this chapter.

The Voters' Behavior

There are two possible implications of surge and decline for our understanding of voting behavior. The first concerns the general matters of the

competence and interest of the public in fulfilling their electoral responsibilities. The second concerns a more specific matter touched upon
earlier, the effects of ticket-splitting.

Voter competence in the presidential surge. The revised theory of surge
and decline has several implications for evaluations of voter competence.
What, if anything, does the process of surge and decline reveal about the
competence and concerns of the American voter?

The popular view of presidential coattails or the presidential surge is
that they do not speak well of the voter. Presidential coattails are presumed to be evidence that voters are uninterested in politics and irra-
tional in their decision making. By this view, voters unthinkingly cast
their votes for candidates below the presidency, almost as an afterthought. Like the charge of "guilt by association," coattail voters are
suspected of giving congressional candidates credit for association with a
presidential candidate without good cause.

There are two reasons why this denigration of coattails may be in
error. First, generally speaking, there is good cause to link the presidential and congressional votes. The candidates are linked by their common
party, and though they are diverse organizations, American political
parties still mean something.[2] The labels Democrat and Republican are
brand names that communicate different perspectives about government. There are real differences between the parties. A voter who judges
one party's presidential candidate to be superior to the opposition's
might well want to vote for a congressional candidate who shares a
similar perspective and would be more inclined to support that presidential candidate, if elected.[3] Edwards (1989, 40-41), for one, finds that voters
are on pretty solid ground if they assume that a congressional candidate
of the same party as their presidential candidate is going to be more likely
to give that president greater support if elected. Given commonalities
within parties and differences between parties, the straight-ticket voter,
whether loyally voting a straight ticket or defecting to vote a straight-
ticket for the opposition, is casting a coherent vote.

The above argument suggests a reasoned basis for straight-ticket
voting, whether partisans remain loyal to their parties' presidential and
congressional candidates or defect to the opposition on both votes. Of
course, presidential coattails do not reflect simple partisan loyalties and,
as the evidence of chapters 5 and 8 indicate, they also are not based on
partisan defections. Thus, regardless of whether it would be reasonable
to defect in congressional voting or whether it would be blindly casting a
congressional vote as an afterthought to the presidential vote, the presidential surge is simply not based on either.

The view that presidential coattails indicate that voters simplemindedly cast a congressional vote for the same party as their presidential choice for no good reason is wrong on two counts. First, there are good reasons for straight-ticket voting. Second, while independents contribute to surge and decline by changes in their vote choice, partisans do not. While it is generally believed that partisans contribute to surge and decline by defecting in both their presidential and their congressional votes, the analysis indicates that this is not true. Partisans, who constitute the vast majority of potential voters, contribute to surge and decline by their decision of whether to vote or not.

Given that surge and decline effects depend on the turnout decisions of partisans, what does this suggest about the competence and attentiveness of the American voter? In a way the revised theory draws a distinction between the charge of voter incompetence and the charge of voter apathy. The theory suggests that the electorate may be rightly charged with apathy but cannot be so easily charged with incompetence.

The basis of the presidential surge in the different turnout rates of partisans suggests voter apathy. Partisans cross-pressured in their presidential choice could choose to turn out to vote in the congressional race and simply abstain in their presidential voting. While some may do just that, many more just fail to vote at all, by which they indicate both their indifference to the presidential choice and a lack of interest in subpresidential politics. The presidential surge and its midterm decline simply reflects the greater salience of presidential politics for many potential voters.

Ticket-Splitting and the revised presidential surge. The fact that presidential coattails are in large measure a function of different turnout rates of partisans also has an implication for the significance commonly attached to split-ticket voting. The rise of split-ticket voting poses a far less serious threat to a presidential surge based on partisan turnout differences (like the revised theory) than one based on partisan defection differences. The rise in split-ticket voting is of marginal relevance to the presidential surge because the presidential surge never depended on straight-ticket defections from the opposition party.[4] The basis of the presidential surge in partisan turnout rates explains how significant presidential surge effects can be found alongside higher rates of ticket-splitting.

As mentioned in chapter 2, it is generally believed that split-ticket voting is a sign of the uncoupling of presidential and congressional politics by the public. While I have already discussed reasons why this may be a misunderstanding of the phenomena, it is now clear that the vote choice, split or unsplit, is only a part of presidential surge or coattail effects.

The trend in ticket-splitting says nothing about what portion of the potential electorate votes or does not vote. *To be counted as a ticket-splitter you must have voted, but non-voters as well as voters are important to the presidential surge and the midterm decline.* A partisan encouraged by short-term forces to vote generally is a gain for his or her party's congressional candidate. Even in a period of partisan dealignment a congressional candidate generally can count on the votes of three out of four of his or her partisans that turn out (Ornstein, Mann, and Malbin 1990, 65). Even though their numbers have risen since the 1960s, ticket-splitters are still a distinct minority (Stanley and Niemi 1988, 112). Just as important, a partisan discouraged from voting usually is a loss to his or her party's congressional candidate, though he or she is neither a straight-ticket nor a split-ticket voter.

The Vitality of Political Parties

Most views of representative government attribute to political parties a central role in the functioning of the political process. Parties provide stability for the political system by both restraining and reflecting social conflict. They simplify the vote choice. They provide access for activists. They recruit, help to elect, and organize political leaders. While perhaps omitting a few premises, Clinton Rossiter (1960) stated the importance of parties most strongly: "No America without democracy, no democracy without politics, no politics without parties, no parties without compromise and moderation" (1960, 1). Given the prominence of political parties, their health should be of some concern. This concern was quite clear with the apparent decline of parties in the 1970s (Nie, Verba, and Petrocik 1979; Burnham 1970; Broder 1971). The question here is: does the presidential surge and its midterm decline affect the vitality of political parties? As in the case of electoral accountability, the suspected effects of surge and decline are mixed.

The presidential surge should strengthen political parties. The presidential surge links the fates of congressional candidates and their party's presidential candidate. Since the outcomes of congressional elections are affected by national as well as local forces, congressional candidates should have less incentive to run their own campaigns removed from the national party's presidential campaign. While incentives to exploit incumbency and to develop a personal vote are always present (Cain, Ferejohn, and Fiorina 1987), the presidential campaign places some constraints on congressional campaigns.

The presence of the presidential campaign ought to cause congressional candidates to rely more heavily on their parties. Entrepreneurial congressional candidates of a party with a popular presidential candidate might try to maximize the benefits of the presidential surge by coordinating their campaign with the presidential campaign. And while congressional candidates running with an unpopular presidential candidate may try to dissociate themselves from the national ticket, this is usually futile or, worse yet, counterproductive. A congressional candidate may lose his partisan base of support if he or she is regarded as repudiating the party's presidential candidate.

A closer association of congressional candidates to their parties engendered by the presidential surge should also affect the policy coherence of political parties. If, as a result of the presidential surge, congressional candidates become more closely linked to their parties in running for office, they may also become more partisan while serving in office. Both should make political parties more meaningful to voters and of even greater relevance in deciding how to vote. Thus the presidential surge should not only strengthen political parties; it should make them more unified on matters of public policy.

Unlike the presidential surge, the midterm decline most probably weakens political parties. Midterm elections fail to discourage congressional candidates from casting their campaigns in purely local terms. Congressional candidates are quite free to emphasize or deemphasize party affiliations according to the needs of their individual campaigns. In a sense, greater partisanship is imposed on congressional campaigns in presidential years by the presidential campaign for it establishes a partisan context from which congressional candidates cannot escape. This is not so much the case in midterms. In midterms, even more so than in presidential years, congressional candidates must fend for themselves. While the incumbent president is a factor in midterms, without a presidential campaign, midterms may be somewhat less partisan than on-year elections. Moreover, the independence of candidates from the party in running midterm campaigns may cause them to take policy positions at variance with their party's in order to get elected and, once elected, may make them less beholden to the party and its policy agenda. Without the unifying influence of the national party as in the presidential campaign, a party's congressional candidates are free to go off in almost any direction, restrained only by their local party's sensibilities. This blurs what it means to be a Democrat or a Republican and gradually weakens all partisan allegiances.[5]

It seems quite plausible that the weakening of partisan attachments in the midterm campaign has repercussions beyond midterm elections alone. If candidates know that they must rely on themselves to get elected in every other election, it is very much in their self-interest to build a personal following in all elections. Congressional candidates even in presidential years have a great incentive "to run their own show" since they know that, if they are lucky enough to win election, they will be more or less on their own in the next election only two years away. They should strongly feel the need to develop a personal following because, while sometimes their fate is dependent on the party's success, oftentimes it is not. Generally speaking, the development of the personal vote is at the expense of the partisan vote (Cain, Ferejohn, and Fiorina 1987).

Congressional Support for Presidents

Does surge and decline affect the behavior of legislators? More specifically, do presidents receive greater support for their legislative programs from Congress as a result of the presidential surge helping their party's congressional candidates? And like the congressional vote itself, do presidents suffer a loss of congressional support for their program in the second half of their terms following the decline in the midterm elections?

Undoubtedly the presidential surge helps the president gain greater cooperation from Congress. If nothing else, it carries some congressional candidates of the president's party into office who would not otherwise be there. This makes a difference (Weinbaum and Judd 1970; Brady and Lynn 1973; Asher and Weisberg 1978). Representatives of the president's party generally are much more inclined to vote with the president's position, whether for bills he endorses or against those he opposes, than are representatives from the opposition party. The difference is evident in Congressional Quarterly's index of presidential support on congressional roll-call votes. In the thirty-four sessions of Congress from 1954 (when the index was first recorded for both parties in the House) to 1988, the opposition party has not once provided a president the same level of support provided him by members of his own party.[6] In most sessions the partisan gap in presidential support has been quite large. In the typical session, representatives of the president's party have supported the president's position about 70 percent of the time. Members of the opposition party typically support the president only about 45 percent of the time. While a representative from the president's party is not a sure bet to support the president on all matters, there can be little doubt that presidents can get more of what they want from members of their own party (Bond and Fleisher 1990; Pritchard 1983).

Whether the partisan difference in presidential support results from congressmen and presidents having shared or opposed perspectives on government or simply from pure partisanship, the important point is that a partisan difference in presidential support exists (Edwards 1989, 98).[7] Thus the effects of the presidential surge on partisan election outcomes in congressional districts affect decision making in Congress or more specifically, the level of congressional support for the president's program. By determining who will vote on the president's program, the presidential surge affects how those votes will be cast. Moreover, the degree to which the surge favors the president depends upon the size of his victory or the strength of the presidential surge. Presidents who won by larger margins should carry more candidates into office and, therefore, should have a more receptive legislature to work with.

In addition to enjoying more cordial relations with Congress after their coattails have affected its partisan composition, presidents may also gain greater congressional support from running well in districts where their help was not decisive in determining which party won the seat. Both Buck (1972) and Edwards (1980, 100-115) find that the president receives greater support from members representing districts in which the president received a larger share of the vote.[8] Edwards examined the effects of the district's presidential vote on the member's presidential support score, controlling for the member's party affiliation, in each of the twenty-one sessions of the House from 1953 to 1973. Although the coefficients in his analysis varied from year to year, in each case the estimated effect was positive. Two reasons for this effect seem plausible. First, as Edwards (1980, 101) suggests, a representative may read the presidential vote as reflecting their constituents' orientation toward the president; the presidential vote in the district is either an endorsement or a repudiation of the candidate winning nationally by the members constituency. If the member wishes to reflect constituent opinion, he may use the presidential vote to guide his own roll-call votes. Alternatively, the presidential vote in the district may affect the representative's support for the president because of an electoral calculation. In districts in which the president ran well, representatives from the president's party may cozy up to the president out of gratitude for prior electoral help or in anticipation of future help. Representatives may be more inclined than otherwise to support a popular president of the opposing party to blunt any future opposition from the president's party. The support that President Reagan received early in his first term from the so-called boll weevil Southern Democrats may reflect a motivation of this sort. In any case, however arrived at, there is at least reason to suspect that a president can draw more support from congressmen who represent districts in which the president received a strong vote.[9]

Of course, the decline follows the surge. If the presidential surge produces a Congress more hospitable to the president, the midterm decline should produce a more hostile Congress. Following a midterm election, the president certainly faces a Congress with fewer friendly partisan faces. Fewer fellow partisans generally translates into less presidential support. Also, while a popular president may help some congressional candidates in their midterm election, it is less certain that their association with him is helpful, and not being on the ballot, whatever help the president is able to offer is likely to be both of lesser value and less evident to the representative. In short, for a variety of reasons, presidents are likely to be more frustrated in their dealings with Congress in the second half of their terms.

The impact of surge and decline on legislative support for the president may account, in part, for the so-called honeymoon period that presidents enjoy. While all politicians may give a president the benefit of the doubt at the beginning of a new administration, representatives who had just recently won with the president's help may be especially inclined to look favorably on his requests. Both circumstances and people change after the midterm election. Both changes are to the disadvantage of the president.

Effects on Constitutional Arrangements

The process of surge and decline is possible only because of constitutional arrangements. It is a by-product of the presidential and congressional terms of office established by the Constitution and the extraconstitutional development of political parties accompanied by popular election campaigning. The Constitution arranged an electoral sequence in which congressmen are elected in one election during a presidential campaign and in the next elected without one. Mixed with the marginal political interest of many citizens and the greater intensity of the presidential campaign, this electoral schedule provides the setting for surge and decline.

While surge and decline is in part a product of constitutional structures, it may also have consequences for other constitutional arrangements. This is the question I now turn to: How might surge and decline affect the constitutional system?

At least since the publication of *The Federalist Papers*, there have been several issues concerning the proper constitutional structures of government (Sundquist 1986). Two of the more basic structural issues have been the balance of power between the president and Congress and the degree of cooperation between these two branches.

The first of these issues is concerned primarily with whether the Congress or the president has excessive powers relative to the other branch. While the framers did not intend branches of perfectly equal powers, they did intend that each branch would have sufficient powers to fulfill its responsibilities and to fend off incursions from the other branches. The issue is: does one branch of government have excessive powers, either as originally granted to it by the Constitution or as it has evolved throughout our history?

The second issue concerns whether the Constitution divided powers within government too broadly. Applying the principles of "separation of powers" and "checks and balances," the framers intended to disperse powers to prevent arbitrary government and the abuse of governmental powers and also to ensure deliberation, but did not intend to make cooperation between the branches so difficult that the government could not readily adopt coherent and responsible public policies. This was the balance that Justice Jackson observed, "While the Constitution diffuses power the better to secure liberty, it also contemplates that the practice will integrate the dispersed powers into a workable government. It enjoins upon its branches separateness but interdependence, autonomy but reciprocity" (Fisher 1978, 9). This is the issue: has the Constitution so dispersed powers that their integration into a workable government is too rarely achieved? Has the separation of powers led to deadlock, inefficiency, and unaccountability in policy-making?

The presidential surge and the following midterm decline may bear upon both of these issues. Moreover, whatever influence surge and decline may have over the balance of power and extent of interbranch cooperation was entirely unforeseen by the framers. Unable to envision the role of political parties in the process and the popular campaigns for the presidency, they were certainly not cognizant of how the cycle of linking and delinking the presidential and congressional elections might affect electoral outcomes, the relations between the two branches, and the relative power of the executive and legislative branches.

The balance of power. Is there an imbalance of power favoring one branch over the other? This question is as old as the Constitution itself. Within a decade of the ratification of the Constitution, Hamilton (writing as "Pacificus") and Madison (writing as "Helvidius") debated the extent of executive and legislative authorities. While the relative strengths of the president and Congress have undoubtedly changed and continue to change throughout history (Fisher 1972, 1978, 1991), sometimes casting Congress with the upper hand and sometimes the president (Sundquist 1981), there remains the question of whether one branch generally dominates the other.

Not surprisingly, the complaint of an improper balance of power between the president and Congress comes from both sides. Some argue that the president has excessive power; others conclude that Congress was given or has assumed too much power.

It is certainly not unusual to hear it argued that the presidency is too powerful. Events and precedents throughout our history, so the argument goes, have gradually accumulated tremendous powers in the hands of the president. Among other things, critics of presidential power point to the extensive regulatory authority of the executive, the presidential ability to appeal directly to the public through the mass media, and the ability to commit armed forces to battle without prior congressional approval as evidence of the broad powers of the office. This view is expressed most strongly by Schlesinger: "The Imperial Presidency was essentially the creation of foreign policy. A combination of doctrines and emotions—belief in permanent and universal crisis, fear of communism, faith in the duty and the right of the United States to intervene swiftly in every part of the world—had brought about the unprecedented centralization of decisions over war and peace in the presidency. . . . And, as it overwhelmed the traditional separation of powers in foreign affairs, it began to aspire toward an equivalent centralization of power in the domestic polity" (1973, 208).

By this view, presidential scandals from Teapot Dome to Watergate to the Iran-Contra affair are frequently cited as evidence that the presidency has an unhealthy amount of power (see Fisher 1991, 281). The arrogance engendered by an excessively powerful presidency tempts some presidents to abuse power and usurp further power. The only safe president, from this view, is a restrained president, restrained by a more assertive legislature and judiciary.

Others view the politics of executive-legislative relations quite differently. Where Schlesinger sees the growth of the "Imperial Presidency," Lippmann sees the "Enfeebled Executive." From Lippmann's vantage point, the superficial attraction of mass democracy broke the delicate balance between wisdom and consent, between executive leadership and representative responsiveness. It created what he termed a "derangement of powers" in which the legislature usurped executive prerogatives. In *The Public Philosophy*, Lippmann states the case eloquently:

The power of the executive has become enfeebled, often to the verge of impotence, by the pressures of the representative assembly and of mass opinions. This derangement of the governing power has forced the democratic states to commit disastrous and, it could be, fatal mistakes. . . .

The evaporation of the imponderable powers, a total dependence upon the assemblies and the mass electorates, has upset the balance of powers between the two functions of the state. The executive has lost both its material and its ethereal powers. The assemblies and the mass electorates have acquired the monopoly of effective powers.

This is the internal revolution which has deranged the constitutional system of the liberal democracies (1955, 48-50).

Although Lippmann wrote these words more than three decades ago, there are undoubtedly some who would still agree with the gist of his evaluation. Many see Congress, particularly after the Vietnam war, as not simply reasserting itself but usurping presidential prerogatives, especially in matters of foreign affairs. Defenders of the executive argue that Congress tries to micromanage foreign policy. The War Powers resolution, the Boland Amendment aimed at restricting U.S. aid to the Nicaraguan Contras, even the earmarking of foreign aid for specified countries are commonly cited, among many other things, as instances of legislative intrusions on executive turf.

Beyond the increased decisiveness and policy coherence, a more powerful executive might also provide greater political accountability in the system. A guiding principle of the framers in writing the Constitution was to match the responsibility of the office with its powers. As Hamilton wrote in the twenty-third *Federalist*, "the *means* ought to be proportioned to the *end*; the persons from whose agency the attainment of any *end* is expected ought to possess the *means* by which it is to be attained." Today, the president is generally held responsible for many things over which he has little power to control. Many of these powers are with Congress. If the president held greater political sway with Congress, he would get greater cooperation on matters for which they could both then be held jointly accountable at the polls.

Interbranch cooperation. The second Constitutional issue concerns the dispersion of powers throughout the government. Some argue that the framers devised a system that was too prone to conflict, often to the point of deadlock. Madison (Hamilton, Madison, and Jay 1961, 322) wrote in the fifty-first Federalist that "you must first enable the government to control the governed; and in the next place oblige it to control itself." However, the two matters may be related. In obliging the government to control itself, we may impede its ability to control the governed. What happens if, in Madison's terms, government becomes *primarily* ambition counteracting ambition? Madison understood this dilemma. He judged that the dispersion was necessary to protect constitutional assignments of powers but also understood that this dispersion should be only "commensurate to the danger of attack." Separation of powers was not without costs. The dispersion of powers is functional only to a point. The question is whether the framers hit that point or went beyond it.

Critics of the Madisonian system of separation of powers argue that the framers went beyond the proper point, that powers of government in the American system are too dispersed, that the government is too fragmented. Among other problems, this excessive dispersion of power fails to encourage cooperation between the executive and legislative branches. Presidents, congressmen, and political observers regularly lament the lack of cooperation across the separation of powers (Cutler 1986). James Q. Wilson summarizes the case: "The chief criticism of the separation of powers is that it inhibits the capacity of the government, especially the president, to enact policies that are bold, timely, and comprehensive and reduces the ability of the citizenry to hold the government—again, especially the president—accountable for those policies" (1986, 18).

The argument against the excessive dispersion of powers created by the separation of powers doctrine has been most thoroughly made by Burns in *The Deadlock of Democracy* (1967, see also Burns 1949; Mezey 1989). Burns argues that effective government in the Madisonian system required the development of political coalitions across institutional boundaries in order to win the widespread support necessary in the system to pursue any coherent policy. Political parties were developed to maintain these political coalitions. They were a response to the fragmentation of the Madisonian system of separation of powers. The purpose of parties was to bridge the institutional divisions, to provide common political interests to override conflicting institutional interests.[10] However, according to Burns, parties have proven inadequate to the task. The institutional divide is simply too wide.

This view judges the dispersion of power to be disproportionate to the threat to the Constitution and that sufficient deliberation would take place in a government in which powers were less dispersed. While the notion of a critically deadlocked or stalemated system may be overdrawn (Quirk 1991), the system may more accurately suffer from a chronic problem of drift, of a lack of leadership and direction. This is evident in excessive delays in addressing public problems and in the need to create extraordinary majorities requiring excessive compromises giving minorities an effective veto over majority policy preferences. The system tends to produce an incoherent patchwork of least common denominator policies rather than the somewhat more coherent policies that could win the approval of a simple majority.[11]

Concern about the relationship between the executive and legislative branches is built into the system by the separation of powers. However, this concern has grown in recent years because of the increasingly common circumstance of divided partisan control of government. Table 10.1 presents the frequency of divided government following presidential and midterm elections in three time periods since 1864. As the table indicates, although divided government was a fairly common occurrence in the later half of the nineteenth century, it rarely occurred in this century until the mid-1960s. Fewer than one in five elections from 1896 to 1966 produced divided government and divided government was almost unheard of following a presidential election (a result of the presidential surge). Since 1968 divided government has become commonplace. Once the exception, divided government, even in presidential years, is now the rule.[12]

Table 10.1. The Occurrence of Divided Government Following Presidential and Midterm Elections, 1864-1992

| Election years | Elections resulting in divided government | | |
	% Presidential elections	% Midterm elections	% All elections
1864-1894	25 (2/8)	75 (6/8)	50 (8/16)
1896-1966	6 (1/18)	28 (5/18)	17 (6/36)
1968-1992	71 (5/7)	83 (5/6)	77 (10/13)

NOTE: The numbers in parentheses are the actual number of elections in the category that resulted in divided government and the total number of presidential or midterm elections held in that period.

The concern is that, under the prevailing conditions of divided government, the one possible cure for the excessive dispersion of power—common partisanship across institutional boundaries—is absent. Moreover in divided government, partisanship not only fails to ameliorate the divisions created by the separation of power—as Burns had hoped it would—it may actually exacerbate that conflict. In divided government, as Sundquist observes,

the normal tendency of the U.S. system toward deadlock becomes all but irresistible. The president and congressional majorities are compelled to quarrel, for mutual opposition is the parties' reason for existence. Democratic majorities in Congress cannot approve a Republican president's program without raising his stature as a leader and increasing his prospects for defeating them in the next election. For the same reason, the president has to reject congressionally-initiated programs; he cannot concede wisdom and leadership to the opponents he is seeking to discredit and defeat (1982:52).

As a consequence, the costs of separation of powers may have been magnified by divided government. Although Mayhew (1991a, 1991b) and Davidson (1991) find no evidence that divided government makes "deadlock" more likely or that divided government has caused the parties to be any more likely to use institutional powers (such as highly public congressional committee investigations) for partisan purposes, there may be other real dysfunctional consequences of divided government (Pfiffner 1991, 48).[13] The highly dispersed arrangement of powers in the American system, magnified under conditions of divided government, may have made drift, "least common denominator" policies, and avoidance of significant but bipartisan issues (e.g., the budget deficit, the savings and loan fiasco) the mark of late twentieth-century American politics.[14]

There are several defenses of the framers' constitutional arrangements for dispersing powers among the branches. The system's very survival over two centuries is a major argument in its favor. As Madison intended, the dispersion of powers has protected the constitutional order. Neither branch is entirely subservient to the other, otherwise the very question of institutional deadlock would not arise. Ceaser (1986) quotes Edmund Burke to this effect: "It is with infinite caution that any man ought to venture upon pulling down an edifice which has answered in any tolerable degree for ages the common purposes of society" (p.168). In modern slang, "if it ain't broke, don't fix it."

Defenders of the system also argue that the dispersion of powers permits the expression of different opinions that might not be expressed if powers were more concentrated. Different institutions have different constituencies and offer additional access points allowing citizen views to be heard by the government and expressed within government. This increases the prospects for full deliberation prior to adopting a public policy. While separation of powers may slow down the process, this inefficiency is a small price of representative government.

Separation of powers can also be defended as a necessary evil. While the system may chronically bog down in partisan squabbles, this is certainly a lesser evil than the usurpation of constitutional powers and resulting unchecked government. If it takes separation of powers, deadlock and all, to avoid arbitrary or unrestrained government, then it is a price well worth paying.

Finally, defenders of the current separation of powers argue that complaints of deadlock exaggerate the conflict between the president and Congress (Mayhew 1991a, 1991b). As Ceaser (1986,187) observes, from time to time the electorate gives the reins of government clearly to one party. A mandate for change, however clear or unclear the nature of that preferred change, generally accompanies partisan realignments. On these occasions, when the public is sure about their favored course of government, there is no deadlock.

While the system does not necessitate deadlock, its propensity for directionless drift, least common denominator compromises, and excessive interbranch conflict remain serious problems.[15] Moreover, these problems may have grown in recent decades because of the reduced effects of the presidential surge and the resulting more common occurrence of divided government.

The constitutional consequences of surge and decline. What difference does the process of surge and decline make to these constitutional issues?

Figure 10.2. The Suspected Institutional Consequences of the
Presidential Surge and Its Midterm Decline

	Suspected consequences	
	Interbranch cooperation (conflict vs. cooperation)	Balance of power (President vs. Congress)
The presidential surge	More cooperation	Favorable to the President
The midterm decline	Greater conflict	Favorable to Congress

Election cycle

Again, as in the issues of electoral accountability and congressional
support for the president, the probable effects of the presidential surge on
both constitutional matters are quite opposite to those of the midterm
decline. Both sets of effects can be deduced from the suspected effects of
surge and decline on congressional support for the president. The suspected effects of the presidential surge and the midterm decline are
depicted in figure 10.2.

As suggested above, the presidential surge should increase congressional support for the president and the midterm decline should reduce
that support. If this is the case, the presidential surge should add to the
power of the presidency. Following the presidential surge, the president
should face a more friendly Congress, one more willing to pass his
program. As a consequence, the presidential surge should also reduce
the severity of conflict between the Congress and the president. This is in
accord with Sundquist: "The indispensable requisite for fruitful collaboration is that the president and the congressional majority be of the same
party. When the two branches are in the hands of partisan adversaries,
the president will not consult freely and share with congressional leaders
his crucial decisions, which is essential to preventing the abuse of power.
Nor, in those circumstances, will Congress accept the presidential leadership that is needed to compensate for the diffusion of its own internal
structure" (1977, 241). Since the presidential surge increases the likelihood of the president and the congressional majority being of the same
party, it should also increase the chances of "fruitful collaboration" or
harmony between the branches. The presidential surge can provide a
bridge of common partisanship across the separation of powers.

The impact of the midterm decline should be the opposite on both
scores. By setting congressional elections apart from the presidential

election, Congress is made more electorally independent of the president. This electoral independence allows for greater congressional independence in government, greater congressional power. Moreover, with fewer common partisan bonds to unite where institutional rivalries divide, greater conflict in government naturally results.

From this analysis it should be clear that the two constitutional issues of the relative powers of the president and Congress and the relationship between the two branches are intertwined. Synchronizing presidential and congressional elections in order to foster interbranch cooperation increases presidential power in the bargain. Desynchronizing presidential and congressional elections, holding all congressional elections at the midterm, would increase congressional power but would also yield greater conflict within the government.

By structuring terms of office as they did, the framers avoided the pure effects of either the presidential surge or the midterm decline. As constituted, the system has both the advantages and the disadvantages of the presidential surge and the midterm decline. In synchronizing presidential and congressional elections, they provided for a presidential surge that unified government and strengthened the executive. At the same time, by also desynchronizing elections, they provided for a midterm decline that reinforced the separation of powers and strengthened the congressional role. While there is absolutely no evidence that the effects of the current election structure were anticipated by the framers, they may have nevertheless stumbled into a kind of unintentional "mixed" electoral system that they set about to structure by design in other regards.

Constitutional Reform and Midterm Elections

Once we understand the implications of structuring presidential and congressional elections in different ways, whether the mixed electoral system produced unintentionally by the framers is desirable or not becomes a matter of values. Whether the elections to the two offices should be synchronized (allowing the presidential surge) or whether they should be a completely uncoupled or whether the status quo should be preserved depends on the desirability of conflict and of cooperation in governing and perspectives about the proper mix of executive and legislative influence.

It is beyond the scope of this research to claim what constitutes the optimal mix of conflict and cooperation or of executive and legislative powers. Nevertheless, there is much to be said for eliminating the midterm election and thereby also eliminating the midterm decline for the president's party. Cutler (1987, 56-57), Sundquist (1986, 111 and 133), and the Committee on the Constitutional System (1992, 85) have all suggested eliminating the midterm by setting House terms at four years concurrent with the presidential term and Senate terms at eight years.[16] Cutler also considered eliminating the midterm by setting presidential and congressional terms at six years (1986, 15).

What might be accomplished by eliminating the midterm election and, as a consequence, the midterm decline for the president's party? The analysis above suggests four possible benefits from this constitutional reform: (1) stronger and more well-defined political parties, (2) greater ability of the public to hold government accountable through elections, (3) a strengthened presidency, and (4) greater cooperation between Congress and the president. These consequences are only desirable if one judges the American political system to suffer from excessive inefficiency and conflict resulting in incoherence or insufficiently directed public policies. The elimination of the midterm election may be a cure for these ills, a cure that does not diminish the voice of the people in the process.

Of course, like most reforms, there are potential tradeoffs in eliminating the midterm election. For one, the length of the presidential or, more likely, the congressional term would have to be lengthened. Some might find the changed incentives for responsiveness (a lengthened House term encouraging less responsiveness to the constituency) to be an objectionable consequence. For many the question will boil down undoubtedly to a matter of presidential power. Are the advantages of more vigorous parties worth the possible danger of a more powerful president? I think they are. Eliminating the midterm election is a moderate reform, as constitutional reforms go. It leaves the separation of powers and the various institutional checks undisturbed and strengthens another existing check on the abuse governmental powers, the electoral process.[17]

In devising the constitutional system, the framers were guided by two central tenets in the granting of power. First, the grant of powers to government must be sufficient to its responsibilities. If they are not, government will be either ineffective or leaders will usurp powers they deem necessary to be effective. Second, means must be provided, both internal to the government and with the public, to maintain grants of power within the limits of the constitution and the public's will. By both tenets, the establishment of the midterm election was a mistake.[18] Midterm elections strip presidents of valuable support in Congress midway through their term and thus, quite arbitrarily, make it less possible for them to possess the powers necessary to enact their programs and meet their responsibilities to the voters that elected them. Midterm elections accommodate candidate-centered politics and weakened parties and make government less accountable to the voters, the ultimate check of power in a democratic republic.

Epilogue

The 1992 elections are now part of history. For the first time since 1978, the voters have placed the reigns of presidential and congressional power in the hands of a single party. Democratic Governor Bill Clinton of Arkansas won a presidential victory of moderate proportions over incumbent Republican President George Bush. Clinton received 53.5 percent of the national two-party presidential vote to the 46.5 percent cast for Bush. The election left the party split in the Senate unchanged, with 57 Democrats and 43 Republicans.[1] In the House, Republicans registered seat gains despite the Democratic presidential victory. Republicans gained 10 seats to raise their numbers to 176. These minor Republican gains left a Democratic majority of 258 seats, continuing their unprecedented forty-year majority in the House. Before addressing how the 1992 results bear upon the theory of the presidential pulse, a brief review of the campaign is in order.

The 1992 elections were probably more peculiar than any in recent memory. On the presidential election side, President Bush was challenged for his own renomination by conservative columnist and commentator Pat Buchanan. While Buchanan's candidacy met with some initial success, capturing a quarter to a third of the Republican primary vote in many states, it was swamped by the task of mounting an effective campaign against the incumbent across the several Super Tuesday primary states. The Democratic race also had its peculiarities. With Bush's stratospheric approval ratings following the Gulf War, a number of prominent potential Democratic candidates (Cuomo, Nunn, Bradley, Gephardt, and Gore) declined to make the run. Still, the Democratic field was initially crowded, with Brown, Harkin, Kerrey, and Tsongas as well as Clinton seeking the nomination. While no front-runner immediately emerged, the race eventually narrowed to Tsongas and Clinton.[2] The Clinton campaign managed to survive several scandals that had sunk campaigns in the past. Charges of marital infidelity and a complicated story about his draft status during the Vietnam War plagued the campaign. Yet Clinton managed to survive to the Southern Super Tuesday primaries, where a string of victories for the Southern governor set him squarely on the road to the nomination.[3]

All of this was unusual, but there was more to the story of the 1992 presidential race. There was the on-again, off-again presidential candidacy of feisty and petulant billionaire Texas businessman Ross Perot. If nothing else, the Perot candidacy was certainly out of the ordinary. Perot kicked off the campaign on a television talk show and then spent millions of his own money financing petition drives by volunteers to qualify for the ballots in all fifty states. Although somewhat of an unknown quantity to many Americans, polls through early July suggested that Perot might be a formidable third-party candidate. Despite his lack of political experience, the known volatility of polls early in the campaign and the long history of third-party candidates fading in the campaign stretch run, Perot's candidacy was taken quite seriously. Most polls throughout June indicated that better than a third of the public at that time favored Perot over his major-party opponents. At that point in the campaign, Perot was running slightly ahead of Bush, and Clinton ran a distant third. Then in mid-July, Perot abruptly dropped out of the race.[4] Six weeks later, he reconsidered his decision and reactivated his campaign.

In the end, despite his erratic, unconventional, and sometimes controversial campaign, Perot exceeded all expectations. He won 19 percent of the national popular vote and, though he failed to win any electoral votes, he won a quarter or more of the vote in nine states. Perot's national showing was the second strongest of any non-major-party candidate in this century. He drew a greater share of popular votes than Senator Robert La Follette received in 1924 and more than Governor George Wallace received in 1968. Only former president Teddy Roosevelt, running on the Bull Moose ticket in 1912 against Wilson and Taft, outpolled Perot as a third-party candidate in this century. Because of this success, Perot denied Clinton a popular vote majority. In the three-way split of the 1992 vote, Clinton received 43.3 percent to Bush's 37.7 percent and Perot's 19.0 percent.[5]

The 1992 congressional campaign was every bit as unusual as the presidential contest. The House banking scandal set the stage. A GAO report in September 1991 had reported a pattern of widespread abuse of check overdrafts by congressmen in their House bank accounts. This stimulated an investigation by the House Ethics Committee that found that more than half the members of the House had been involved in check overdrafting and several dozen had written overdrafts regularly. The names and numbers of overdrafts were made public after a partisan skirmish with the House leadership that had sought to restrict disclosure. The public was outraged. Public approval of Congress sank to an all-time low. A March 1992 Gallup poll indicated that only 18 percent of the public approved of the way Congress was handling its job. The disgust with Congress found expression in a growing movement to limit legislative terms, a movement that later succeeded in winning approval in all four-teen states posing ballot initiatives for congressional term limits.

Congressional elections were further shaken up in 1992 by reappor-tionment and redistricting.[6] Reapportionment shifted nineteen seats, with the biggest changes moving seats from mid-Atlantic and Mid-western industrial states to Southern states and California. Redistricting, with a special concern to create districts in which minorities stood a good chance at winning election, caused many districts to be redrawn dramat-ically and in a number of cases created bizarrely drawn districts that bore little resemblance to established communities or governmental units. The combination of the bank scandal, reapportionment, and redistricting contributed to a large number of incumbent retirements and decisions to seek other offices. A total of sixty-four incumbents (forty-one Democrats and twenty-three Republicans) decided to retire or run for another office, fifteen more than the previous high in at least the last forty years. This was twice the average number of voluntary departures from the House in elections since 1946. Another nineteen incumbents were defeated in their party's primary.[7]

Republicans had two reasons to take heart from the developments of the congressional campaign. First, as the minority party in the House, they expected to gain from the troubles of incumbents, a majority of whom were Democrats. Anything that reduces the value of incumbency and the number of Democratic incumbents seeking reelection should benefit Republicans as a party. Thus, Republicans stood to gain from increased retirements and the anti-incumbent sentiment in the electorate. At the very least, the troubles of incumbents presented Republicans with substantial opportunities to make inroads. Second, Republicans had reason to believe that redistricting would be to their advantage. Seats were redistributed from more Democratic states to competitive or Repub-lican-oriented states. Districts as a rule would become more suburban and less urban, again to the benefit of Republicans. The protection of minority voting rights also should have benefited Republicans. The impe-tus to create districts in which minorities would be more viable would also create more Republican districts. By packing minority Democrats into districts that would likely elect minority Democrats, Democratic voters would be taken from adjoining districts, tilting some districts from favor-ing a white Democratic candidate to a Republican.

Based on the bank scandal and redistricting, Republicans entered the election year with high hopes.[8] Bob Benenson (1992, 3580) of *Congres-sional Quarterly* wrote that "as they planned for the 1992 elections, Repub-lican strategists were confident that redistricting would be a wedge helping GOP candidates cut deeply into the Democrats' enduring House majority." Although few seriously entertained the possibility that Republicans could displace the Democratic majority, many thought that Republicans could make major inroads, picking up as many as twenty-five or thirty seats. In this light then, the Republican gain of ten seats is generally regarded as disappointingly small.

How do these results mesh with the theory of the presidential pulse? Do Republican seat gains in the face of a Democratic presidential victory indicate the end of the presidential pulse? Based on the presidential pulse, and before considering any of the peculiarities surrounding the 1992 election, we should have expected minor gains for the Democrats rather than for the Republicans. Based on the Democratic presidential two-party vote (53.4 percent), their seat holdings going into the election (267), and the estimated regressions in Tables 6.6 and 6.8, the Democrats were expected to pick up eight or nine seats. The minor gains were expected because the Democrats entered the election with a large number of seats but, more important, because the Democratic presidential victory was in the moderate rather than landslide range. As Table 3.2 shows, when the presidential victory is in the narrow to moderate range, the party more often than not gains seats. However, it is by no means unusual for a party winning by a moderate margin to sustain minor seat losses. Of elections in this century in which the winning presidential candidate received less than 55 percent of the vote, the party lost seats in four of the nine elections. The 1992 results are certainly within these bounds.

Of course, the presence of Perot also complicates matters. At the very least, a significant third-party candidate trims presidential coattails. A comparison of presidential vote coefficients in elections with and without cases of significant third-party activity (Tables 6.2 and 6.6) suggests that significant third-party voting mutes surge-and-decline effects. Whereas in a normal election year disadvantaged would-be Republican partisans might have been discouraged from voting (thus hurting Republican congressional candidates), in 1992 some may have opted instead to turn out and vote for Perot. In chapter 5, the theory was predicated on cross-pressured partisans facing three possible choices—reluctant loyalty, reluctant defection and abstention. In 1992, a fourth option was available, a Perot vote. Apparently many disadvantaged partisans took the Perot option. The fact that overall turnout rose significantly, from 50 percent to nearly 55 percent of the voting age population, the biggest increase in over thirty years, suggests that some significant number of disgruntled would-be Republicans took advantage of the Perot option rather than stay home. In addition, exit polls indicated that more than a quarter of voters who identified themselves as Republicans defected to vote for Clinton (12 percent) or Perot (16 percent). The percentage of Republicans voting for a non-Republican presidential candidate in 1992 was extremely high by historical standards.[9] This suggests that the usual cross-pressure abstention effect of disadvantaged partisans, the effect that drags down the party's congressional candidates, may have been short-circuited by Perot. Once at the polls, these disgruntled Republicans could vote for Perot but cast their vote in the congressional race according to their normal partisan disposition.

How should the 1992 results be interpreted? First, in normal times, Democrats should have gained a small number of seats given Clinton's modest popular vote victory and the large number of seats Democrats held going into the election. Second, these modest Democratic gains from the presidential surge should have been further reduced by the success of the Perot candidacy. The success of the Perot candidacy diluted the effects of the presidential surge. Third, redistricting and the anti-incumbency mood of the electorate should have been at least moderately to the Republicans' advantage. With small presidential surge effects, further dampened by the Perot factor, the Republican congressional advantage in redistricting and anti-incumbency was sufficient to produce minor Republican seat gains. In short, the story of the 1992 election, while taking a number of unexpected twists and turns, still reflected the presidential pulse of congressional elections.

Appendix 1. Presidential Vote and Seat Regressions

The following two tables (tables A1.1 and A1.2) report regression results for the midterm vote and seat change equations oriented in terms of the incumbent president's party rather than the Democratic party as in tables 6.1 and 6.2. Readers should be aware, however, of the significant problems associated with structuring the analysis in this way. Orienting variables in terms of the presidential party versus out-party artificially truncates or restricts variation in both the dependent and independent variables. This is especially true in the midterm analysis where the presidential party's share of the prior presidential two-party vote virtually by definition must be greater than 50 percent. For a more detailed discussion of these problems see the first note in chapter 6.

Table A1.1. The Presidential Vote's Effect on Midterm Change in the Presidential Party's Congressional Vote, 1902-1990

Dependent variable: Change in the presidential party's congressional vote from the presidential to the midterm election

Independent variables	Elections included				
	1902-1990				1950-1990
	All elections		Excluding 3rd party elections		
	1	2	3	4	5
Prior presidential vote	−.16	−.18	−.30	−.33	−.25
	(1.60)	(1.81)	(2.63)	(3.20)	(2.24)
New Deal	—	3.65	—	4.19	—
		(1.58)		(2.20)	
Constant	5.79	6.56	13.08	14.77	10.34
Number of cases	23	23	19	19	11
R^2	.11	.21	.29	.45	.36
Adjusted R^2	.07	.13	.25	.39	.29
Std. error	2.32	2.24	2.03	1.83	1.50

NOTE: The presidential and congressional votes are the presidential party's share of the two-party vote. The New Deal variable is a dummy taking on a value of 1 for 1934 and zero otherwise. The significant third-party elections excluded from regressions 3 and 4 are 1912, 1924, 1968, and 1980. The coefficients' t-ratios are in parentheses.

Table A1.2. The Presidential Vote's Effect on Midterm Change in the Presidential Party's House Seats, 1902-1990

Dependent variable: Change in the presidential party's congressional seats from the presidential to the midterm election

Independent variables	All elections		Excluding 3rd party elections		1950-1990
	Elections included				
	1902-1990				1950-1990
	1	2	3	4	5
Prior presidential	−2.32	−2.56	−3.00	−3.46	−2.79
vote	(2.27)	(2.77)	(2.36)	(3.24)	(2.72)
New Deal	—	52.02	—	57.15	—
		(2.49)		(2.92)	
Constant	99.74	110.72	136.03	159.16	130.62
Number of cases	23	23	19	19	11
R^2	.20	.39	.25	.51	.45
Adjusted R^2	.16	.33	.20	.45	.39
Std. error	22.69	20.31	22.65	18.87	13.71

NOTE: The presidential vote is the presidential party's share of the two-party vote. The number of seats have been adjusted to a constant House size of 435 seats. Seats held by third parties have been divided equally between the two major parties for comparability across years. The New Deal variable is a dummy taking on a value of 1 for 1934 and zero otherwise. The significant third-party elections excluded from regressions 3 and 4 are 1912, 1924, 1968, and 1980. The coefficients' t-ratios are in parentheses.

Appendix 2. Robust Regression of National Evidence

While the alternative regressions provide considerable confidence in the national level midterm findings of chapter 6 (tables 6.1 and 6.2), in this appendix I employ a more systematic technique for dealing with possibly aberrant elections: robust regression analysis. Robust regression techniques are relatively insensitive to the influence of aberrant cases.

As Rousseeuw and Leroy (1987) demonstrate, OLS estimation has a low breakdown point, indicating that a few aberrant cases or outliers can drastically change coefficient estimates. Moreover, they show that these aberrant cases, or more accurately "influence points," cannot always be determined from a simple residual analysis. To remedy this problem, a problem that may be especially troublesome for analyses of small data sets, Rousseeuw (1984; Rousseeuw and Leroy 1987) developed the robust regression technique of least median squares (LMS). The least median squares technique is an iterative estimation procedure that minimizes the median squared error. Based on the LMS solution, cases that are influence points are diagnosed with a diagnostic statistic (the "resistant diagnostic") and dropped from a second OLS regression, termed a reweighted least squares solution (RLS).

Robust Regression Analyses of the Midterm Decline

Both the LMS and RLS estimated equations were used to reassess the effects of the Democratic presidential vote on subsequent midterm Democratic vote and seat losses. These regressions are presented in table A2.1.

The robust regression estimates of table A2.1 confirm the general findings of the conventional regression analysis. These estimates differ only in their indication of somewhat stronger midterm decline effects than the initial coefficients suggested. Whereas the OLS estimates in table 6.1 placed congressional vote loss repercussion effects at between -0.45 and -0.6 percentage points for every additional percentage point of the previous presidential vote, the robust solutions estimate the effects at between -0.6 and -0.8 percentage points. Similarly, the seat loss repercussion effects initially appeared in the range of minus four to five seats according to OLS, the robust estimates place them between minus five and six seats for every percentage point gain in the presidential vote. The overall fit of the robust regressions were also comparable or better than the OLS regressions. The prior presidential vote explained 80 percent to 85 percent of the variance in

Table A2.1. Least Median Squares Estimates of the Presidential Vote's Effect on Midterm Change in Democratic Congressional Votes and Seats, 1902-1990

Independent variable	Dependent variable			
	Midterm change in Democratic votes		Midterm change in Democratic votes	
	1 LMS	2 RLS	3 LMS	4 RLS
Prior Democratic presidential vote	− .79	− .59 (9.91)	− 6.04	− 5.14 (13.52)
Constant	37.32	28.56	293.74	250.44
R^2	.80	.85	.89	.91
Median abs. error	1.15	1.52	8.03	12.08
Median deviation from the mean	3.27	3.27	28.70	28.70

NOTE: (N = 23) LMS equations 1 and 3 are least median squares estimates. RLS equations 2 and 4 are reweighted least squares estimates based on the least median squares solution. See, Rousseeuw and Leroy (1987). The Democratic presidential vote is the Democratic share of the two-party vote. The t-ratios for the RLS solutions are in parentheses.

midterm vote changes and about 90 percent of the variance in midterm seat changes.

The LMS analysis detected three influence points or aberrant elections in the vote change analysis and four in the seat change regression. Two influence points were common to both analyses, the expected outlier of the 1934 New Deal midterm and the 1926 midterm, following a significant third-party presidential candidacy (of LaFollette) in 1924. In addition to 1926 and 1934, the vote loss regression diagnosed the 1914 midterm as aberrant. The initial analysis anticipated 1914 as a problem case since it followed the 1912 presidential election in which the third-party candidacy of Teddy Roosevelt drew approximately 28 percent of the popular vote and Socialist Eugene Debs drew an additional 6 percent away from the major parties.

Although 1914 did not present a problem in the seat loss analysis, two other cases in addition to 1934 did. The two additional outliers in the seat change regression were 1910 and 1986. In 1910 the Democrats made unusually large seat gains that were not expected by the estimated seat change equation. The reason for this particular discrepancy would appear to be the emerging third-party activity for House seats in the 1910 election, the precursor of Teddy Roosevelt's Bull Moose Progressive party challenge in 1912. Third-party congressional candidates siphoned-off 5 percent or more of the vote in 31 percent of the districts in 1910 (35 percent of districts with any competition) and received more than 10 percent of the vote in nearly 13 percent of the districts (49 of 391). For purposes of comparison, about one-half as many districts had significant (5 percent or more) third-party candidates in the 1908 presidential election year. Third-party candidates received 10 percent or more of the 1908 vote in only twenty districts, compared to forty-nine in 1910. Although its not certain where the 1910 third-party votes would have gone between the major parties, they might have been at the expense of Republican congressional candidates. The problems with the 1986 case are not quite so clear. According to the seat change regressions, the Democrats did not gain as many seats as they should have in 1986. Two reasons for this can be advanced. First, there were signs of a developing realignment in the mid-1980's that may have cut into Democratic gains. Second, and probably more important given the gradual nature of the suspected realignment, there is some evidence that House incumbents have been able to insulate themselves from national forces to a greater degree. This would attenuate changes of any sort, including the expected 1986 Democratic seat gains.

Robust Regression Analyses of the Presidential Surge

Vote and seat change in presidential election years were also reanalyzed with LMS robust regression. The LMS regression results and the RLS results are presented in table A2.2. The robust regression results support the prior analysis reported in tables 6.5 and 6.6 of chapter 6. The presidential vote's estimated

Table A2.2. Least Median Squares Estimates of the Presidential Vote's Effect on Presidential Year Change in Democratic Congressional Votes and Seats, 1990-1988

	Dependent variable			
	Presidential year change in Democratic votes		Presidential year change in Democratic seats	
Independent Variable	1 LMS	2 RLS	3 LMS	4 RLS
Democratic presidential vote	.35	.40 (7.11)	4.39	4.08 (8.65)
Initial Democratic seats or votes	− .45	− .44 (4.09)	− .33	− .25 (2.71)
Constant	6.44	3.43	− 147.42	− 149.92
R²	.71	.76	.35	.63
Median abs. error	.94	1.16	9.20	15.27
Median deviation from the mean	1.99	1.99	20.48	20.48

NOTE: (N = 23) LMS equations 1 and 3 are least median squares estimates. RLS equations 2 and 4 are reweighted least squares estimates based on the least median squares solution. See, Rousseeuw and Leroy (1987). The Democratic presidential vote is the Democratic share of the two-party vote. The t-ratios for the RLS solutions are in parentheses.

effects on congressional vote change are nearly identical to the earlier estimates. The seat change regressions differ in one respect from the earlier analysis: the presidential vote appears to have an even stronger impact on seat changes than the earlier estimates indicated. An additional percentage point of the presidential vote, according to the LMS estimates, typically adds more than four seats for a party. The LMS generated diagnostics indicated one influence point in the vote change equation (1920) and two in the seat change equations (1932 and 1948, the New Deal and a third-party election).

Notes

Chapter 1. The Midterm Question

1. See John Bartlett, *Bartlett's Familiar Quotations, 14th edition*. (Boston: Little, Brown and Company, 1968) p. 423.

2. The data on seat changes are drawn from Norman J. Ornstein, Thomas E. Mann, and Michael J. Malbin (1990, 51). Note that in the 1902 midterm the president's party nominally gained nine seats but that this was not a true gain since the total number of seats in the House grew by twenty-nine from 1900 to 1902. See George B. Galloway (1976, Appendix C).

3. The original statement of surge and decline was published by Angus Campbell in *Public Opinion Quarterly* in the Fall 1960 issue. The article was reprinted as chapter 3 of Angus Campbell, Philip E. Converse, Warren E. Miller, and Donald E. Stokes, *Elections and the Political Order* (1966).

4. The notions of surge and decline, as originally used, are relative. An election may be a high-stimulus or surge election compared to one election while at the same time being a relatively low-stimulus or decline election when compared to a third election. This permitted Campbell to speak of 1948 as a low-stimulus presidential election, even though it would be considered high-stimulus if compared to any midterm election of recent history.

5. This figure is based on a definition of a peripheral voter as a voter in a presidential election and a nonvoter in a midterm election. Assuming that the potential electorate is roughly static in a two-year period, the percentage of the presidential electorate composed of peripheral voters can be computed by comparing adjoining presidential and midterm election turnout rates. These calculations using table 2.1 in Ornstein et al. (1990) suggest that peripherals have comprised anywhere from 21 percent to 30 percent of recent presidential electorates.

6. This distinction may be clarified by reference to a three-variable causal model including (1) general circumstances of political relevance, (2) evaluations of presidential candidates, and (3) evaluations of the congressional candidates (listed in their causal order). The coattail model focuses on the direct effects of the presidential evaluations on the congressional evaluations. The surge-and-decline model, in recognizing all short-term forces to the advantage of the president's party, includes this direct effect and the systematic common cause effect of general political circumstances boosting both presidential and congressional evaluations.

Chapter 2. The Premises of Surge and Decline

1. One could reasonably suppose that personality traits would also affect the stability of attitudes, partisan or otherwise. An obstinate personality might be quite definite in his or her opinions even though they may be based on little

information. Conversely, a very flexible personality may be excessively open to persuasion even though his or her opinions have been formed from a wealth of information. Although not considered explicitly in the theory, one might assume that these personality traits are uncorrelated with information gathering and storage and, therefore, do not disturb the theory's argument.

2. In a statistical sense, equating deviations from the normal vote with the direction of short-term forces is committing the mistake of regression on residuals (King 1986, 669; Achen 1979; Fiorina 1981, 189; Page and Jones 1979, 1078).

3. An example may clarify this point. Assume that the majority party's normal vote is 55 percent. That is, in the absence of short-term forces the majority party should normally receive 55 percent of the vote based on long-standing partisan commitments. What can we conclude about the net impact of short-term forces if the majority party's presidential candidate receives exactly 55 percent of the vote, the same as the normal vote? The proper conclusion is that short-term forces are as positive for the majority party as the long-term forces are. However one blends short-term and long-term considerations, short-term forces algebraically must benefit the majority party by a margin of 55 to 45, given the 55 percent normal vote, the 55 percent final vote, and the existence of short-term forces [solve for Y, the net effect of short-term forces: $55 = (1 - x)55 + xY$ where x, the weight attached to short-term forces is greater than 0 and not greater than 1]. One might wrongly conclude that short-term forces are neutral in this case. If short-term forces were in fact neutral, the actual vote would necessarily be less than the normal vote. The drop from the normal vote when short-term forces are neutral would depend on the relative weights voters attach to long-term and short-term forces. The fact that short-term forces can be positive when the majority party receives less than its normal vote is an important consideration in examining national election results, but may be even more important in examining district level results where the normal vote may deviate a good bit from an even division.

4. Stokes (1962) used the normal vote estimates to assess the likelihood of deviating elections and, thereby, the relative importance of long-term and short-term factors in the presidential vote. His analysis indicated a moderate variance around the normal vote, suggesting strong but not determinative partisanship effects. In retrospect, the analysis appeared to understate the variability of the presidential vote. Later studies attempting to predict the vote, for instance, have found the normal vote to be a poor predictor (Rosenstone, 1983, 73). Also, the Stokes study wrongly assumed that short-term forces must cause deviations from the normal vote, when they very well could reinforce that vote (see Achen 1979).

5. *The American Voter* group has elsewhere also explicitly identified evaluations of short-term forces as the principal "attitudes immediately supporting the vote choice" (Stokes, Campbell, and Miller 1958, 368).

6. Two measurement strategies have been used in the measurement of short-term forces: forced-choice questions and open-ended questions. Both have problems that would cause them to underestimate short-term forces. Open-ended questions may understate short-term influences because voters inability to articulate or even to recall on demand reasons for the vote. The reliability of open-ended measures may also suffer with the length of the survey itself. Respondents may cut short a lengthy interview by indicating no responses to any open-ended question (as many as 11 percent of respondents offer no responses to any of the eight candidate or party-image open-ended questions). Forced-choice questions have different problems. They may structure issues and candidate images in ways

that may not coincide with the thinking of different voters. Some voters may be concerned with issues other than those posed on the survey or may structure alternatives differently, seeing issues as prospective rather than retrospective or seeing candidate differences in commitment to solving a problem rather than simple policy differences and so forth. Anecdotally, at a 1976 election-night party, I asked the fellow I was sitting next to, a medical doctor, who he had voted for and why? He responded that he had voted for Carter because President Ford had vetoed the "arthritis bill." Of course, there was no "arthritis bill" per se, but funding for related medical programs were a small part of a much larger bill that Ford had vetoed. Needless to say, there was not a single "arthritis bill" question on the 1976 NES survey.

7. Previous counts of NES likes and dislikes questions, such as those reported by Miller and Traugott (1989, 117) and Flanigan and Zingale (1987, 143), also generally supported the hypothesis that short-term forces in the aggregate favored the winning presidential candidate. However, two anomalies were apparent: 1960 and 1984. Short-term forces appeared slightly to favor Republicans in 1960 and were neutral or slightly favored Democrats in 1984. Given the closeness of the vote in 1960, it is perfectly understandable that any Democratic short-term advantage would be difficult to discern in a general survey. However, compounding this problem is the fact that the 1960 NES survey included more Nixon than Kennedy voters (Miller and Traugott, 1989, 315). A similar problem confronts the 1984 results. The 1984 NES study undercounts Reagan voters, thus contributing to the anomalous finding of pro-Mondale short-term forces (even so, the thermometer scale differences favor Reagan).

8. In the preelection survey, nearly 55 percent of respondents indicated an inclination to vote for Nixon. This compares to the postelection survey in which about 51 percent indicated that they had voted for Nixon.

9. It is the high volume of short-term forces in presidential elections that explains why long-term forces mediated by short-term evaluations play a role in the presidential surge and midterm decline. While the usual partisan themes may be evident in both presidential and midterm campaigns, they may be highlighted in a presidential contest and then fade in the relatively toned-down midterm campaign. It may be the same old partisan song, but it is played a lot louder in the presidential race.

10. It might be suggested that the pattern of declining presidential approval ratings indicates a negative tilt of short-term forces for the president's party in midterms. However, there are at least two reasons to be wary of this pattern. First, the pattern of declining approval ratings takes as its starting point the presidential inauguration rather the presidential election itself. Presidents generally enjoy high initial approval ratings as a "honeymoon" effect when the country reunites behind a new president after a divisive campaign. Second, while there seems to be a drop in these ratings from the first months of an administration, the drop is not necessarily into the negative range. Indeed, a number of president's have had quite positive ratings at the midterm. Kennedy's approval ratings in November of 1962 and Reagan's ratings in November of 1986 were both in the plus 65 percent region. Others, including Eisenhower in 1954 and Nixon in 1970 were quite respectable (around 57 percent). In short, there is little evidence to suggest a dependable systematic tilt in midterm short-term forces against the president's party.

11. The theory of surge and decline also assumes that the party system is stable. As Campbell originally noted, the theory holds "(a)s long as there is no

significant shift in the standing party attachments within the electorate" (Campbell et al. 1966, 61). A realignment of the underlying support of the parties could overwhelm surge and decline effects. This is especially true of critical realignments and would account for the 1934 New Deal realignment deviation from the regular pattern of presidential party midterm losses. Secular realignments of sufficient magnitude might also mask the consequences of surge and decline.

12. Wattenberg's findings are consistent with those reported by Miller and Traugott (1989, 338) and with an earlier analysis by Hadley and Howell (1979, 261) that examined ticket-splitting from 1952 to 1976. Nie, Verba, and Petrocik (1979, 53) also examined ticket-splitting with survey data and found an increase in the period from 1952 to 1972. Their data however counts a split-ticket as a vote anywhere below the presidential level that differs from the party of the presidential vote. Their figures thus portray a larger number of split-tickets than Hadley and Howell's count of tickets split on the presidential and congressional levels. In comparing the figures of Nie, Verba, and Petrocik to those of Hadley and Howell, it may be useful to recall that Campbell and Miller (1957, 294) found that most ticket-splitting occurs below the congressional level, though there may have been some change in this pattern since their study.

13. The four hypothetical situations described in figure 2.5 do not exhaust all possible circumstances. There are numerous scenarios of both straight-ticket and split-ticket voting that are not depicted. There are three variations in these diagrams: the starting points or initial dispositions toward both candidate choices, the ability of short-term forces to move those preferences in a common or opposite direction, and the end result of a straight or split ticket. A fourth factor might also be added: the relative magnitude of preference shift in voting for the two offices. We might expect congressional incumbency to reduce the effects (shorten the arrows) of short-term forces in congressional voting.

Chapter 3. The Propositions and Evidence of Surge

1. This original analysis also examined a pair of elections (1948 and 1956) which did not include a midterm election.

2. The most notable finding that runs contrary to Campbell's expectation is with respect to the effects of the turnout decline of the peripherals in the 1958 midterm. As Campbell noted, "the dropout of the peripheral voters in 1958 had very little effect on the distribution of congressional votes in that year" (Campbell et al. 1966, 59).

3. The validity of this assertion rests on the premise that the national normal vote for any party has not strayed too far from the 50 percent mark. If the normal vote of a party at some point was, say, 75 percent, its presidential candidate might win a landslide with short-term forces actually opposing him.

4. Hinckley's analysis is entirely in terms of seat losses not vote losses. This fact and the crudeness of the vote gap measure may also account for the failure to find that distance that the president ran ahead of the congressional candidate made any appreciable difference (1963, 698). Hinckley's relative partisan strength measure would seem to correspond roughly to a measure of the deviation from the normal vote. As both Achen (1979) and King (1986) point out, deviations from the normal vote cannot properly be equated with the effects of short-term forces. King refers to this error as an instance of the more general error of "regression on residuals." Put more simply, the effects of long-term forces and short-term forces should be estimated simultaneously and not sequentially. It should not be as-

sumed, as the normal vote deviation measure implicitly does, that short-term forces have effects if they differ or deviate from the effects that long-term forces might have had.

5. Strictly speaking, partisan short-term forces encompass more than just presidential coattails. However, presidential coattails, or at least those factors included as presidential coattail effects, capture a healthy portion of the short-term forces present in a presidential election year. Many short-term forces or conditions that might jointly affect both presidential and congressional contests, and are thus not truly coattail effects, are likely nonetheless to be attributed to coattails.

6. Edwards (1979) was criticized by Born (1984, 68) for examining outcomes rather than the vote and using OLS regression with the dichotomous dependent variable. Edwards also did not explicitly take the incumbent party into account, though he did consider what seems to amount to a district normal vote (the average prior vote in the district for president, senator and congressman). Finally, it should be noted that while Edwards found that coattail effects had "declined to the vanishing point" (1979, 94), presidential coattail effects were at least statistically significant in five of the six elections Edwards examined.

7. Campbell (Campbell et al. 1966) also noted differences in occupational status and income, those in the midterm electorates being of somewhat higher status and income than those in the presidential electorates. Subsequent research by Wolfinger and Rosenstone (1980) suggests that the bivariate association of turnout to income and occupational status is in large part due to their correlation with education. That is, the greater presence of higher income and occupational status voter in midterm electorates is largely spurious. Age and education, on the other hand, are thought to affect turnout, though much of their impact is indirect through various civic orientations such as political interest and sense of civic duty.

8. Fiorina (1981, 91) actually terms the link between age and strength of partisanship "an artifact." Fiorina's point is that the experiences accumulated with age do not necessarily reinforce partisanship. It is possible that experiences pull the voter in different directions. However in normal political times, parties stand for the same things over a voter's lifetime, and established partisanship colors perceptions of experience. Thus experience tends to reinforce partisanship and accounts for the correlation of age and strength of partisanship.

9. The data for this analysis are from the National Election Studies. Two problems with these survey data were encountered. First, NES surveys, like other surveys, consistently overreport turnout. The gap between reported and actual turnout is consistent and considerable, ranging between fifteen and twenty-four percentage points of the voting-age population. To correct for this problem as much as possible, NES voter validation studies were used when available. Although this does not fully address the problem, prior research suggests that the consequences of the problem should not be very serious (Wolfinger and Rosenstone 1980, 118). Moreover, since the study is concerned with comparisons between electorates, whatever bias is introduced by the presence of misreporters should be common to both presidential and midterm electorates and its impact reduced in examining differences. Second, there is a disparity between the NES reported and the true partisan division of the congressional vote. NES data consistently overreport the Democratic party's share of the congressional vote. The overreports ranged from one to eight percentage points with a median of three percentage points. This discrepancy was corrected by a simple weighting procedure. Cases were weighted by a factor of the true percentage having voted

for a party divided by the reported percentage having so voted. The weighted reported partisan division thus equals the true partisan division of the vote.

10. By definition, characteristics of core voters can be equated with the characteristics of the midterm electorate. Given the characteristics of core voters, the known percentages of the presidential electorate composed of core and peripheral voters, and the characteristics of the presidential electorate, the characteristics of the peripherals can be determined algebraically. For example, if we know that a presidential electorate is 75 percent core and 25 percent peripheral, that the average age of midterm of core voters is fifty and that the average age in the presidential electorate is forty-five, the average age of peripheral voters can be calculated to be 30. This is the solution for X in the equation: $45 = (.75 * 50) + (.25 * X)$.

11. Since the comparison of presidential and midterm electorates simply understates differences between core and peripheral voters (core voters are equivalent to the midterm electorate and presidential electorates mix core and peripherals together), I will report the algebraically determined difference between core and peripherals only when a difference between the electorates suggests that the theory's proposition might be supported. When differences between the electorates are contrary to expectations, the differences between core and peripherals would be only more so and we can safely conclude that the proposition is not significantly supported by the data.

12. Patrick Kenney (1988) has examined a different measure of political interest that may be less contaminated by campaign stimulation than the commonly consulted "interest in the presidential campaign" measure. Kenney examined a measure of interest in the *congressional* elections. Unfortunately, this question was only first asked in 1980 and Kenney's analysis does not compare responses of presidential election voters to voters in the midterm. In any case, while this alternative measure might be preferable to the explicitly presidential measure, one would suspect that any form of a political interest question asked in the midst of a presidential campaign would be contaminated by that campaign's stimulation.

13. While the difference between the 1972 presidential electorate's and the 1974 midterm electorate's interest in public affairs appears quite minor, it suggests a somewhat larger difference between core and peripheral voters. If you accept the midterm electorate as a core voters and algebraically calculate (as in note 10) the interest of peripheral voters, a fourteen percentage point gap is indicated (37 percent interested among peripheral voters and 51 percent interested among core voters). However, given the other inconsistent evidence and the fact that this difference is derived from observed differences that are close to sampling error, the findings ought to be interpreted with great caution.

14. It has been convincingly demonstrated by several studies (see Keith et. al. 1986; and Asher 1983, n. 7) that independents leaning in favor of either of the parties are equivalent in most respects to weak partisans of that party.

15. There is no evidence that bears directly on the theory's underlying theory of political information (discussed in chapter 2). However, we can speculate about a possible problem with that theory that may have led to problems for surge and decline. The nature of this problem is most easily explained with reference to the causal model presented in figure 2.4. As the model suggests, the suspected positive association between a citizen's political involvement and his party loyalty (as well as the stability of partisan attitudes) depends upon the positive indirect effects of political involvement on party loyalty (through stored or accumulated

information) greatly outweighing the negative indirect effects (through the acquisition of new information). It is quite plausible that the two indirect effects of opposite signs would cancel each other, in the whole or in large part.

16. As a control group, I examined the association between the midterm congressional vote of the independents and the prior presidential surge as indicated by the overall presidential vote. As expected, there was no significant association.

17. A related question of variance concerns the variance of the congressional vote across districts in a given year. One might suppose that there would be greater variation in a presidential election year because of the supposed volatility produced by strong short-term forces. However, greater volatility in presidential election years does not necessarily entail greater variation in the congressional vote across districts. In fact, to the extent that presidential short-term forces are uniform across the country, there should be less variation in the congressional vote. In the extreme case, if a presidential candidate were to receive all the votes and all congressional votes were "coattail" votes, each congressional candidate of the winning presidential party would receive 100 percent of the district's votes and there would be zero variance in the congressional vote across districts.

18. A related question of variance is the debate over the "nationalization" versus the "localization" of the vote. A sizeable body of literature has developed on this topic since it was first addressed by Stokes (1967). As Claggett, Flanigan, and Zingale (1984) properly observe, "nationalization" of the vote can be used in two different senses: (1) the attention to "national" level candidates, issues, and conditions; or (2) uniformity in responses to these stimuli across the nation. The distinction is that differential responses to a common stimuli are possible as are apparently uniform responses to different (local) stimuli. As in the case of the analysis of the simple magnitude of the congressional vote variance, it might be suggested that surge and decline requires a high level of nationalization in both senses of the term. This hypothesis, however, would seem not to be suggested by the theory. While greater nationalization would presumably magnify surge effects, these effects do not require a highly nationalized electorate. Congressional elections can be primarily local in character and influenced at the margin, though significantly, by national forces. While substantial nationalization is not a requirement, one might infer from the theory that the degree of nationalization in the congressional vote (in both senses) would be somewhat greater in presidential election years than in midterms. Although, again, the theory does not rest on the validity of this claim.

Chapter 4. The Theory of Midterm Referendum

1. Tufte reports that building the normal vote into the dependent variable is not problematic. Tufte analyzed an equation explaining the actual party vote, rather than the standardized vote loss, using the normal vote as an explanatory variable. This analysis yielded an unstandardized coefficient for the normal vote that was "very close to unity." Thus transferring the normal vote to the left-hand side of the equation is equivalent to learning the normal vote on the right-hand side as an independent variable. The reason then for his choosing to analyze the standardized vote loss equation rather than using the simple vote as the dependent variable is to save one degree of freedom in a study with a very small number of cases. There are, however, good reasons why this specification should not be used in subsequent research. Achen (1979) notes biases that are possibly signifi-

cant in estimates of the normal vote and the improper specification of analyses that examine deviations from the normal vote. King (1986) refers to this as the error of regression on residuals. Even if this did not create a problem in Tufte's original analysis, because of his estimate that the normal vote would have had a coefficient of 1, there is no guarantee that the normal vote would have coefficient of 1 with the addition of new elections. Moreover, with the addition of new elections to the analysis is the reason to examine the standardized vote loss rather than the vote itself becomes less important. That is, the advantage of saving a degree of freedom decreases as the number of cases in the analysis increases. In table 4.1 equation 4 will be estimated with the normal vote specified as an independent variable rather than incorporated into the dependent variable.

2. Erikson's objection to the simple referendum explanation of midterm losses is of a very different sort. "The size of the penalty given the presidential party is far too large and far too regular to attribute to a pattern of persistently adverse circumstances for presidents at midterm," according to Erikson (1988, 1020). He argues that the referendum explanation is implausible because, as estimated, the president's party would suffer losses even at the highest levels of presidential popularity and in the most thriving economy.

3. A substantial body of work now takes exception to the idea that there is a necessary or regular decline in presidential popularity by the midterm (see Ostrom and Simon 1985, 1988, 1989; MacKuen 1983).

4. Calvert and Isaac (1981) offer an interesting twist to the negative voting thesis. They argue that congressional candidates of the president's party are at a disadvantage in the midterm because they are associated with a set of issue positions developed to appeal to a national constituency by the president while their opponent may more freely tailor his or her issue positions to appeal to the district constituency. An optimal issue strategy for national politics is likely to be suboptimal in any given district. Although intriguing, they unfortunately offer no direct test of this thesis.

5. In addition to doubts about the negativity hypotheses raised by Cover's analysis, the negativity hypotheses pose a troubling question. If voters are more prone to perceive and act on the negative when focused on a single politician, why are congressional incumbents reelected at such high rates?

6. A third problem in Erikson's analysis is that, to the extent that he offers strong tests of the various theories, his analysis examines each theory in isolation from the others. It is quite plausible, as Tufte suggested and as I will advocate in chapter 5, that some combination of the theories best explains the pattern of midterm losses.

7. Alesina and Rosenthal (1989) offer what might be construed as an interesting variation of the negativity thesis. They argue that moderate voters are faced with an unsatisfactory choice between polarized economic programs by the two parties in presidential elections. In order to moderate government policies, so the argument goes, these moderate voters decide to split their tickets in the presidential election and to vote against the president's party in the midterm. While intriguing, their test of the thesis is fairly weak. Their entire analysis is conducted on only aggregate congressional election results from 1950 to 1984. There are two points to their evidence, both of which are subject to criticism: (1) Like Erikson (1988), they read unwarranted meaning into the statistical significance of a midterm dummy variable. All it really means is that midterm losses have not been explained by other variables in their model; an unexplained difference between midterms and presidential years remains. (2) They test their thesis *only* against

retrospective economic voting models. While their model of voters favoring stable economic growth outperforms other retrospective economic models that posit "the faster growth, the better" voters, the fit of the equations are quite poor relative to analyses of similar election series. The unadjusted R^2 in their final equation is only .44 (with five variables) (p. 392).

8. Jacobson (1989, 785-86) offered an interesting additional component to the thesis: that there is an interaction between candidate quality and the political climate, and that quality challengers are more capable of exploiting favorable conditions. Also, although the notion of strategic politician has only been applied to the referenda theory of midterms, it may also be applied to the presidential election theories of midterms. In chapter 5, a strategic politician component to the revised theory of surge and decline is suggested.

9. In addition to mediating the effects of the economy and presidential popularity, party competence evaluations may mediate other considerations bearing on the vote. Kinder and Kiewiet (1979) found that party identification strongly affected evaluations of party competence. Peffley, Feldman, and Sigelman (1987) found strong corroborating evidence that party identification and prior beliefs about economic conditions exert a much stronger influence on party competence evaluations than perceived economic conditions.

10. The party competence and attribution of responsibility arguments, of course, do not apply in the same way to the presidential performance variable. The evaluation of presidential performance is quite clear in its political implications and, unlike the economic conditions variable, does not require translation into a subjective political assessment by the voter.

11. Erikson's (1988, 1019-20) analysis rejects the "regression to the mean" or exposure explanation on different grounds. He finds that the congressional vote in presidential years is positively associated with the following midterm vote (b about +1) and that a negative coefficient should be expected if there was regression to the mean. He thus concludes that there is no "regression to the mean" or midterm decline to the normal vote. There are several problems in this analysis: (1) It implicitly assumes a constant normal vote throughout this century, when the normal vote has obviously varied a lot. The effects of this can be detected in Erikson's plot of the Democratic congressional midterm and presidential votes (1988, 1021). In this plot, the smaller Democratic midterm congressional votes are, with just a few exceptions, in the pre-New Deal realignment midterms. (2) The equilibrium or exposure thesis cannot be fairly tested without explicitly examining the difference between both the presidential year and midterm congressional votes and the normal vote. Without taking the normal vote into account, a positive association between the two votes should be expected because both are presumably affected by the normal vote. The coefficient for the presidential year congressional vote is, therefore, positively biased as a result of specification error, the exclusion of a common causal variable.

12. Oppenheimer, Stimson, and Waterman conduct a very brief analysis of the theory of surge and decline in considering the exposure thesis (1986, 236-39). Their analysis is in two steps. They estimated and compared the simple exposure equation with an equation accounting for seat change in terms of both exposure and a dummy variable for midterm elections. The analysis indicated that the addition of the midterm dummy variable significantly improved the model's fit (adjusted R^2 of .46 vs. .57). Rather than concluding that one should distinguish on-year from off-year congressional elections, a distinction made by surge and decline, they proceeded to the second step: an analysis of residuals. After dis-

counting the first four midterms in their series as being held in an unstable partisan transition period (1938-50), they examined the pattern of errors in the "exposure only" equation for the eight more recent midtems. The residuals varied in signs, indicating that the exposure equation did not consistently underestimate midterm losses. On the basis of the alternating signs of these eight residuals, Oppenheimer, Stimson, and Waterman conclude that "surge and decline should be set aside as merely a special case of exposure" and that the theory "is no longer necessary" (p. 239). There are several flaws in this analysis and the inferences they draw from it. First, they proposed a weak specification of the surge and decline theory. By measuring the strength of the theory by the effects attributed to a simple midterm dummy variable they have wrongly assumed, like Tufte, that surge and decline has a fixed effect, that it explains the consistency but not variability of midterm losses. Even as poorly measured, however, the variable is statistically significant and has a sizeable effect. Second, the second part of their analysis offers a weak test of the exposure explanation, a simple alternation in signs of the residual. Unless autocorrelation is present, the regression analysis should not yield residuals with the same sign. Third, by not estimating the exposure equation on midterm elections alone, they fail to note that the exposure variable accounts for no variance in midterm losses. Finally, to the extent that exposure may help account for the consistency of midterm losses, it does not invalidate surge and decline. Instead, exposure is an intervening variable within the theory of surge and decline. Surge and decline explains why the president's party is regularly overexposed in midterms. In fact, Cover (1985, 617) suggested the regression-to-the-mean or exposure perspective as an element of surge and decline prior to the Oppenheimer, Stimson, and Waterman analysis. In their most recent analysis (Waterman, Oppenheimer, and Stimson 1991), they examine the exposure thesis and the surge and decline theory over a more extended time period. Throughout most of their new analysis, they no longer assume fixed surge and decline effects and appropriately use the presidential vote as a measure of the presidential surge. Examining Democratic seat gain in presidential years, they find strong evidence of the presidential surge (1991, 381). They also find evidence of a midterm decline effect (p. 385) over and above that which might be indirectly generated by coattails causing the presidential party to go into the midterm overexposed. They only fail to find supporting evidence for surge and decline in recent years when they reorient their analysis to examine the presidential party versus its opposition rather than the Democratic versus Republican parties. In reorienting the analysis, the Oppenheimer group truncates variation in surge and decline effects. If they had left the analysis as originally oriented, estimates of surge and decline effects would have remained significant.

13. The weakness of the exposure thesis in explaining midterm losses is also suggested by a comparison of midterm losses in table 1.1. As it happens, Republicans were equally exposed going into three recent midterms. Republicans held the presidency and 192 House seats in 1968, in 1972, and in 1980. The exposure thesis suggests similar losses, adjusted to some extent by referenda evaluations, in each of the subsequent midterms. However, the losses differed tremendously. Republicans lost just twelve seats in 1970 but twenty-six seats in 1982 and forty-eight seats in 1974.

14. In the eleven midterms from 1946 to 1986, the president's party was overexposed in every midterm except for 1946 when it was underexposed (using the Oppenheimer, Stimson, and Waterman base of 254) by twelve seats. The mean exposure of the president's party in these midterms was sixteen or more

seats and the median was eleven or more seats. In the 1990 midterm, the president's party was slightly underexposed.

15. Marra and Ostrom (1989) have developed a modified exposure model to explain seat change in both presidential and midterm elections, although they measure exposure from an eight-election moving average rather than the average of the entire period. Like the other referenda models, they include presidential approval and economic conditions. Unlike the other referenda models, Marra and Ostrom include a "political events" variable, an aggregated party identification variable, and a variable that measures the change in presidential approval since the presidential election (actually six months into office). Five criticisms of the Marra and Ostrom model can be offered: (1) As in the original exposure model, the authors do not attribute the midterm overexposure of the president's party to the prior presidential surge, though they observe "the fact that the president's party is typically under its historical average during on-year elections and over its historical average during midterm elections accounts for an additional 9.4 seat difference between the two elections" (p. 564). In fact, as with Oppenheimer, Stimson, and Waterman's exposure measure, the president's party was overexposed using the moving average measure in nine of the last ten midterms and was underexposed in the single exception (1958) by only four seats. As in the case of the original exposure thesis, seat exposure might be best construed as an intervening variable between the presidential surge and midterm seat losses. (2) The change in approval from the past presidential election is tantamount to sneaking the presidential vote into the equation, a measure of the prior presidential surge. A very close surrogate for the presidential vote would be the simple difference between the midterm approval and the change in presidential approval measures. As Marra and Ostrom note, "the change in approval over the two years leading up to the election accounts for a difference of 19 seats between the two types of elections" (p. 564). Given this and the fact that change in approval was one of the strongest variables in the equation, the model might well be interpreted as evidence in behalf of surge and decline. (3) The inclusion of an index of political events is highly subjective in the choice of events and their specification in the equation. Marra and Ostrom chose the strongest fit of eight different variable forms. The high degree of subjectivity in this variable makes it suspect as a general explanation of seat change. (4) Although the economic variable produced a coefficient in the wrong direction, it was kept in the equation. While this would not normally be a problem, the economic variable was quite near conventional levels of statistical significance and thus may have added to the explained variance even though it unambiguously failed to exert its expected effect. (5) Finally, by their own account, the Marra and Ostrom model better fits presidential elections than midterms (table 2, p. 557).

Chapter 5. The Revised Theory of Surge and Decline

1. Tufte's reference to "the midterm model" is to his referenda model of midterm elections.

2. Born (1990, 633) also implicitly recognizes the coexistence of the surge and decline and the referenda theories.

3. Nonparametric correlations were examined rather than Pearson's r because of the dichotomous turnout variable. However, Pearson's r was also examined and yielded the same substantive results. Somer's d was deemed preferable to gamma since the dependent variable was clearly the turnout variable. For a

discussion of the advantage of the Somer's d correlation, see Bohrnstedt and Knoke (1988, 325). Also, in this particular instance, the zero-order association between partisanship and turnout is of theoretical interest rather than the actual effect of partisanship on turnout in a multivariate context.

4. Sperlich (1971, 32-38) offers an excellent overview of cognitive consistency theories in general and the cognitive dissonance theory in particular.

5. The willingness and ability to tolerate cross-pressure stress in an election were measured by a variety of variables including: education, sense of civic duty, care about the election outcome, and personality integration (Sperlich 1971, chaps. 7 and 8).

6. At the most superficial levels of demographic or socioeconomic status there appears to be little or no evidence that cross-pressures produce greater abstention. As Wolfinger and Rosenstone (1980) observe in their analysis of socioeconomic status and turnout: "We found absolutely no evidence for any variant of the cross-pressure hypothesis. While the effect of increments of any single status variable was not always additive, no inconsistent combinations were ever related to lower turnout" (p. 35). In Sperlich's (1971) terms, demographic and socioeconomic cross-pressures may not be central in most voter decision-making and are easily tolerated by potential voters.

7. Sperlich (1971, 30) also identifies two explanations of cross-pressures effects: a rational or logical explanation and a psychological explanation. The logical explanation associates cross-pressures with an increase in decision costs. The psychological explanation draws on the psychological stress and discomfort linked to conflict by cognitive consistency theories. The two explanations of cross-pressure effects that I offer are in some respects similar to those identified by Sperlich but do not draw a sharp distinction between the rational and the psychological aspects of an individual's decision making.

8. Frohlich et al. (1978, 191), however, also found no evidence of cross-pressure effects and claimed that the cross-pressure thesis is inconsistent with Downs' theory of voter rationality: "such a hypothesis contradicts his formulation of the rational-choice calculus" (p. 191). However, aside from cross-pressures resulting in indifference, they may also increase uncertainty which certainly may be incorporated into the rational voter calculus (Downs 1957, chaps. 5 and 6).

9. Erikson (1981) in his examination of the influences on voter registration and turnout in 1964 examines the strength of the party differential (based on the likes/dislikes questions) and found it to have no statistically significant direct effects on registration or turnout in either the primary or general election. These findings may in part reflect indirect effects of cross-pressures through his index of voter "opinionation" and "political activity" as well as political involvement.

10. Weisberg and Grofman (1981) also examine cross-pressures more specifically. They identified cross-pressures in several ways (p. 206). In most simple terms, cross-pressured partisans were identified as those rating their own party's candidate below 50 degrees on the thermometer scale or those rating the opposing candidate above 50 degrees. They place greater confidence in a third measure, which identified cross-pressured partisans as those rating the opposing party's candidate more highly than their own. Using this measure, they found a very slight cross-pressure abstention effect. Aside from the lack of controls for the usual array of background factors affecting turnout, there are two problems with the Weisberg and Grofman analysis. First, their measure does not examine gradations in the magnitude or extent of cross-pressures. More important, they use the thermometer difference as an indication of short-term forces rather than

the overall evaluation based on both long-term and short-term considerations. If they are viewed as summary evaluations, a cross-pressured partisan may continue to rate his or her own party's candidate more highly than the opposition's, just not as highly as he or she would if short-term considerations supported his or her party's candidate.

11. In a somewhat different argument Ferejohn and Fiorina (1974) have argued that uncertainty about the voter's vote deciding the election stimulates turnout. The uncertainty that they consider involves uncertainty of the election outcome. The uncertainty raised here concerns what information should be considered by the voter and to what extent in deciding to vote for one candidate rather than another.

12. If cues are consistent the weights attached to them are less important to the decision. If, for instance, domestic policies lead the vote to slightly favor the Republican and foreign policies also slightly favor the Republican, whatever weights are attached to the two issue areas would lead to a voter with a slight preference for the Republican candidate.

13. Fiorina (1976) also addresses a number of secondary hypotheses about the turnout of cross-pressured voters. That is, rather than test the main effect of cross-pressures depressing turnout, he examined within the context of the Riker and Ordeshook (1968) Downsian economic model of turnout the related factors that would make a cross-pressured voter more or less likely to vote. He considers a variety of hypotheses involving the vote preference and turnout of cross-pressured citizens under conditions of varying short-term evaluations (a.k.a., party differentials), strength of partisanship, perceptions of the closeness of the election, and intentions of party loyalty or disloyalty in the vote, if cast. The preliminary analysis of the turnout hypotheses was generally inconclusive.

14. Neutral evaluations of short-term forces is not equivalent to neutral reactions to the candidates since those reactions would be composed of both long-term and short-term views. Thus if a partisan were indifferent to the candidates it would suggest that short-term negative evaluations had offset long-term positive evaluations toward the party.

15. Since the "goodness" of news for a party is not judged by all by the same criteria and since news is usually somewhat ambiguous, those welcoming campaign information as supportive of their party may actually come from both parties. However, to the degree that commonalities in criteria exist, one would expect the partisans of one party to be more generally pleased with campaign news than partisans of the opposing party.

16. Most general causal models of the vote choice would seem to support this view. The direct effects of issues and candidate image evaluations on the vote choice are generally greater than party identification's direct effects on the vote. Most of the impact of party identification on the vote appears to be exerted indirectly through issues and candidate image evaluations rather than directly (see Campbell et al. 1986).

17. Theoretically partisanship and independence are ranges on a continuum rather than discrete categories. However, as conventionally measured in the National Election Studies, individuals are placed into one of seven categories. Given previous work on the measurement of party identification, most notably that of Keith et al. (1986), the most accurate categorization of individuals would count strong partisans, weak partisans, and independents leaning in favor of a party as partisans. Independents are exclusively those who claim no leaning toward either party. While weak partisans and leaning "independents" are more

partisan than independents, they are apparently less partisan than those who claim a strong attachment to a party.

18. Converse (1966b) acknowleged the possible partisan turnout effects of short-term forces but dismissed them. According to Converse: "It can be shown that in some instances strong partisan forces affect the turnout of different classes of identifiers increasing the turnout of the advantaged party and depressing the turnout among its opponents. However, these instances are rarer than is commonly assumed" (p. 18).

19. The revised theory also differs with the age (proposition 5) and education (proposition 6) hypotheses of the original theory. The age and educational backgrounds of the presidential and midterm electorates, according to the revised theory, are not relevant to their reaction to presidential election year short-term forces since it is the net partisan slant of these forces, rather than their gross magnitude, that affects turnout.

20. It should be noted that it is hypothetically possible for elite and mass decisions to be in conflict *if* there is a radical change in the political climate between the time that potential candidates decide whether to run and the time when potential voters reach their vote decisions.

Chapter 6. Evidence from National Elections

1. The appropriate orientation of variables in this analysis is in terms of Democratic and Republican parties rather than the presidential and opposition parties since an important variable in the analysis, the presidential vote, itself determines which party is the presidential party (see note 11 in chapter 4 on the exposure thesis research). Thus orienting the analysis in terms of the presidential party and then examining for effects of the presidential vote is tantamount to controlling twice for the presidential vote. The first control, albeit a crude one, is in the orientation in terms of the presidential party and the second control (the independent variable in the regression) determines the effects of the presidential vote over and above those already achieved by the party winning the presidential election. Thus, because of the orientation of the variables, the regression coefficients only estimate part of the effects of the presidential vote. From a different perspective, orienting the analysis in terms of the presidential vote artificially restricts variance. Variance is most clearly restricted in the presidential vote, which has a lower bound of about 50 percent (since winning candidates in order to be winners virtually must receive about 50 percent of the two-party vote, though this is not strictly required by the Electoral College system) but is also artificially restricted on the dependent variable since the upper bound of seat and vote change for the president's party in midterms has been a negative number. While strictly speaking it would be inappropriate to orient the analysis in terms of the presidential party, for those who might be interested in the results of such an analysis, I present such results in appendix 1.

2. Because the dependent variable is a change variable, consideration of change in the normal vote only makes a significant difference to estimates when the normal vote change is substantial and abrupt. When change is more gradual, any change in a party's base vote within the two-year interval should be fairly small and should not obscure the surge and decline effects.

3. There is a definite pattern of narrowing variance in both midterm vote and seat changes since 1900. In the eight midterms prior to the 1900 election, the standard deviation of presidential party vote losses was 3.8 and the standard

deviation of presidential party seat losses was 54.7. This variation declined quite consistently throughout the century. In the eight midterms prior to the 1984 election, the standard deviation of the presidential party's vote losses was only 1.5 and the standard deviation of its seat losses had declined to just 18.3. An identical pattern of reduced variance was found in an examination of a series of eleven (rather than eight) midterms. To examine whether this pattern of variance affected the OLS regressions, the regressions were reexamined after dividing the Democratic seat and vote losses by their variability at the time, measured as the standard deviation of losses for the president's party in the prior eight midterms. This adjustment in the dependent variable made little difference. The prior Democratic presidential vote accounted for 62 percent of the variance in the adjusted congressional vote losses and 69 percent of the variance in the adjusted seat losses. If the narrowing variance pattern were severe enough through the century to cause distortions in the estimates, we would expect these equations to significantly underestimate early presidential party midterm losses and overestimate later losses. Neither the vote loss nor seat loss residuals displayed trends of this sort.

4. Negative autocorrelation indicates nonrandom errors that tend to alternate in sign (e.g., positive errors following negative errors). This may inflate standard errors thus biasing significance testing against inferring statistically significant coefficients. Also, the proportion of variance explained cannot be compared between the OLS and "first difference" equations since the initial variances of the dependent variables differ and the first case in the series is dropped from the first difference estimates since there was no prior election from which to take a difference.

5. These estimates are a good bit smaller than those in tables 6.1 and 6.2. While one might suspect this reduction is a result of including the midterm popularity consideration into the multivariate analysis, this is not the case. A president's vote and later popularity during this period have been remarkably unrelated ($r = .001$). The difference is due to some decline in effects in recent years but mostly to the attenuation caused by orienting variables in terms of the winning and losing presidential parties rather than the Democratic and Republican parties.

6. Initial vote and seat holdings were not included in the midterm analysis because presidential coattails had already built in "slack" for midterm vote and seat change. Also, since a party's holdings prior to a midterm are partially a result of presidential coattails, proportionate to the presidential vote, including initial holdings would complicate the analysis. In any case, adding the initial vote in seat holdings in the midterm analysis, to equation 2 in tables 6.1 and 6.2, does not yield significant effects. In the seat change equation, the initial seat holdings have the expected negative effects but do not reach statistical significance ($b = -.21$, $t = 1.41$). The initial vote share, the Democratic congressional vote percentage in the presidential election year, does not have the expected negative effect ($b = .03$, $t = .20$).

7. Despite Eisenhower's solid victory in 1952, Republicans added only one-tenth of a percent of their national congressional vote. The small increment would seem to reflect the fact that Eisenhower's victory was short of a landslide and the fact that the party's initial vote base from 1950 was fairly strong (49.9 percent). Also, though to a far lesser degree than Nixon in 1972, some of Ike's potential coattail strength in 1952 was wasted in Southern states (he carried Virginia, Texas, and Florida) where Republicans had few congressional candi-

dates. Both the recent and long-term LMS estimates expected the small vote change.

8. Republican coattails may also have been wasted in Southern districts in other elections, though the waste may not have been as great as in 1972. For instance, the equations indicate greater Republican seat gains in Reagan's 1984 landslide than were actually won. Like 1972, the shortfall may be due, in part, to wasted Republican coattails in the South. The problem of the unusually great waste of coattails would seem to depend on how quickly Southern Republicans can recruit more and stronger congressional candidates.

9. From Tufte's analysis of the swing-ratio, Jacobson (1976, 197-98) offers essentially two explanations for why Republicans failed to gain more seats in 1972. First, as the number of marginal seats has declined (Mayhew 1974), the swing-ratio has also declined. That is, since incumbents win by bigger margins, it now takes a bigger change in the vote to switch a seat from one party to the other. Second, there is a bias against the Republicans in the distribution of seats, presumably due to lower turnout rates in predominantly Democratic districts but also, perhaps, to Democratic control of redistricting in a majority of states. While these factors probably played a role in the 1972 shortfall in Republican seat gains, they probably do not account for much of it. Recall that one set of the regression estimates used here are based on a recent series of elections. The reduced swing-ratio and pro-Democratic bias is a trend in which 1972 is not unusual within this series. Moreover, the regressions include the previous party holdings which address the matter of increased incumbency advantage. Also, the swing-ratio explanation does not account in any way for the shortfall in actual vote gains.

10. Surge and decline between 1972 and 1974 also may be illustrated in four Indiana districts: the second, sixth, tenth, and eleventh. In these four districts the identical pairs of Republican and Democratic congressional candidates opposed each other in both 1972 and 1974. In each case, the Republican won in 1972, Nixon carried the district easily (between 66 percent and 74 percent) and the Democrat defeated the incumbent Republican in 1974. While the midterm referenda, undoubtedly based heavily on the Watergate scandal, contributed a good deal to these Republican losses, it would appear that the coattail help they received in 1972 also contributed.

Chapter 7. Evidence in Congressional Districts

1. Congressional votes are recorded as percentage points of the two-party vote.

2. One might question the assumption of only one-way causation in the relationship between the presidential and congressional votes. That is, the analysis assumes that the presidential vote affects the congressional vote but is not affected by the congressional vote. In a separate analysis of the relationship between the presidential and Senate votes (Campbell and Sumners 1990) it was determined in a two-stage least squares nonrecursive analysis that the presidential vote affected the Senate vote but that the Senate vote did not affect the presidential vote. Given this finding and the generally greater prominence of Senate elections (compared to House contests), it is quite reasonable to assume that House contests do not affect presidential voting.

3. The factor analyses were conducted on all 435 districts. For the purpose of obtaining a normal vote, uncontested districts were coded as a 90 percent win

for the party holding the seat. The rationale for this is that the normal vote measurement should be devoid of candidate-specific influence and that it is safe to assume that a major party in nearly all districts should be able to win 10 percent of the vote if it puts up an active candidate. The 1968 Democratic presidential vote had to be estimated for several districts. *The Almanac of American Politics 1976* (Barone, Ujifusa, and Matthews 1975) did not indicate the 1968 presidential vote for four districts in New York (12-15) and for the seven districts in Washington. Rather than lose these cases for the analysis, 1968 presidential votes were estimated. The Washington cases were estimated by apportioning the known 1968 state presidential vote by the known 1968 district turnout in the congressional races. The four New York district votes were estimated from the preredistricting 1968 presidential votes as indicated in *The Almanac of American Politics 1972* (Barone, Ujifusa, and Matthews 1970). The 1976-78 normal vote factor score coefficients are .34 for the 1968 presidential vote; .32 for the 1974 congressional vote; .29 for the 1972 congressional vote; and .28 for the 1972 presidential vote. The 1984-86 normal vote factor score coefficients are .34 for the 1982 congressional vote; .38 for the 1980 presidential vote; and .39 for the 1976 presidential vote.

4. To illustrate this property of the index, take two hypothetical districts. In one district, each of the candidates has $100,000. In the other district, each candidate has $500,000. In both cases, given the equality of finances, the index would take a value of zero. Suppose further that the presidential party's candidates in these districts received an additional $40,000. In the first (low spending) district, the addition of $40,000 toward the presidential party's candidate would raise the index to .17 (40,000/240,000). In the second (high spending) district where greater diminishing returns should have set in, the addition of $40,000 toward the presidential party's candidate would raise the index to only .04 (40,000/1,040,000).

5. The district analysis, in fact, identified all fifteen districts actually gained by the Republicans in 1984 since one of the sixteen gains counted in this analysis was Indiana's eighth district, although this outcome was later reversed in a bitter and very controversial partisan vote of the House.

6. The absence of a zero-order association between the prior presidential vote and midterm vote loss is probably a consequence of midterm presidential popularity. As argued in the text, the president presumably remains most popular and therefore restricts midterm losses in many of the same districts which he won in the presidential election.

7. The drop following the presidential gains is more pronounced if all districts, not just those seriously contested, are examined. The bivariate coefficients are $-.34$ ($t = 6.03$) in 1978 and $-.28$ ($t = 5.92$) in 1986.

8. The 1980 presidential vote used in obtaining the 1978 presidential popularity measure is the Carter vote alone. For the purpose of estimating approval of President Carter, votes for independent presidential candidate John Anderson are interpreted as indicating disapproval. The 1988 presidential vote is also the Bush vote, and there was little third-party activity in 1988 to complicate the measure.

9. Even if change in presidential approval is not at a constant rate, the average of the two presidential votes may serve as a good measurement of midterm popularity if deviations from the constant rate of popularity change are uniform across districts. If, for instance, the surrogate measurement underestimated midterm presidential approval by ten percentage points in all districts, it

would still control fully for the effects of popularity since it would be perfectly correlated with actual midterm popularity.

10. Estimates of the base vote's effects may have been attenuated by the exclusion of cases that were not contested at both elections.

11. Including seats not seriously contested actually strengthens the surge and decline case. The coefficients are more strongly negative when all 435 districts are included in the analysis. Reestimating the additive equations in table 7.5 (equations 2,4,6, and 8) for all districts yields the following coefficients for the prior congressional vote gain variable: $-.28$ and $-.45$ in 1978; $-.25$ and $-.22$ in 1986 (each p $\langle.01$).

12. As in the case of the presidential year analysis, some effects of the withdrawal of the presidential surge may be indirect in nature. Assuming that the presidential gains may affect the incumbency and the campaign spending advantages in the following election, the indirect effects of the presidential surge can be estimated and added to the direct effects. The total effects of the prior presidential vote were somewhat more negative than the direct effects alone ($-.31$ and $-.48$ in 1978's equations 2 and 4; $-.10$ and $-.13$ in 1986's equations 6 and 8).

13. A number of the 1978 losses seem traceable to distinctly local district factors. For instance, Republicans were able to win several seats with well-financed challengers in Republican leaning districts vacated by Democratic incumbents (e.g., the fourth in South Carolina; the twenty-first in Texas; and Wyoming).

14. Fowler and McClure (1989, 195) in their district case study speculated that coattails were "nonexistent" in Eckert's 1984 election in New York's thirtieth district. This analysis, however, indicates that coattails were decisive in both the Republican's 1984 victory and, by their absence, his subsequent loss in the 1986 midterm.

15. The effects of surge and decline also may be illustrated in the 1972 and 1974 elections in four Indiana congressional districts: the second, sixth, tenth, and eleventh. In these four districts the identical pairs of Republican and Democratic congressional candidates opposed each other in both the presidential (1972) and midterm (1974) elections. If we accept that the major local conditions capable of causing electoral change are linked to the quality of the candidates, we might think of these pairs of races as twins and, like biological twin studies disentangling the effects of nature and nurture, use the constancy of the factors in these cases to separate local and national forces on the vote. The electoral pattern in each of these four "twin" districts is identical to one another's and conforms to the surge and decline pattern. In 1972 the congressional Republican won in each district while Nixon easily carried each district in the presidential vote (with between 66 percent and 74 percent of the vote). In 1974, though each Republican now had the advantages of incumbency on his side, each congressional Democrat was elected. Although the midterm referenda, undoubtedly based heavily on the Watergate scandal, contributed a good deal to these Republican losses and overrode the Republican candidates' incumbency advantages, the coattail help they received in 1972 and then ran without in 1974 also appears to have contributed to this pattern.

16. Information regarding these two case studies have been obtained from the pertinent selections of Ehrenhalt's *Politics in America* and Barone, Ujifusa, and Matthew's *Almanac of American Politics.*

17. There were no Senate or governorship races in Nevada in 1984, which

might have complicated the interpretation of the surge as something other than a consequence of the presidential campaign.

18. Vucanovich's 1988 vote failed to rise above her 1986 midterm vote. She received 57 percent of the 1988 vote electing her to her fourth term. Two reasons would seem to account for the 1988 vote failing to rise: first, George Bush did not win as convincingly in Nevada as Reagan had in the two previous elections (a smaller surge); and second, unlike 1984 and 1986, in 1988 Vucanovich faced a very well financed opponent.

Chapter 8. Evidence in the Electorate

1. The impact of short-term forces on the independent congressional vote, although positive, is somewhat weaker than expected and falls short of conventional levels of statistical significance. The explanation for this may be the small number of voting independents in some surveys. After weighting (to the reported N) to correct for the known partisan division of the vote, the number of pure independent reported voters in some surveys was less than fifty (e,g., 1958, 1962, and 1966). This might reduce the reliability of the division of the independent vote.

2. A second disaffection index was also calculated from the NES "feeling thermometer" scales. These scales ask respondents to rate candidates from zero to 100 degrees or points, with 100 being most favorable. While the use of any single thermometer scale may be problematic (is one person's fifty degrees the same as another's seventy-five degrees? see Knight 1984), a comparison of ratings indicates a respondent's relative satisfaction with a candidate. This second party disaffection index is calculated by the equation:

$$INDEX2 = OtherTherm - OwnTherm$$

Like the first index, this measure indicates a respondent's overall relative dissatisfaction with his own party's presidential candidate. Among partisans of the same party, this indicates the presence and extent of pressures running against a vote for the party. INDEX2 conceivably could range from $+100$ to -100. As in the case of the likes/dislikes index, more positive values indicate stronger pressures against the partisan's "standing decision." Findings using INDEX2 are consistent with those using the likes/dislikes index and since the measure was not included in the early election surveys, I report only the likes/dislikes measure findings.

3. Born (1990) found turnout to play no role in surge and decline. However, this was probably a result of several problems with his analysis: (1) As an indicator of the presidential short-term evaluations, Born used the NES "thermometer" scales for the presidential candidates. Rather than examine the difference in the ratings of the two candidates, Born instead used the simple raw score for each candidate separately. In determining the effects of these evaluations, Born made the highly dubious assumption that the fifty-degree mark was a true neutral evaluation for all voters, despite evidence of substantial individual differences in using the scale and a general positivity bias in its use (Knight 1984). This decision probably led Born to classify many as neutral who might more appropriately be classified as negatively disposed toward a candidate. Also, with respect to the thermometer index, Born failed to link partisanship with the candidate evaluations and, thus, cannot actually test for cross-pressure effects. (2) Born conducted

his analysis with a nested multinomial logit technique that does not assume a definite order to the three choices of a loyal vote, an abstention, and a defecting vote. The above analysis examines the ordering presumed by the theory. (3) In testing whether the midterm decline stemmed from the presidential surge, Born makes two very restrictive assumptions: that the coattail voter must have cast a straight ticket in the presidential election (see chapter 2) and that the voter had positively evaluated (fifty degrees plus) the presidential candidate in the on-year election (rather than just evaluated the presidential candidate more positively than his opponent). He then simply coded voters by a dummy variable, entirely disregarding the extent of their disaffection and again relying on the supposed neutrality of a fifty-degree rating. (4) Finally, Born's analysis does not consider the turnout effect of cross-pressures on the losing or disadvantaged presidential party. In his analysis of the 1974 midterm Republican vote loss, Born fails to consider whether Democrats discouraged from voting in 1972 because of their disaffection from the McGovern presidential campaign later returned to the 1974 electorate.

4. Multinomial logit analysis is the more appropriate technique to examine the trichotomous dependent variable, though it is also less readily interpretable. Nevertheless, the logit results concurred with the regression results. Each coefficient was negative and statistically significant (p $\langle$.01). The logit coefficients distinguishing between defectors and abstainers ranged from $-.43$ to $-.63$. The logit coefficients distinguishing between abstainers and loyal partisan voters ranged from $-.14$ to $-.28$.

5. A multivariate analysis taking educational level, age, political efficacy, political interest, and other possible influences on turnout was also conducted. Strong cross-pressure effects were evident in that analysis as well (see Campbell 1989). However, since the theory only requires a bivariate relationship, that is what is reported in table 8.3.

6. As the regressions in table 8.4 indicate, partisan disaffection has a much larger effect on voting behavior regarding presidential candidates than congressional candidates. This is expected, given the presidential focus of the questions used in constructing the disaffection index. The magnitude of the difference between the congressional and presidential vote regression coefficients was larger than expected (especially in 1972) and may reflect the lack of controls for circumstances relevant to congressional voting, such as the party of the incumbent and the quality of the challenger.

7. The reported congressional votes for the parties in the NES studies differ from their known actual partisan division of the national congressional votes (Ornstein, Mann, and Malbin 1990, 47-48). For instance, the 1988 NES study indicates nearly 59 percent of voters cast ballot for Democratic congressional candidates whereas we know from the actual national congressional vote that Democrats only received about 54 percent of the vote. Given the narrow range in which the actual congressional vote varies (from 1956 to 1990 it ranged from 50.9 percent to 58.5 percent and had a standard deviation of only 2.4 percent), these discrepancies are quite large and uncorrected may play havoc with longitudinal studies relying on aggregated NES data (see the following note). To correct for this known unrepresentative characteristic of the sample, the cases were weighted to produce the actual division of congressional vote. The weights used on reported Democratic and Republican congressional voters in each election are as follows: 1952, D = 1.026 and R = .976; 1956, D = .977 and R = 1.025; 1958, D = .949 and R = 1.074; 1960, D = .982 and R = 1.021; 1962, D = .893 and R = 1.152; 1964, D = .899

and R = 1.240; 1966, D = .900 and R = 1.135; 1968, D = .991 and R = 1.014; 1970, D = .996 and R = 1.005; 1972, D = 1.037 and R = .979; 1974, D = .982 and R = 1.029; 1976, D = 1.010 and R = .987; 1978, D = .933 and R = 1.094; 1980, D = .928 and R = 1.112; 1982, D = .975 and R = 1.033; 1984, D = .954 and R = 1.056; 1986, D = .914 and R = 1.131; 1988, D = .916 and R = 1.120; and 1990, D = .844 and R = 1.279. The 1972, 1974, and 1976 data are drawn from the panel study.

8. Bivariate results are very similar to those including the trend variable. The bivariate unstandardized coefficients of the Democratic presidential vote with the presidential year presence of partisans were + .38 for Democrats and − .28 for Republicans. The bivariate coefficients for partisan presence in midterm electorates were − .07 for Democrats and + .02 for Republicans. The bivariate coefficients for change in the partisan composition of midterm electorates were − .48 for Democrats and + .30 for Republicans.

9. Born (1990, 642) criticizes an earlier report (Campbell 1987) of this aggregated analysis of partisan turnout on two grounds: (1) that I find that more advantaged partisans turn out to vote because party identification itself is sensitive to short-term forces and this inflates the number of voters claiming to be identified with the advantaged party, and (2) that my analysis was based on the partisan percentages of the electorate rather than the partisan percentage of the voting-age population which then should have been examined within each party over the series of elections. Three responses may be offered to Born's criticisms: (1) The partisan complexion of the electorate does not appear to be a consequence of party identification changing to reflect short-term forces since most such change is among the degrees of partisanship categories rather than between the nominal parties (and I used only the collapsed or nominal categories of Democratic or Republican identification). Moreover, as Born notes, I used lagged party identification measures where they were available (see the following note). (2) I examined the variation in the partisan percentages of the electorates rather than their turnout rates because the partisan composition of the electorates is important to the theory and a proper analysis of partisan turnout would entail more complicated controls for the secular decline in turnout across the series of elections. (3) Finally, Born ignores the known unrepresentativeness of the NES samples on the very important congressional vote distribution (see note 7 above). While this unrepresentativeness may not be problematic for individual level analyses, it can seriously distort aggregated analyses and, therefore, should be corrected by reweighting cases to the known national vote distribution.

10. In an earlier analysis (Campbell 1987), I examined lagged party identification for several years, to test the possibility that partisans were changing identification between elections. In that analysis, also using the broad categorization of partisans, I found no systematic evidence of a surge and decline effect on partisan identification itself.

11. The steeper slope found for Democrats is consistent with previous findings. First, DeNardo (1980) found evidence that Democrats hold a greater advantage among peripherals than among core voters. Pro-Democratic forces should stimulate more Democratic peripherals to vote. Second, from a different angle, Verba and Nie (1972, 214) found that Republicans participate more often than Democrats, even when other characteristics are controlled.

12. Although there was no realignment for the whole series, a separate analysis suggests a modest shift to Republicans in the 1980s, about 2 to 3 percentage points.

Chapter 9. Surge and Decline in Subpresidential Elections

1. In a subsequent and more fully specified equation of pooled state legislative election results of non-Southern states in elections from 1940 to 1982, Chubb (1988) also found evidence of substantial presidential coattail effects. By Chubb's estimates, a party gains 1 percent of state legislative seats for every 3 percent of the presidential vote, though he also estimated that this effect was greater in earlier years and has declined in more recent elections. With a separate turnout change variable, Chubb also examined what he labeled "surge and decline" effects. As the discussion of Angus Campbell's original theory in chapter 3 indicates, this is an inappropriate specification of surge and decline effects. A rise in turnout was not suspected of having a simple additive effect but was supposed to amplify support for the party benefiting from the short-term forces that had stimulated the turnout.

2. Key (1958, 592-99) and Hinckley (1970) also found evidence of presidential coattails in Senate elections. More recently, Stewart (1987) found that presidential coattails significantly affected the numbers of voters turning out to vote for both incumbents and challengers.

3. The number of seats won or lost by a party obviously depends in part on the number of seats it has at stake. This, along with the other complications already mentioned, would account for some deviations from the surge and decline pattern of midterm losses. It might also explain why the president's party did not, in all cases, register large gains in landslides. For instance, the Democrats gained only one seat in Johnson's 1964 landslide because Democrats had registered very large gains in that class of Senate seats in 1958 (more than fifteen seats).

4. The complications raised by the disparity between the national presidential vote and the subset of states holding Senate elections and by the different size of the state electorates may possibly cause an overestimation of surge and decline effects in any given election. Although these complications suggest likely random error in the measurement of short-term forces in the national presidential vote, the general effect should be an underestimation of surge and decline effects.

5. Although there is still some controversy about whether the 1980s witnessed a realignment favorable to Republicans, Ladd (1985), Petrocik (1987), Bullock (1988), and Wolfinger (1985) present compelling evidence that the allegiances of Southern white voters have shifted toward the Republican party. Stanley (1988) also notes the favorable shift but leaves open the possibility that it is a result of dealigning Southern Democrats who may or may not procede to align themselves with the Republicans. Carmines and Stimson (1989) agree with the secular realignment interpretation but trace its origins to the 1960s when black voters were mobilized into the Democratic ranks.

6. The rise of the number of Southern uncontested Democratic districts carried by Republican presidential candidates was not the only congressional development in the South. The number of competitive congressional districts in the South also increased significantly in this period. In the 1952, 1956, and 1960 presidential elections, only elevem to fifteen (between 10 percent and 14 percent) southern districts were competitive (won by 60 percent or less). In the 1980, 1984, and 1988 elections, from twenty-one to as many as thirty-six (20 percent to 34 percent) Southern districts were competitive. Accompanying this rise in competition in parts of the South was a growth in Republican representation. Whereas Republicans held only two seats in 1950, they were able to expand their ranks to forty-three Southern seats by 1984. These two trends, increased competition and

increased Republican seat holdings in the South, partially offset the effects of wasted Republican coattails in the South as well as the reduced level of congressional competition outside the South. Given the countervailing trends within the South itself, the wasted coattail explanation should not be understood as simply a matter of the South as a whole compared to the rest of the nation.

7. The uncontested district index scores for each year are: 1952 = 30; 1956 = 25; 1960 = 39; 1964 = −4; 1968 = 18; 1972 = −32; 1976 = 31; 1980 = 15; 1984 = −34; and 1988 = −2.

8. The analysis reported here considers only uncontested districts held by Democrats. There are also uncontested seats held by Republicans, though they have never numbered as many as twenty in any recent election and have been consistently carried by Republican presidential candidates. However, since the number of these uncontested Republican districts has increased in recent years, the analysis was rerun counting these districts as ones that would inflate the presidential pulse. These districts would appear in the lower left-hand quadrant of figure 9.3. The reanalysis including uncontested Republican districts reconfirms the above results. The adjusted R-square was .62; the uncontested seats term took its expected negative sign (b = −.34 and t = 2.00) and the presidential vote coefficient was stronger than in the equation without the uncontested seats variable (b = 2.56 and t = 3.97).

9. The wasted coattail explanation explains why the decline in coattail effects appears more severe in aggregate national analyses than in district level analyses that exclude uncontested districts. Born's (1984) analysis of presidential coattails in districts from 1952 to 1980 shows a weakening of coattails of about 20 percent (from .37 for 1952-64 to .29 for 1968-80) rather than the approximately 50 percent drop in the national-level analysis. It is important to note that Born's district analysis excludes uncontested districts, precisely where most (but not all) coattail support would appear diminished in more recent elections. If merely token Republican candidacies were also excluded from the district analysis, it is quite likely that there would be even a smaller decline in estimated coattail effects.

Chapter 10. Reflections on the Presidential Pulse

1. Sundquist (1986) notes a variety of other methods by which divided government might be avoided and accountability thereby enhanced. These provisions include having a team ticket or package vote for president and Congress, delayed voting for Congress, and a set number of bonus seats awarded to the party winning the presidency. While these proposals would reduce the chance of divided government, many of these reforms would accomplish this without much input from voters and all would entail constitutional reform.

2. The party linkage is meaningful even when confronting congressional candidates of similar ideologies. If nothing else, the congressional candidate of the chosen presidential party can be counted on to vote with the party in the straight party-line roll call vote to organize the House, thus elevating fellow partisans to institutional positions in which they can further assist the president.

3. Of course, whether the voter initially has sound reasons for voting one way or the other for president is a matter beyond the pale of this analysis. The point here is merely that extending reasons for voting for a party's presidential candidate to its congressional candidates is defensible as a coherent vote. The burden of proving "reasonableness" in the vote decision ought to lie with those splitting their tickets.

4. A number of prior analyses (e.g., Edwards 1980, 70-77) have assumed wrongly that coattail effects require straight-ticket voting. These studies have ignored the possibility of coattails based in partisan turnout differences.

5. It is no mere coincidence that majority parties in the states often attempt to divorce themselves from their national party that is less popular locally by holding gubernatorial elections in midterms or even odd-numbered years. They want voters to distinguish between national Democrats and Republicans and state Democrats and Republicans so that local elections will be less influenced by national politics. While this may serve the needs of some local politicians, it may have substantial costs for political parties and consistency in national public policies. As a result of the disjunction between presidential and subpresidential elections, some research indicates that some voters develop a dual partisanship (Hadley 1985; Niemi, Wright, and Powell 1987). A Southern conservative, for instance, may identify with the Democrats as far as state and local politics is concerned but with the Republicans when it comes to presidential politics.

6. The closest case of bipartisan support for the president was in Eisenhower's second term. In the 1958 session of the House, House Republicans were only two percentage points more likely than House Democrats to support Eisenhower's positions (65 percent vs. 63 percent). This was quite unusual. In thirty of the thirty-four sessions examined, presidential support scores in the president's party were at least ten percentage points higher than in the opposition party.

7. Surprisingly, in an earlier study Edwards (1980, 105) did not find consistent evidence that representatives of the president's party are more inclined to support him. In regressions with overall policy support of the president as the dependent variable explained by the party affiliation of the representative and the presidential vote in the district, Edwards found the expected positive coefficients for the party of the representative in only nine of the twenty-one sessions examined. Quite plausibly, part of these contrary findings may be due to the lack of controls for other factors such as the region or ideological leanings of the district represented. Conservative Southern Democrats might be expected to support Republican presidents at the same rates as Republicans. This explanation would be consistent with the fact that all negative coefficients occurred under Republican administrations.

8. Buck's (1972) analysis unfortunately uses a simple comparison of the congressional and presidential vote in the district. A presidential vote exceeding the congressional vote, however, does not necessarily reflect presidential coattails. A presidential candidate who trailed a congressional candidate may actually have provided greater coattail help to that candidate than another congressional candidate that he lead, depending on the congressional votes involved. See note 3 in chapter 2.

9. Asher and Weisberg's (1978) analysis of roll-call voting raises serious doubts about presidential influence in shifting congressional behavior from previous positions, but would appear to be consistent with the notion that surge effects increase roll-call support for the president by adding seats to the presidential party's side of the aisle.

10. In fact, Burns argues that parties have been more affected by institutional arrangements (both separation of powers and federalism) than an influence shaping the operation of those institutions.

11. Producing a more harmonious relationship between the president and Congress was the purpose of more than a half dozen constitutional reforms

examined by Sundquist (1986, chaps. 4 and 7), Cutler (1986, 13-16), and the Committee on the Constitutional System. These proposed reforms ranged from including the drawing the cabinet from members of Congress to giving the winning presidential party bonus seats in Congress (Petracca 1990, 1991; Sundquist 1990).

12. Numerous explanations for the increase in divided government have been proposed. They include the Democratic party's congressional incumbency advantage, the partisan bias from low-turnout districts favoring Democratic House candidates, the Democratic advantages in recruiting quality challengers, the Democratic advantage in uncontested districts, Democratic gerrymandering, party dealignment, greater split-ticket voting with reduced presidential surge and decline effects, party realignment, the Republican's advantage in the Electoral College, and the public's sentiment to elect Republican presidents to represent broad national interests and Democratic congressional candidates to represent particular local interests. See, Jacobson (1990, 1991), Thurber (1991), Ornstein (1990), and Campbell (1991a). Also, Fiorina (1992) demonstrates that divided government is now also more frequent in state governments.

13. Mayhew (1991a, 1991b) finds no association in the period from 1946 to 1990 between dysfunctionally high partisan conflict within government (as measured by either the inability to pass major legislation or the conduct of high-publicity investigations) and divided government. My own analysis of presidential vetos from 1946 to 1984 (data from King and Ragsdale 1988, table 2.20) tends to mesh with Mayhew. While the mean presidential vetoes per year were, as one might expect, more frequent under divided government, the difference of means was not very large (17.6 under divided government and 14.9 under unified government). It seems, however, that the lack of association between divided government and dysfunctional partisan conflict may be due to the size of the working majority in Congress. If it is either so large as to be nearly veto-proof or if it is so small as to be frequently defeated, dysfunctional partisan conflict may be minimal — either the president or the majority leadership in Congress will "see the writing on the wall" and avoid a battle they anticipate losing. Dysfunctional partisan conflict (deadlock, bidding wars, shameless compromises, and the like) might be most likely in divided government when the majority congressional party is neither so weak that the president can pick off a few votes to defeat it nor so strong that presidents concede defeat without a fight. Rhode (1991, 140) also suggests that the level of partisanship in unified and divided governments depends upon the homogeneity of the parties and the president's inclination to compromise.

14. It should be clear that the debate over whether divided government substantially reduces cooperation between the Congress and the president is only part of the larger debate over whether the system of separation of powers, under either unified or divided government, provides sufficient incentives for cooperation.

15. Anderson (1986, 153) rightly notes that the idea of checks and balances is meant to prevent deadlock rather than to create it. The president, for instance, is given the veto power to increase incentives for compromise and agreement between the branches. However, the principal objection to constitutional structures is not that powers are insufficiently separated but that they are excessively separated. In other words, the complaint is more with the principle of separation of powers than with the principle of checks and balances.

16. Stephen Bailey (1964, 12-13) also recommended a constitutional reform to

a four-year term for members of the House, but called for half the seats to be synchronized and half desynchronized with presidential elections. Although congressmen might gain some independence from lengthened terms, the fact that Bailey's proposal amounts to another "mixed system" would appear to do little to increase party responsibility or interbranch cooperation.

17. As a constitutional reform, eliminating the midterm election would not suffer as many public doubts about its legitimacy as a "democratic" structure as several other suggested reforms, such as a forced presidential and congressional team ticket in which voters would be structurally denied the choice of splitting their tickets (Sundquist 1986). Moreover, the elimination of the midterm reform has the advantage of letting the public decide how much cooperation they desire between the branches and how much power they wish to invest in a particular president. It is also a less artificial or mechanistic reform than the term limits currently being debated. Moreover, it may be a more effective restraint on congressional power while also providing more coherence to the system.

18. While I regard the establishment of midterm elections as a mistake, I am not suggesting that the framers intended to create midterm elections or foresaw either the costs or the benefits of synchronizing or desynchronizing elections. The two tenets I discuss are mentioned at several points in *The Federalist Papers* (see especially, Hamilton, Madison, and Jay, p. 196, 321-22, and 350, *Federalist Papers* 31, 51, and 57).

Epilogue

1. There was no net party shift in the Senate. Democratic seat gains in California and Wisconsin offset Republican gains in North Carolina and Georgia.

2. Former California governor Jerry Brown continued in the race to the end, running his own unconventional, neo-populist campaign. Although Brown did well in places, finishing first, for instance, in the Connecticut primary, his campaign was never considered much of a threat to Clinton's nomination.

3. The Southern Super Tuesday primaries worked as they were intended to in 1992. That is the grouping of most Southern presidential primaries on a single day increased the influence of the Southern states in the selection of the Democratic presidential candidate. It did not have this effect in helping Southern Senator Al Gore's 1988 candidacy, since he split the Southern primary vote with front-running Governor Michael Dukakis and civil rights activist Reverend Jesse Jackson. Clinton faced the competition with neither a clear front-runner nor a candidate who siphoned off black voters. Clinton also may have benefited from Tsongas's decision to drop out in mid-March, a decision that appeared premature. Even though he suspended his campaigning, Tsongas continued to receive a significant share of the primary vote. In early April he considered reentry, but by that time recapturing his position in the nomination race appeared to be a long shot.

4. Perot claimed within days of the election that one reason he had dropped out in July was a report that the Republican campaign was planning to disrupt his daughter's impending wedding!

5. The 1992 election is the sixteenth (of forty-three since 1824) in which a president was elected with less than a majority of the popular vote. Only three of these presidents (John Quincy Adams, Lincoln, and Wilson) were elected with a smaller popular vote percentage than Clinton's. Clinton's vote percentage was slightly smaller than Nixon's in 1968.

6. An additional incentive to leave Congress in 1992 was provided by a change in campaign finance laws. Campaign finance reforms permitted the conversion of accumulated campaign contributions to personal use if the representative left Congress before the 1992 elections. This conversion would not be permitted after the 1992 campaign.

7. The defeat of nineteen incumbents in primaries is the largest number defeated in a single election year since 1946. In elections from 1946 to 1990, the mean number of incumbents defeated in primaries was only seven.

8. The expectations of substantial Republican gains were reflected in post-election reporting by a variety of newspapers. The morning after the election, the *New York Times* (Clymer, 1992) ran a story "On Clinton's Coattails, Democrats Overcome Anti-Incumbent Anger." Two days after the election, *USA Today* (Wolf, 1992) wrote that Democrats "had feared much larger losses in the House." Three days after the election, the *Washington Post* (Cooper, Babcock and Lee, 1992) concluded that larger Republican gains were widely expected and that their pickup of nine or ten seats was a "mediocre showing." *Congressional Quarterly* (Benenson, 1992), given the context, called the gains "meager."

9. Republican presidential defection rates in recent years have generally been under 15 percent. Not since the Goldwater landslide loss to Johnson in 1964 have so many Republican voters cast ballots for non-Republican presidential candidates.

References

Abramowitz, Alan I. 1983. "Partisan Redistricting and the 1982 Congressional Elections." *Journal of Politics* 45:767-70.

―――. 1985. "Economic Conditions, Presidential Popularity, and Voting Behavior in Midterm Congressional Elections." *Journal of Politics* 47:31-43.

―――. 1988. "Explaining Senate Election Outcomes." *American Political Science Review* 82:385-403.

Abramowitz, Alan I., Albert D. Cover, and Helmut Norpoth. 1986. "The President's Party in Midterm Elections: Going from Bad to Worse." *American Journal of Political Science* 30:562-76.

Abramowitz, Alan I., and Jeffrey Segal. 1986. "Determinants of the Outcomes of U.S. Senate Elections." *Journal of Politics* 48:433-9.

Abramson, Paul R. 1983. *Political Attitudes in America*. San Francisco, Calif.: W.H. Freeman.

Achen, Christopher H. 1979. "The Bias in Normal Vote Estimates." *Political Methodology* 5:343-56.

Alesina, Alberto, and Howard Rosenthal. 1989. "Partisan Cycles in Congressional Elections and the Macroeconomy." *American Political Science Review* 83:373-98.

Allsop, Dee, and Herbert F. Weisberg. 1988. "Measuring Change in Party Identification in an Election Campaign." *American Journal of Political Science* 32:996-1017.

Anderson, Ann Stuart. 1986. "A 1787 Perspective on Separation of Powers." In *Separation of Powers—Does It Still Work?* ed. Robert A. Goldwin and Art Kaufman, 138-67. Washington, D.C.: American Enterprise Institute.

Arcelus, Francisco, and Allan H. Meltzer. 1975. "The Effects of Aggregate Economic Variables on Congressional Elections." *American Political Science Review* 69:232-39.

Arseneau, Robert B., and Raymond E. Wolfinger. 1973. "Voting Behavior in Congressional Elections." Paper presented to the annual meeting of the American Political Science Association.

Asher, Herbert B. 1983. "Voting Behavior Research in the 1980s: An Examination of Some Old and New Problem Areas." In *Political Science: The State of the Discipline*, ed. Ada W. Finifter, 339-88. Washington, D.C.: American Political Science Association.

―――. 1992. *Presidential Elections and American Politics*. Pacific Grove, Calif.: Brooks/Cole.

Asher, Herbert B., and Herbert F. Weisberg. 1978. "Voting Change in Congress: Some Dynamic Perpectives on an Evolutionary Process." *American Journal of Political Science* 22:391-425.

Axelrod, Robert. 1972. "Where the Votes Come From: An Analysis of Electoral Coalitions, 1952-1968." *American Political Science Review* 66:11-20.

Bailey, Stephen K. 1964. "Our National Political Parties." In *Political Parties, U.S.A.*, ed. Robert A. Goldwin, 1-20. Chicago: Rand McNally.

Barone, Michael, and Grant Ujifusa. 1981. *The Almanac of American Politics 1982*. Washington, D.C.: Barone.

———. 1989. *The Almanac of American Politics 1990*. Washington, D.C.: National Journal.

Barone, Michael, Grant Ujifusa, and Douglas Matthews. 1972. *The Almanac of American Politics 1972*. Boston: Gambit.

———. 1975. *The Almanac of American Politics 1976*. New York: Dutton.

———. 1979. *The Almanac of American Politics 1980*. New York: Dutton.

Bauer, Monica, and John R. Hibbing. 1989. "Which Incumbents Lose in House Elections: A Response to Jacobson's 'The Marginals Never Vanished.'" *American Journal of Political Science* 33:262-71.

Bean, Louis H. 1948. *How to Predict Elections*. New York: Knopf.

———. 1950. *The Mid-Term Battle*. Washington, D.C.: Cantillion Books.

———. 1972. *How to Predict the 1972 Election*. New York: Quadrangle Books.

Benenson, Bob. 1992. "GOP's Dreams of a Comeback via the New Map Dissolve." *Congressional Quarterly Weekly Report*, 50:3580-81.

Berelson, Bernard B., Paul F. Lazarsfeld, and William N. McPhee. 1954. *Voting*. Chicago: Univ. of Chicago Press.

Bibby, John F. 1983a. "Patterns in Midterm Gubernatorial and State Legislative Elections." *Public Opinion* 6:41-46.

———. 1983b. "State House Elections at Midterm." In *The American National Elections of 1982*, ed. Thomas E. Mann and Norman J. Ornstein, 111-32. Washington, D.C.: American Enterprise Institute.

Bishop, George F., Robert W. Oldendick, and Alfred J. Tuchfarber. 1984. "Interest in Political Campaigns: The Influence of Question Order and Electoral Context." *Political Behavior* 6:159-69.

Bloom, Howard S., and H. Douglas Price. 1975. "Voter Response to Short-run Economic Conditions: The Asymmetric Effect of Prosperity and Recession." *American Political Science Review* 69:1240-54.

Bohrnstedt, George W., and David Knoke. 1988. *Statistics for Social Data Analysis*. 2nd ed. Itasca, Ill.: F.E. Peacock.

Bond, Jon R., Cary Covington, and Richard Fleisher. 1985. "Explaining Challenger Quality in Congressional Elections." *Journal of Politics* 47:510-29.

Bond, Jon R., and Richard Fleisher. 1990. *The President in the Legislative Arena*. Chicago: Univ. of Chicago Press.

Born, Richard. 1984. "Reassessing the Decline of Presidential Coattails: U.S. House Elections from 1952-1980." *Journal of Politics* 46:60-79.

———. 1986. "Strategic Politicians and Unresponsive Voters." *American Political Science Review* 80:599-612.

———. 1990. "Surge and Decline, Negative Voting, and the Midterm Loss Phenomenon: A Simultaneous Choice Analysis." *American Journal of Political Science* 34: 615-45.

Boyd, Richard W. 1969. "Presidential Elections: An Explanation of Voting Defection." *American Political Science Review* 63:498-514.

Brady, David W., and Naomi B. Lynn. 1973. "Switched-Seat Congressional Districts: The Effect on Party Voting and Public Policy." *American Journal of Political Science* 17:528-43.

Broder, David S. 1971. *The Party's Over*. New York: Harper.

Brody, Richard A. 1978. "The Puzzle of Political Participation in America." In *The New American Political System*, ed. Anthony King, 287-324. Washington, D.C.: American Enterprise Institute.

Brody, Richard A., and Benjamin I. Page. 1973. "Indifference, Alienation and Rational Decisions: The Effects of Candidate Evaluations on Turnout and the Vote." *Public Choice* 15:1-17.

Broh, C. Anthony, and Mark S. Levine. 1978. "Patterns of Party Competition." *American Politics Quarterly* 6:357-84.

Buck, J. Vincent. 1972. "Presidential Coattails and Congressional Loyalty." *Midwest Journal of Political Science* 16:460-72.

Bullock, Charles S., III. 1988. "Regional Realignment from an Officeholding Perspective." *Journal of Politics* 50:553-74.

Burnham, Walter Dean. 1970. *Critical Elections and the Mainsprings of American Politics*. New York: W.W. Norton.

———. 1975. "Insulation and Responsiveness in Congressional Elections." *Political Science Quarterly* 90:411-35.

Burns, James MacGregor. 1949. *Congress on Trial*. New York: Harper.

———. 1967. *The Deadlock of Democracy*. Englewood Cliffs, NJ: Prentice-Hall.

Cain, Bruce, John Ferejohn, and Morris Fiorina. 1987. *The Personal Vote*. Cambridge: Harvard Univ. Press.

Caldeira, Gregory A., and Samuel C. Patterson. 1982a. "Contextual Influences on Participation in U.S. State Legislative Elections." *Legislative Studies Quarterly* 7:359-81.

———. 1982b. "Bringing Home the Votes: Electoral Outcomes in State Legislative Races." *Political Behavior* 4:33-67.

Caldeira, Gregory A., Samuel C. Patterson, and Gregory A. Markko. 1985. "The Mobilization of Voters in Congressional Elections." *Journal of Politics* 47:490-509.

Calvert, Randall L., and John A. Ferejohn. 1983. "Coattail Voting in Recent Presidential Elections." *American Political Science Review* 77:407-19.

Calvert, Randall L., and R. Mark Isaac. 1981. "The Inherent Disadvantage of the Presidential Party in Midterm Congressional Elections." *Public Choice* 36:141-46.

Campbell, Angus. 1960. "Surge and Decline: A Study of Electoral Change." *Public Opinion Quarterly* 24:397-418.

———. 1964. "Voters and Elections: Past and Present." *Journal of Politics* 26:745-57.

Campbell, Angus, Philip E. Converse, Warren E. Miller, and Donald E. Stokes, eds. 1960. *The American Voter*. New York: Wiley.

———. 1966. *Elections and the Political Order*. New York: Wiley.

Campbell, Angus, and Warren E. Miller. 1957. "The Motivational Basis of Straight and Split Ticket Voting." *American Political Science Review* 51:293-312.

Campbell, James E. 1985. "Explaining Presidential Losses in Midterm Congressional Elections." *Journal of Politics* 47:1140-57.

———. 1986a. "Forecasting the 1986 Midterm Elections to the House of Representatives." *PS* 19:83-87.

———. 1986b. "Predicting Seat Gains from Presidential Coattails." *American Journal of Political Science* 30:165-83.

———. 1986c. "Presidential Coattails and Midterm Losses in State Legislative Elections." *American Political Science Review* 80:45-63.

———. 1987. "The Revised Theory of Surge and Decline." *American Journal of Political Science* 31:965-79.

———. 1989. "The Cross-Pressured Partisan." Paper presented at the annual meeting of the American Political Science Association.

———. 1990. "The Presidential Pulse of Congressional Elections: National Evidence from 1868 to 1988." Paper presented at the Carl Albert Center's Conference on the Bicentennial of the United States Congress, University of Oklahoma, Norman.

———. 1991a. "Divided Government, Partisan Bias and Turnout in Congressional Elections: Do Democrats Sit in the 'Cheap Seats'?" Paper delivered to the annual meeting of the American Political Science Association.

———. 1991b. "The Presidential Surge and Its Midterm Decline in Congressional Elections, 1868-1988." *Journal of Politics* 53:477-87.

———. 1992. "The Presidential Pulse of Congressional Elections, 1868-1988." In *The Atomistic Congress,* ed. Allen D. Hertzke and Ronald M. Peters, Jr., 49-72. Armonk, N.Y.: M.E. Sharpe.

Campbell, James E., John R. Alford, and Keith Henry. 1984. "Television Markets and Congressional Elections." *Legislative Studies Quarterly* 9:665-78.

Campbell, James E., and Kenneth J. Meier. 1979. "Issue Voting: An Empirical Examination of Individually Necessary and Jointly Sufficient Conditions." *American Politics Quarterly* 7:21-50.

Campbell, James E., Mary Munro, John R. Alford, and Bruce A. Campbell. 1986. "Partisanship and Voting." In *Research in Micropolitics,* volume 1: *Voting Behavior,* ed. Samuel Long, 99-126. Greenwich, Conn.: JAI.

Campbell, James E., and Joe A. Sumners. 1990. "The Presidential Coattails in Senate Elections." *American Political Science Review* 84:513-24.

Carmines, Edward G., and James A. Stimson. 1989. *Issue Evolution: Race and the Transformation of American Politics.* Princeton, N.J.: Princeton Univ. Press.

Ceaser, James W. 1986. "In Defense of Separation of Powers." In *Separation of Powers—Does It Still Work?* ed. Robert A. Goldwin and Art Kaufman, 168-73. Washington, D.C.: American Enterprise Institute.

Chatterjee, Sangit, and Frederick Wiseman. 1983. "Use of Regression Diagnostics in Political Science Research." *American Journal of Political Science* 27:601-13.

Chubb, John E. 1988. "Institutions, the Economy, and the Dynamics of State Elections." *American Political Science Review* 82:133-54.

Claggett, William, William Flanigan, and Nancy Zingale. 1984. "Nationalization of the American Electorate." *American Political Science Review* 78:77-91.

Clymer, Adam. 1992. "On Clinton's Coattails, Democrats Overcome Anti-Incumbent Anger." *New York Times,* November 4, B1.

Committee on the Constitutional System. 1992. "A Bicentennial Analysis of the American Political Structure." In *Parliamentary Versus Presidential Government,* ed. Arend Lijphart, 78-89. New York: Oxford Univ. Press.

Congressional Quarterly. 1975. *Presidential Elections since 1789.* Washington, D.C.: Congressional Quarterly, Inc.

———. 1981. "Official 1980 Presidential Election Results." *Congressional Quarterly Weekly Report* 39:138.

———. 1984. "Official 1984 Presidential Election Results." *Congressional Quarterly Weekly Report* 42:2931.

———. 1985. *Guide to U.S. Elections*, 2nd ed. Washington, D.C.: Congressional Quarterly, Inc.

Converse, Philip E., 1966a. "Information Flow and the Stability of Partisan Attitudes." In *Elections and the Political Order*, ed. Angus Campbell, Philip E. Converse, Warren E. Miller, and Donald E. Stokes, 136-57. New York: John Wiley and Sons.

———. 1966b. "The Concept of the 'Normal Vote.'" In *Elections and the Political Order*, ed. Angus Campbell, Philip E. Converse, Warren E. Miller, and Donald E. Stokes, 9-39. New York: John Wiley and Sons.

———. 1976. *The Dynamics of Party Support*. Beverly Hills, Calif.: Sage Publications.

Cook, Rhodes. 1976. "Carter Squeezes Out a Popular Majority." *Congressional Quarterly Weekly Report* 34:3332-36.

———. 1985. "Will the 'Six-Year Itch' Strike Again in 1986?" *Congressional Quarterly Weekly Report* 43:1284-86.

———. 1991. "Incumbents' National Status Breeds Local Distrust." *Congressional Quarterly Weekly Report* 49:483-87.

Cooper, Kenneth J., Charles R. Babcock, and Gary Lee. 1992. "Election Scorecard." *Washington Post*, November 6, A18.

Council of State Governments. 1942-82. *The Book of the States*. Lexington, Ky.

Cover, Albert D. 1985. "Surge and Decline in Congressional Elections." *Western Political Quarterly* 38:606-19.

———. 1986a. "Party Competence Evaluations and Voting for Congress." *Western Political Quarterly* 39:304-12.

———. 1986b. "Presidential Evaluations and Voting for Congress." *American Journal of Political Science* 30:786-801.

Cummings, Milton C., Jr. 1966. *Congressmen and the Electorate*. New York: Free Press.

Cutler, Lloyd N. 1986. "To Form a Government." In *Separation of Powers—Does It Still Work?* ed. Robert A. Goldwin and Art Kaufman, 1-17. Washington, D.C.: American Enterprise Institute.

———. 1987. "Political Parties and a Workable Government." In *A Workable Government?* ed. Burke Marshall, 49-58. New York: W.W. Norton.

Davidson, Roger H. 1991. "The Presidency and Three Eras of the Modern Congress." In *Divided Democracy*, ed. James A. Thurber, 61-78. Washington, D.C.: CQ Press.

Declerq, Eugene, Thomas L. Hurley, and Norman R. Luttbeg. 1975. "Voting in American Presidential Elections, 1956-1972." *American Politics Quarterly* 3:222-46.

DeNardo, James. 1980. "Turnout and the Vote: The Joke's on the Democrats." *American Political Science Review* 74:406-20.

———. 1986. "Does Heavy Turnout Help Democrats in Presidential Elections?" *American Political Science Review* 80:1298-1304.

DeVoursney, Robert M. 1977. *Issues and Electoral Instability: A Test of Alternative Explanations for Voting Defection in the 1968 American Presidential Election*. Ph.D. diss., University of North Carolina, Chapel Hill.

Donnelly, Harrison. 1984. "Republicans Score Gains in State Legislatures." *Congressional Quarterly Weekly Report* 42:2943-45.

Downs, Anthony. 1957. *An Economic Theory of Democracy*. New York: Harper and Row.

Duncan, Phil, ed. 1989. *Politics in America*, Washington, D.C.: Congressional Quarterly.

Edwards, George C., III. 1979. "The Impact of Presidential Coattails on Outcomes of Congressional Elections." *American Politics Quarterly* 7:94-107.

———. 1980. *Presidential Influence in Congress*, San Francisco, Calif.: W.H. Freeman.

———. 1983. *The Public Presidency*. New York: St. Martin's Press.

———. 1989. *At the Margins: Presidential Leadership of Congress*, New Haven, Conn.: Yale Univ. Press.

Ehrenhalt, Alan. ed. 1983, 1985, 1987. *Politics in America*. Washington, D.C.: CQ Press.

———. 1985. "House GOP Jittery about Midterm Elections." *Congressional Quarterly Weekly Report* 43:1851.

Erikson, Robert S. 1971. "The Advantage of Incumbency in Congressional Elections." *Polity* 3:395-405.

———. 1981. "Why Do People Vote? Because They Are Registered." *American Politics Quarterly* 8:259-76.

———. 1988. "The Puzzle of Midterm Loss." *Journal of Politics* 50: 1011-29.

———. 1990. "Economic Conditions and the Congressional Vote: A Review of Macrolevel Evidence." *American Journal of Political Science* 34:373-99.

Eubank, Robert B., and David John Gow. 1983. "The Pro-Incumbent Bias in the 1978 and 1980 National Election Studies." *American Journal of Political Science* 27: 122-39.

Fair, Ray C. 1978. "The Effect of Economic Events on Votes for President." *Review of Economics and Statistics* 60:159-73.

Feigert, Frank B. 1979. "Illusions of Ticket-Splitting." *American Politics Quarterly* 7:470-88.

Ferejohn, John A., and Randall L. Calvert. 1984. "Presidential Coattails in Historical Perspective." *American Journal of Political Science* 28:127-46.

Ferejohn, John A., and Morris P. Fiorina. 1974. "The Paradox of Not Voting: A Decision Theoretic Analysis." *American Political Science Review* 68:525-36.

———. 1985. "Incumbency and Realignment in Congressional Elections." In *The New Direction in American Politics*, ed. John E. Chubb and Paul E. Peterson, 91-115. Washington, D.C.: Brookings.

Festinger, Leon. 1957. *A Theory of Cognitive Dissonance*. Evanston, Ill.: Row, Peterson.

Fiorina, Morris P. 1976. "The Voting Decision: Instrumental and Expressive Aspects." *Journal of Politics* 38:390-413.

———. 1981. *Retrospective Voting in American National Elections*. New Haven, Conn.: Yale Univ. Press.

———. 1983. "Who Is Held Responsible? Further Evidence of the Hibbing-Alford Thesis." *American Journal of Political Science* 27:158-64.

———. 1990. "The Electorate in the Voting Booth." In *The Parties Respond*, ed. L. Sandy Maisel, 116-33. Boulder, Colo.: Westview Press.

———. 1992. *Divided Government*. New York: Macmillan.

Fisher, Louis. 1972. *President and Congress*. New York: Free Press.

———. 1978. *The Constitution between Friends.* New York: St. Martin's Press.

———. 1991. *Constitutional Conflicts between Congress and the President.* 3rd ed., rev. Lawrence, Kans.: Univ. Press of Kansas.

Flanigan, William H., and Nancy H. Zingale. 1987. *Political Behavior of the American Electorate.* Boston, Mass.: Allyn and Bacon.

Fowler, Linda, and Robert McClure. 1989. *Political Ambition.* New Haven, Conn.: Yale Univ. Press.

Frohlich, Norman, Joe A. Oppenheimer, Jefferey Smith, and Oran R. Young. 1978. "A Test of Downsian Voter Rationality: 1964 Presidential Voting." *American Political Science Review* 72:178-97.

Galloway, George B. 1976. *History of the House of Representatives.* 2nd ed. New York: Crowell.

Gant, Michael. 1983. "Citizen Uncertainty and Turnout in the 1980 Presidential Campaign." *Political Behavior* 5:257-75.

Goldenberg, Edie N., and Michael W. Traugott. 1981. "Normal Vote Analysis of U.S. Congressional Elections." *Legislative Studies Quarterly* 6:247-57.

———. 1984. *Campaigning for Congress.* Washington, D.C.: CQ Press.

Goodman, Saul, and Gerald H. Kramer. 1975. "Comment on Arcelus and Meltzer, the Effect of Aggregate Economic Conditions on Congressional Elections." *American Political Science Review* 69:255-65.

Green, Donald Philip, and Jonathan S. Krasno. 1988. "Salvation for the Spendthrift Incumbent: Reestimating the Effects of Campaign Spending in House Elections." *American Journal of Political Science* 32:884-907.

Hadley, Charles D. 1985. "Dual Partisan Identification in the South." *Journal of Politics* 47:254-68.

Hadley, Charles D., and Susan E. Howell. 1979. "Partisan Conversion in the Northeast: An Analysis of Split Ticket Voting, 1952-1976." *American Politics Quarterly* 7:259-83 and 8:129-34.

Hamilton, Alexander, James Madison, and John Jay. 1961. *The Federalist Papers.* ed. Clinton Rossiter. New York, New American Library.

Hibbing, John R., and John R. Alford. 1981. "The Electoral Impact of Economic Conditions: Who is Held Responsible?" *American Journal of Political Science* 25:423-39.

Hibbs, Douglas A., Jr. 1982. "President Reagan's Mandate from 1980 Elections: A Shift to the Right?" *American Politics Quarterly* 10:387-420.

Hinckley, Barbara. 1967. "Interpreting House Midterm Elections: Toward a Measurement of the In-party's 'Expected' Loss of Seats." *American Political Science Review* 61:694-700.

———. 1970. "Incumbency and the Presidential Vote in Senate Elections." *American Political Science Review* 64:836-42.

———. 1971. *Stability and Change in Congress.* New York: Harper and Row.

———. 1981. *Congressional Elections.* Washington, D.C.: CQ Press.

Hinckley, Barbara, C. Richard Hofstetter, and John H. Kessel 1974. "Information and the Vote: A Comparative Election Study." *American Politics Quarterly* 2:131-58.

Howell, Susan. 1981. "Short-term Forces and Changing Partisanship." *Political Behavior* 3:163-80.

Jacobson, Gary C. 1976. "Presidential Coattails in 1972." *Public Opinion Quarterly* 40:194-200.

———. 1980. *Money in Congressional Elections.* New Haven, Conn.: Yale Univ. Press.

———. 1982. "Strategy and Choice in the 1982 Congressional Elections." *PS* 15:423-30.

———. 1983a. *The Politics of Congressional Elections.* Boston, Mass.: Little, Brown.

———. 1983b. "Reagan, Reagonomics, and Strategic Politics in 1982: A Test of Alternative Theories of Midterm Congressional Elections." Paper presented at the annual meeting of the American Political Science Association.

———. 1986. "National Forces in Congressional Elections." Paper presented at the annual meeting of the American Political Science Association.

———. 1989. "Strategic Politicians and the Dynamics of U.S. House Elections." *American Political Science Review* 83:773-93.

———. 1990a. *The Electoral Origins of Divided Government.* Boulder, Colo.: Westview Press.

———. 1990b. "Does the Economy Matter in Midterm Elections?" *American Journal of Political Science* 34:400-404.

———. 1991. "Explaining Divided Government: Why Can't the Republicans Win the House?" *PS* 24:640-43.

Jacobson, Gary C., and Samuel Kernell. 1981. *Strategy and Choice in Congressional Elections.* New Haven, Conn.: Yale Univ. Press.

———. 1986. "Interpreting the 1974 Congressional Election." *American Political Science Review* 80:591-93.

Jewell, Malcolm E., and David M. Olson. 1982. *American State Political Parties and Elections.* Rev. ed. Homewood, Ill.: Dorsey Press.

Kaplan, David. 1990. "The Tally: Democrats, Up Nine; Republicans, Down Eight." *Congressional Quarterly Weekly Report* 48:483-87.

Kaplowitz, Stan. 1971. "Using Aggregate Voting Data to Measure Presidential Coattails Effects." *Public Opinion Quarterly* 35:415-19.

Keith, Bruce E., David B. Magleby, Candice J. Nelson, Elizabeth Orr, Mark Westlye, and Raymond Wolfinger. 1986. "The Partisan Affinities of Independent 'Leaners.'" *British Journal of Political Science* 16:155-84.

Kelley, Stanley, Jr. 1983. *Interpreting Elections.* Princeton, N.J.: Princeton Univ. Press.

Kelley, Stanley, Jr., and Thad W. Mirer. 1974. "The Simple Act of Voting." *American Political Science Review* 68:572-91.

Kenney, Patrick J. 1988. "Surge and Decline: Reconsidered." Manuscript on file with author.

Kernell, Samuel. 1977. "Presidential Popularity and Negative Voting: An Alternative Explanation of the Midterm Congressional Decline of the President's Party." *American Political Science Review* 71:44-66.

Key, V.O. 1958. *Politics, Parties and Pressure Groups.* New York: Thomas Y. Crowell.

Kiewiet, D. Roderick. 1983. *Macroeconomics and Microeconomics.* Chicago: Univ. of Chicago Press.

Kinder, Donald R., and D. Roderick Kiewiet. 1979. "Economic Discontent and Political Behavior: The Role of Personal Grievances and Collective Economic Judgments in Congressional Voting." *American Journal of Political Science* 23:495-527.

King, Gary. 1986. "How Not to Lie with Statistics: Avoiding Common Mistakes in Quantitative Political Science." *American Journal of Political Science* 30:666-87.

King, Gary, and Lyn Ragsdale. 1988. *The Elusive Executive.* Washington, D.C.: CQ Press.

Knight, Kathleen, 1984. "The Dimensionality of Partisan and Ideological Affect: The Influence of Positivity." *American Politics Quarterly* 12:305-34.

Kramer, Gerald H. 1971. "Short-term Fluctuations in U.S. Voting Behavior, 1896-1964." *American Political Science Review* 65:131-43.

———. 1983. "The Ecological Fallacy Revisited: Aggregate Versus Individual-level Findings on Economics and Sociotropic Voting." *American Political Science Review* 77:92-111.

Kritzer, Herbert M., and Robert B. Eubank. 1979. "Presidential Coat-tails Revisited: Partisanship and Incumbency Effects." *American Journal of Political Science* 23:615-26.

Ladd, Everett Carll. 1985. "As the Realignment Turns: A Drama in Many Acts." *Public Opinion* 7, no.6:2-7.

Langbein, Laura Irwin, and Allan J. Lichtman. 1978. *Ecological Inference.* Beverly Hills, Calif.: Sage.

Lavine, Harold. 1956. "Riding the Coattails." *Newsweek,* October 22, 31-33.

Lazarsfeld, Paul F., Bernard Berelson, and Hazel Gaudet. 1944. *The People's Choice.* New York: Duell, Sloan and Pearce.

Lewis-Beck, Michael S. 1985. "Election Forecasts in 1984: How Accurate Were They?" *PS* 18:53-62.

Lewis-Beck, Michael S., and Tom W. Rice. 1984. "Forecasting U.S. House Elections." *Legislative Studies Quarterly* 9:475-86.

———. 1985. "Are Senate Elections Predictable?" *PS* 18:745-54.

Lippmann, Walter. 1925. *The Phantom Public.* New York: Harcourt, Brace.

———. 1955. *The Public Philosophy.* New York: New American Library.

Lodge, Milton C., and Ruth Hamill. 1986. "A Partisan Schema for Political Information Processing." *American Political Science Review* 80:505-19.

MacKuen, Michael B. 1983. "Political Drama, Economic Conditions, and the Dynamics of Presidential Popularity." *American Journal of Political Science* 27:165-92.

Mann, Thomas E. 1978. *Unsafe at Any Margin.* Washington, D.C.: American Enterprise Institute.

Mann, Thomas E., and Norman J. Ornstein. 1981. "The 1982 Election: What Will It Mean?" *Public Opinion* 4:48-50.

———. 1983. "Sending a Message: Voters and Congress in 1982." In *The American Elections of 1982*, ed. Thomas E. Mann and Norman J. Ornstein, 133-52. Washington, D.C.: American Enterprise Institute.

Mann, Thomas E., and Raymond E. Wolfinger. 1980. "Candidates and Parties in Congressional Elections." *American Political Science Review* 74:617-32.

Markus, Gregory B., and Philip E. Converse. 1979. "A Dynamic Simultaneous Equation Model of Electoral Choice." *American Political Science Review* 73:1055-70.

Marra, Robin F., and Charles W. Ostrom, Jr. 1989. "Explaining Seat Change in the U.S. House of Representatives, 1950-86." *American Journal of Political Science* 33:541-69.

Mayhew, David R. 1974. *Congress: The Electoral Connection.* New Haven, Conn.: Yale Univ. Press.

———. 1991a. *Divided We Govern.* New Haven: Yale Univ. Press.

———. 1991b. "Divided Party Control: Does It Make a Difference?" *PS* 24:637-40.

McKay, David H., and Graham K. Wilson. 1974. "The U.S. Mid-Term Elections." *Parliamentary Affairs,* 28:216-24.

Meier, Kenneth J. 1975. "Party Identification and Vote Choice." *Western Political Quarterly* 28:496-505.

Meier, Kenneth J., and James E. Campbell. 1979. "Issue Voting: An Empirical Examination of Individually Necessary and Jointly Sufficient Conditions." *American Politics Quarterly* 7:21-50.

Mezey, Michael L. 1989. *Congress, the President, and Public Policy.* Boulder, Colo.: Westview Press.

Miller, Arthur H., and Martin P. Wattenberg. 1983. "Measuring Party Identification: Independent or No Partisan Preference?" *American Journal of Political Science* 27:106-21.

Miller, Warren E. 1955. "Presidential Coattails: A Study in Political Myth and Methodology." *Public Opinion Quarterly* 19:353-68.

Miller, Warren E., and Santa A. Traugott. 1989. *American National Election Studies Data Sourcebook.* Cambridge, Mass.: Harvard Univ. Press.

Mondak, Jeffery J. 1990. "Determinants of Coattail Voting." *Political Behavior* 12:265-88.

Monroe, Kristen. 1979. "'God of Vengeance and of Reward?': The Economy and Presidential Popularity." *Political Behavior* 1:301-29.

Moos, Malcolm. 1952. *Politics, Presidents and Coattails.* Baltimore, Md.: Johns Hopkins Press.

Moreland, William B. 1973. "Angels, Pinpoints and Voters." *American Journal of Political Science* 17:170-76.

Mueller, John E. 1973. *War, Presidents and Public Opinion.* New York: Wiley.

Mughan, Anthony. 1986. "Toward a Political Explanation of Government Losses in Midterm By-Elections." *American Political Science Review* 80:761-75.

———. 1988. "On the By-Election Vote of Governments in Britain." *Legislative Studies Quarterly* 13:29-48.

Neustadt, Richard E. 1964. *Presidential Power.* New York: New American Library.

Nie, Norman H., Sidney Verba, and John R. Petrocik. 1979. *The Changing American Voter.* enl. ed. Cambridge, Mass.: Harvard Univ. Press.

Niemi, Richard G., and Patrick Fett. 1986. "The Swing Ratio: An Explanation and an Assessment." *Legislative Studies Quarterly* 11:75-90.

Niemi, Richard G., Stephen Wright, and Lynda W. Powell. 1987. "Multiple Party Identifiers and the Measurement of Party Identification." *Journal of Politics* 49:1093-103.

Norpoth, Helmut, and Thom Yantek. 1983. "Macroeconomic Conditions and Fluctuations of Presidential Popularity: The Question of Lagged Effects." *American Journal of Political Science* 27:785-807.

Oppenheimer, Bruce I., James A. Stimson, and Richard W. Waterman. 1986. "Interpreting U.S. Congressional Elections: The Exposure Thesis." *Legislative Studies Quarterly* 11:227-47.

Ornstein, Norman J. 1990. "The Permanent Democratic Congress." *Public Interest* 100:24-44.

Ornstein, Norman J., Thomas E. Mann, and Michael J. Malbin. 1990. *Vital Statistics on Congress, 1989-1990 Edition.* Washington, D.C.: CQ Press.

Ornstein, Norman J., Thomas E. Mann, Michael J. Malbin, Allen Schick, and John F. Bibby. 1984. *Vital Statistics on Congress, 1984-1985 Edition.* Washington, D.C.: American Enterprise Institute.

Ostrom, Charles W., Jr. and Dennis M. Simon. 1985. "Promise and Performance: A Dynamic Model of Presidential Popularity." *American Political Science Review* 79:334-58.

———. 1986. "The President's Public." *American Journal of Political Science* 32:1096-119.

———. 1989. "The Man in the Teflon Suit?" *Public Opinion Quarterly* 53:353-87.

Owens, John R. 1984. "Economic Influences on Elections to the U.S. Congress." *Legislative Studies Quarterly* 9:123-50.

Page, Benjamin I., and Calvin C. Jones. 1979. "Reciprocal Effects of Policy Preferences, Party Loyalties and the Vote." *American Political Science Review* 73:1071-89.

Parker, Glenn R. 1986. "Economic Partisan Advantages in Congressional Contests: 1938-1978." *Public Opinion Quarterly* 50:387-401.

Patterson, Samuel C., and Gregory A. Caldeira. 1984. "The Etiology of Partisan Competition." *American Political Science Review* 78:691-707.

Petracca, Mark P. 1991. "Divided Government and the Risks of Reform." *PS* 24:634-37.

Petracca, Mark P., with Lonce Bailey and Pamela Smith. 1990. "Proposals for Constitutional Reform: An Evaluation of the Committee System." *Presidential Studies Quarterly* 20:503-32.

Petrocik, John R. 1981. "Voter Turnout and Electoral Oscillation." *American Politics Quarterly* 9:161-80.

———. 1987. "Realignment: New Party Coalitions and the Nationalization of the South." *Journal of Politics* 49:347-75.

———. 1989. "An Expected Party Vote: New Data for an Old Concept." *American Journal of Political Science* 33:44-66.

Petrocik, John R., and Frederick T. Steeper. 1986. "The Midterm Referendum: The Importance of Attributions of Responsibility." *Political Behavior* 8:206-29.

Piereson, James E. 1975. "Presidential Popularity and Midterm Voting of Different Levels." *American Journal of Political Science*, 19:683-93.

Pfiffner, James P. 1991. "Divided Government and the Problem of Governance." In *Divided Democracy*, ed. James A. Thurber, 39-60. Washington, D.C.: CQ Press.

Pomper, Gerald M. 1975. *Voter's Choice*. New York: Harper and Row.

Press, Charles. 1958. "Voting Statistics and Presidential Coattails." *American Political Science Review* 52:1041-50.

Pritchard, Anita. 1983. "Presidents Do Influence Voting in the U.S. Congress: New Definitions and Measurements." *Legislative Studies Quarterly* 8:691-711.

Prysby, Charles L. 1986. "Electoral Coattails: Clarification and Measurement of an Elusive Concept." Paper presented at the annual meeting of the American Political Science Association.

Quirk, Paul J. 1991. "Domestic Policy: Divided Government and Cooperative Leadership." In *The Bush Presidency: First Appraisals*, ed. Colin Campbell, S.J., and Bert Rockman, 69-91. Chatham, N.J.: Chatham House.

Ranney, Austin. 1962. *The Doctrine of Responsible Party Government*. Urbana, Ill.: Univ. of Illinois Press.

———. 1976. "Parties in State Politics." In *Politics in the American States*, 3rd. ed., ed. Herbert Jacob and Kenneth N. Vines, ch. 3. Boston, Mass.: Little, Brown.

Ray, David, and John Havick. 1981. "A Longitudinal Analysis of Party Competition in State Legislative Elections." *American Journal of Political Science* 25:119-28.

Riker, William, and Peter C. Ordeshook. 1968. "A Theory of the Calculus of Voting." *American Political Science Review* 62:25-42.

Robinson, W.S. 1950. "Ecological Correlations and the Behavior of Individuals." *American Sociological Review* 15:351-57.

Rohde, David W. 1991. *Parties and Leaders in the Postreform House.* Chicago: Univ. of Chicago Press.

Rosenstone, Steven J. 1983. *Forecasting Presidential Elections.* New Haven, Conn.: Yale Univ. Press.

Rossiter, Clinton. 1960. *Parties and Politics in America.* Ithaca, N.Y.: Cornell Univ. Press.

Rousseuw, Peter. J. 1984. "Least Median of Squares Regression." *Journal of the American Statistical Association* 79:871-80.

Rousseuw, Peter J., and Annick M. Leroy. 1987. *Robust Regression and Outlier Detection.* New York: Wiley.

Schattschneider, E.E. 1942. *Party Government.* NewYork: Rinehart.

Schlesinger, Arthur M., Jr. 1973. *The Imperial Presidency.* New York: Houghton Mifflin.

Shaffer, Stephen D. 1981. "Balance Theory and Political Cognitions." *American Politics Quarterly* 9:291-320.

Sigelman, Lee. 1979. "Presidential Popularity and Presidential Elections." *Public Opinion Quarterly* 43:532-34.

———. 1982. "The Nonvoting Voter in Voting Research." *American Journal of Political Science* 26:47-56.

Sigelman, Lee, and Malcolm E. Jewell. 1986. "From Core to Periphery: A Note on the Imagery of Concentric Electorates." *Journal of Politics* 48:440-49.

Sigelman, Lee, and Yung-mei Tsai. 1981. "Personal Finances and Voting Behavior: A Reanalysis." *American Politics Quarterly* 9:371-99.

Southwell, Priscilla L. 1986. "The Politics of Disgruntlement: Nonvoting and Defection among Supporters of Nomination Losers, 1968-1984." *Political Behavior* 8:81-95.

Sperlich, Peter W. 1971. *Conflict and Harmony in Human Affairs: A Study of Cross-Pressures and Political Behavior.* Chicago: Rand McNally.

Stanley, Harold W. 1988. "Southern Partisan Changes: Dealignment, Realignment or Both?" *Journal of Politics* 50:64-88.

Stanley, Harold W., and Richard G. Niemi. 1988. *Vital Statistics on American Politics.* Washington, D.C.: CQ Press.

Stewart, Charles, III. 1987. "Towards a Model of Senate Elections in the States." Paper presented at the annual meeting of the Southern Political Science Association.

Stimson, James A. 1976. "Public Support for American Presidents: A Cyclical Model." *Public Opinion Quarterly* 40:1-21.

Stokes, Donald E. 1962. "Party Loyalty and the Likelihood of Deviating Elections." *Journal of Politics* 24:681-702.

———. 1967. "Parties and the Nationalization of Electoral Forces." In *The American Party Systems,* ed. William N. Chambers and Walter Dean Burnham, 182-202. New York: Oxford Univ. Press.

Stokes, Donald E., Angus Campbell, and Warren E. Miller. 1958. "Components of the Electoral Decision." *American Political Science Review* 52:367-87.

Sundquist, James L. 1977. "Congress and the President: Enemies or Partners?" In

Congress Reconsidered, ed. Lawrence C. Dodd and Bruce I. Oppenheimer, 222-43. New York: Praeger.

————. 1981. *The Decline and Resurgence of Congress.* Washington, D.C.: Brookings.

————. 1982. "Party Decay and the Capacity to Govern." In *The Future of American Political Parties,* ed. Joel L. Fleishman, 42-69. Englewood Cliffs, N.J.: Prentice-Hall.

————. 1986. *Constitutional Reform and Effective Government.* Washington, D.C.: Brookings Institution.

————. 1990. "Response to the Petracca-Bailey-Smith Evaluation of the Committee on the Constitutional System." *Presidential Studies Quarterly* 20:533-43.

Thurber, James A. 1991. "Representation, Accountability, and Efficiency in Divided Party Control of Government." *PS* 24:653-57.

Tucker, Harvey J. 1982. "Interparty Competition in the American States." *American Politics Quarterly* 10:93-116.

Tufte, Edward R. 1973. "The Relationship between Seats and Votes in Two-Party Systems." *American Political Science Review* 67:540-54.

————. 1974. *Data Analysis for Politics and Policy.* Englewood Cliffs, N.J.: Prentice-Hall.

————. 1975. "Determinants of the Outcomes of Midterm Congressional Elections." *American Political Science Review* 69:812-26.

————. 1978. *Political Control of the Economy.* Princeton, N.J.: Princeton Univ. Press.

Uslaner, Eric M., and M. Margaret Conway. 1985. "The Responsible Congressional Electorate: Watergate, the Economy, and Vote Choice in 1974." *American Political Science Review* 79:788-803.

————. 1986. "Interpreting the 1974 Congressional Election." *American Political Science Review* 80:593-95.

Verba, Sidney, and Norman H. Nie. 1972. *Participation in America.* New York: Harper and Row.

Ware, Alan. 1979. "The 1978 U.S. Mid-Term Elections in Historical Perspective" *Parliamentary Affairs* 32:207-21.

Waterman, Richard W. 1990. "Comparing Senate and House Electoral Outcomes: The Exposure Thesis." *Legislative Studies Quarterly* 15:99-114.

Waterman, Richard W., Bruce I. Oppenheimer and James A. Stimson. "Sequence and Equilibrium in Congressional Elections: An Integrated Approach." *Journal of Politics,* 53:373-93.

Watson, Tom. 1985. "House '86 Outlook: Bipartisan Pessimism." *Congressional Quarterly Weekly Report* 43:2049-53.

Wattenberg, Martin P. 1990. "From a Partisan to a Candidate-centered Electorate," In *The New American Political System,* 2nd version, ed. Anthony King, 139-74. Washington, D.C.: AEI Press.

Wayne, Stephen J. 1984. *The Road to the White House.* 2nd ed. New York: St. Martin's Press.

Weatherford, M. Stephen. 1983. "Economic Voting and the 'Symbolic Politics' Argument: A Reinterpretation and Synthesis." *American Political Science Review* 77:158-74.

Weber, Ronald E. 1980. "Gubernatorial Coattails: A Vanishing Phenomenon?" *State Government* 53:153-56.

Weber, Ronald E., and T. Wayne Parent. 1985. "National Versus State Effects on

State and Local Elections." Paper presented at the annual meeting of the Midwest Political Science Association.

Weinbaum, Marvin G., and Dennis R. Judd. 1970. "In Search of a Mandated Congress." *Midwest Journal of Political Science* 14:276-302.

Weisberg, Herbert F., and Bernard Grofman. 1981. "Candidate Evaluations and Turnout." *American Politics Quarterly* 9:197-219.

White, Theodore H. 1973. *The Making of the President 1972.* New York: Bantam Books.

Wilson, James Q. 1986. "Political Parties and the Separation of Powers." In *Separation of Powers—Does It Still Work?* ed. Robert A. Goldwin and Art Kaufman, 18-37. Washington, D.C.: American Enterprise Institute.

Witt, Evans. 1983. "A Model Election?" *Public Opinion* 6:46-49.

Wolf, Richard. 1992. "Most Incumbents Rode out the Storm." *USA Today,* November 5, 15A.

Wolfinger, Raymond E. 1985. "Dealignment, Realignment, and Mandates in the 1984 Election." In *The American Elections of 1984,* ed. Austin Ranney, 277-96. Durham, N.C.: Duke Univ. Press.

Wolfinger, Raymond, and Steven J. Rosenstone. 1980. *Who Votes?* New Haven, Conn.: Yale Univ. Press.

Wolfinger, Raymond, Steven J. Rosenstone, and Richard A. McIntosh. 1981. "Presidential and Congressional Voters Compared." *American Politics Quarterly* 9:245-55.

Zipp, John F. 1985. "Perceived Representativeness and Voting: An Assessment of the Impact of 'Choices' and 'Echoes.'" *American Political Science Review* 79:50-61.

Index